CASTING ABOUT
in the
REEL WORLD

FISHING ON THE FLY

William A. Douglass

RDR Books
Oakland, California

RDR Books
4456 Piedmont
Oakland, CA 94611
Phone: (510) 595-0595
Fax: (510) 595-0598
E-mail: read@rdrbooks.com
Website: www.rdrbooks.com

ISBN 1-57143-093-8
Library of Congress Control Number 2002093602

Editor: Bob Drews
Text Design and Typography: Richard Harris

Cover: *Author encounters black noddy tern in the Florida Keys*
photo by Billy Sydnor

Distributed in Europe by Airlift Book Company,
8 The Arena, Mollison Avenue, Enfield,
Middlesex, England EN37NJ

Distributed in Canada by
Starbooks Distribution
100 Armstrong Way
Georgetown, ON L7G 5S4

Printed in Canada

Dedication

Whenever I take my fishing and myself too seriously, my wife, Jan, is there to help me with perspective. The first time she saw me in my waders and fishing vest she laughed, as she did over the table conversation at her first fishing camp on Turneffe Island (Belize). She could not believe that grown men might sit around and pontificate on the relative advantages of a "Pink Puff" fly over a "Crazy Charlie." If my angling addiction comes up at a cocktail party, she is given to say something like: "My husband spends thousands of dollars to fly thousands of miles to stand in icy water to put feathers on a string to throw at a fish that he photographs and lets go." Ouch! Try saying something intelligible after that introduction.

I dedicate this book to Jan. When it came to my passion for fishing, she tried to care and even come along, but it didn't work. So she gave me the ultimate love offering of patience and understanding—she let me go. Jan did so because she understood that it is the freedom to pursue a passion that provides the best safety valve on sanity.

Contents

Crafting the Angler

For every serious angler there is a particular place that defines fishing, no matter how eclectic his subsequent tastes and experiences. It may be a river, lake or creek, an Atlantic or Pacific pier or even as minute as the juncture of a wayward riffle with a fallen log on a far bank under which lurked the 20-inch wild rainbow that initiated a lucky lad in the joys of real angling. The true north of my fishing compass is the Dean River in central coastal British Columbia. Over the last quarter century, I have made many an autumnal pilgrimage there.

Actually, my affair with the Dean began relatively late in life, in my mid-30s. Having grown up in the American West and been drawn to the mountains and deserts of my native Nevada, in my youth I was a serious fur trapper in winter and reptile collector in summer. Along the way I became a casual (as in inept) hunter and novice fly fisherman. At the age of 19, the fates plucked me from my beloved outdoor sojourns and solitude and plunked me down in the urban university settings of Madrid, Berkeley and Chicago before flinging me at the Spanish Basque Country. There, for two years, I conducted anthropological research into the causes and consequences of emigration from the villages of Echalar and Murelaga. Strangely enough, my vertiginous journey came full cycle when I was spewed out the other end of the academic mill and back into the nascent Desert Research Institute of my own hometown, charged with the task of founding a Basque Studies Program for DRI's Center for Western North American Studies. Like some befuddled and contrarian Martin Guerre, I was home from the Pyrenees.

The next few years were hectic. As antidote to the combined pressures of launching an embryonic professional career, along with program building, I felt certain stirrings. For several winters I dusted off (or, more accurately, derusted) the 150-odd steel traps in my parents' storage room and reenacted my youth. In summers I would occasionally slip off by myself after a particularly stressful day to fish the evening hatch at nearby Mogul on the Truckee River.

It was some years later when my brother John observed that, although we lived in the same town, we rarely saw one another. By then all three of my brothers were in the family casino business. I was the black sheep. John suggested that we institute an annual trip going off somewhere to spend a week together. It wasn't until much later, in 1980, that I was whitened by entering the casino business with them, so at the time I was supporting a growing family on an academic's modest recompense. Not to worry, my better-off kid brother would pick up the tab—choice of destination and activity was mine.

It was a head-scratcher since I'm not much for jet-setter excitement and would perish of apoplexy within 15 minutes left to my own devices on a beach (sans fishing rod, of course). But as a boy I had read of steelhead fishing in several outdoor magazines and filed away the thought of trying it one day. I knew that a schoolmate of mine was a regular steelheader on some Canadian river which turned out to be the Dean. It sounded all right to John, who was practically an angling virgin. The Dean was fully booked, but my friend also had contacts with a lodge on the Babine. By then my teaching duties had all but disappeared, and I was essentially a researcher and program administrator free to use my month of annual leave at any time. So, in mid-October we were off to Smithers and the Babine beyond.

In retrospect I am amazed, given that experience, that my casual interest in angling could have blossomed (or festered) into my current predicament. The Babine should have strangled my baby in its crib. It was so cold that our lines froze in the rod guides. The stream itself was fearsome, posing neophytes with a world-class wading challenge. By actual count as they passed through a weir there were fewer than one thousand steelhead in the river. So if the fishing was slow, the anticipation and dreaming were actually slower. Worst of all, we were in the midst of a classic territorial war (one that we shall revisit in these pages as endemic to today's sport fishing world). Our upstart outfitter, Bob Wickwire, was the former head guide of the pioneering operator ensconced a few miles upriver. The problem was the lack of sufficient fishable water for two eight-guest-per-week operations. This meant that we would arise a couple of hours before dawn each morning in order to beat the other camp to the best runs. After a terrifying boat ride in the dark, John and I would be left on some sandbar well before daylight with the admonition to protect our spot at all costs. It was important advice, since the crowded conditions meant we were destined to spend at least half the day on our beachhead.

As we huddled miserably over our pitiful matinal fire awaiting the beginning of the day's futility, I struggled with guilt over having gotten us into this mess. My mood was not improved when, one pre-dawn, on telling the outfitter that we were on vacation and preferred to sit around the lodge and drink coffee until the sun came out, I was ordered to the dock. "What do you think this is, a summer camp?" "No, Sir. Sorry, Sir. It is obviously of the boot variety!"

It was a long week in Camp Challenge, but not without its moments. We each hooked and then lost a small steelhead. Unlike John, I had spent the entire time fly fishing, an uncommon, though not unknown, technique for the steelheaders of the era in the early 1970s. I did so not out of any sense of elitism, but rather because I possessed neither the gear for, nor knowledge of, spin fishing.

Fishing a wet line, at one point I had a take that instantly conveyed the impossibility of my situation. I was working a short eddy paralleling a maelstrom of white water, and my quarry had but to move out into the current to render me helpless. It was over in about two minutes, leaving me nursing both bruised pride and knee that I had whacked against a boulder in my desperate scramble to follow my dream fish downstream.

My fish was free, but I was hooked. I resolved that one day the outcome would be different, a goal that was reinforced a day later when, standing waist deep in the icy water, I was visited by a phantasmagoria. In a grey dawn's dim light a massive, silver apparition rolled slowly beside me within reach of my rod tip. I was awestruck by the sight of the familiar rainbow trout swollen by a factor of 10.

By winter the memories of one grand tug and flitting glimpse of sheer magnificence had eclipsed the painful recollections of our Babinean daily ordeal. I was up for another steelhead trip, as was my surprisingly compliant brother. Miraculously, there were two slots available at the Dean. My nagging discomfort over being John's kept companion was also allayed. It seems that Canadian quarters and dimes fit his slot machines, but none of the local banks would handle the coin. Brokers went from casino to casino purchasing it at a 20 percent discount. For the next few years John and I would buy the Club Cal Neva's Canadian coin, load it into the trunk of my Volkswagen, drive the 600 or so miles from Reno to Olympia, Washington, in one day, completing the journey to Vancouver the next morning. ("Carrying any firearms, gentlemen?" "No, Sir, just money.") At noon a friend of John's would meet us with a cart in the alley behind his bank, and we lunched together while the coin was counted. It was then off to the Dean, expenses more or less covered.

As a professional purveyor of words, I have often tried to describe (not to mention photograph) the scenery in and around the Dean—but without much success. It is so spectacular and panoramic that attempting to capture its reality in mere utterances and partial images is to walk the razor's edge between understatement and hyperbole. Suffice it to say that Deanland is a mosaic of sheer cliffs, peaks and glaciers, fjords and forests, sparsely inhabited by commercial fishermen and loggers, some derived from the First Nations, others from British Canada and often with ties (recent or remote) to the British Isles themselves, spiced with a dash of "drop-out" Yanks from the lower 48. It is also a land of deer, moose, wolves, grizzly and black bears, mountain goats and bald eagles. In short, if a memorable place, for me the Dean transcends memory's capacity to store information. I seem to experience it anew with each visit's glimpse of sheer sublimity.

John and I made an annual trip to the Dean over the next several years and then became restless to try something new. So it was off to Alaska's Rainbow King Lodge on Lake Iliamna. Eventually, I entered the family business and as our lives at least in part coursed through the same channels, the near daily contacts undermined the need for our fraternal travel. John discovered golf and I saltwater fly fishing—our paths diverged.

After a few years of searching for the proverbial greener grass, my thoughts were turning back to the Dean. In those early years, though he was somewhat my junior, I had become reasonably close to Rob Stewart, owner of the Lower Dean River Lodge. One summer he and I were both undergoing divorces and bonded during many a long streamside conversation over the causes and ramifications of that particular life's failure. So after a silence of several years, I contacted him ("Sorry, Bill, filled up and with a long waiting list. Could you come on short notice as a substitute? Sometimes I get last minute cancellations. I mean maybe twenty-four hours notice. You'd have to drop everything").

Such was the dynamic of my next three trips to the Dean, a last-minute inclusion in three different parties. Then, in 1988, I received a call. It was May (Rob's season started in July) and through a miscommunication the entire second week of September, all nine rods, was available. Did I want them? It meant taking on the responsibility of group leader. John was game to come again and by then I had enough friends in the fishing world to fill the week easily, but I had also witnessed the sorrows of what it means to herd nine very-busy, self-centered cats. So John and I took two rods and Rob put together the rest of our group from his extensive waiting list.

Despite our diversity—a banker, lawyer, proctologist, ophthamologist, two medical professors, an anthropologist, gambler and a retired dentist—we got along famously. By the second year we were uniformed in T-shirts and caps proclaiming our brotherhood in the "Dean River Miscasts." While the group has evolved over time (John went back to golf), it holds together yet. In recent years I have controlled three rods during a prime week on what is arguably North America's premier steelhead stream.

Why have I dwelt upon one river and at such length? In part because it defined the Bill Angler in me. I am of the Dean; it looms large in my life. However, as we shall see, there are also many ways in which the Dean is larger than any one life, a place to experience and ponder virtually all of the complexities and controversies inherent in the world of sport fishing at this commencement of the new millenium. These include environmentalism versus development, elitism versus populism, artificial-lure angling versus bait fishing, the catch-and-release philosophy versus killing, Native-American rights versus everyone else's and private enterprise in the fishing industry versus government regulation of it—all played out within a scenario of high-drama triumph and tragedy.

But first there are different perambulations to consider, the contemplation of which may assist us to better appreciate the many lessons afforded by the Dean. For I would argue that to ignore or misunderstand them is a form of blindness that can only lead today's serious angler into the thicket of frustration and malaise. That would indeed be an ironic outcome of a "sport" that is supposedly designed for relaxation and recreation. In this era of "catch and release" it is critical to appreciate the many implications of the release. As an act it is about much more than simply returning fish alive to the water. Rather, it takes each of us through the looking glass and into our own private angling wonderland.

Floating on Friendship

*I*n 1987, Mikhail Gorbachev was engaged in the ultimately failed
attempt to reform the Communist world's political and economic systems without destroying the Soviet Empire. One evening I happened to
catch the tail end of a news broadcast that reported one of the many
symbolic gestures of the new Soviet attitude toward the West—a group
of fly fishermen were to be allowed to pursue Atlantic salmon somewhere in Russia.

Since I had missed the details, I called Mike Michalak at The Fly Shop
in Redding, California, to see if he'd heard about the opportunity. He had-
n't but said that it must be a Frontiers International initiative, since it was
the behemoth of the angling travel industry. Mike was right—but there
was a caveat. The trip was to be sold through silent auction. Any surplus over
Frontiers' costs was going to Trout Unlimited as a charitable donation.

Faced with the prospect of excessive bidding and possibly dashed
hopes, I demurred. Russia's Kola Peninsula has since become the world's
premier destination for Atlantic salmon fishing, but as it turned out that
first trip was an unmitigated disaster. The luckless "winners" were not

taken to the Kola but were instead left pretty much to their own devices for a week on an immense Arctic river where they hardly caught a thing.

About a year later I received a call from Frontiers. I was in the inquiries file for the Russian trip and the agent wanted to send me literature on an upcoming angling exploratory to northern China. It was also to be a diplomatic mission since our leader would be negotiating the conditions under which Chinese officials might permit Western anglers to enter their country in the future. Was this to be another silent auction? No. I didn't need to see the literature; I reserved my slot on the spot.

I wrote of our adventure in November 1988, several months before the tragic events at Tiananmen Square sidetracked China's aperture to the world. To my knowledge, our group was not only the first to fish China, but to date the last.

Day 1. The waters of the remote Zhan River of northeast China's Heilongjiang province were high and murky as we launched our 10 rubber rafts. Children ran along the banks shouting encouragement, and wives waved farewell to their husbands. Our flotilla consisted of six American rafters and a support staff of 25 made up of three provincial officials, 10 oarsmen, four camptenders, two cooks, two medical doctors, three interpreters and a cameraman. A veteran of float trips in the American West, in which I shared a boat with my guide and maybe one other angler, I was somewhat unnerved by the hoopla.

Before us lay a five-day, 100-mile journey through one of the last remaining wilderness areas of the world's most populous nation. As we passed the point of no return, a sense of trepidation replaced the exhilaration I had felt since securing a place on Frontiers International's inaugural float trip down the Zhan. My apprehension was heightened when Li Qing Hua, deputy director of the Zhan'he Forest Bureau, delivered a streamside lecture on the importance of water safety given the swollen condition of the river. We were assured that our Chinese military rafts were designed to hold 12. However, they seemed filled to capacity, if not downright overloaded, when carrying two passengers, an interpreter, oarsman and gear.

The Americans included Bob and Virginia Scott, from Chimacun, Washington, who, like myself, were simply paying guests in search of a truly unusual fly-fishing experience. A second raft carried Charlie Gaddy, news anchorman from television station WRAL of Raleigh, North Carolina, and his photographer Scott Miskimon. While they intended to film the float trip, it was but a part of a planned half-hour documentary on a region of China virtually unvisited by Westerners. My raft mate was Tom Earnhardt, a 42-year-old law professor at North Carolina Central University and vice chairman of Trout Unlimited's Committee for International Affairs.

We first met Tom several days earlier in the Garden Villas Hotel of Harbin, capital of Heilongjiang (or "Black Dragon River") province. While our group spent its first two days in China doing the mandatory tours of Beijing's Forbidden City, the Ming tombs and the Great Wall at Badaling, Tom had preceded us to Harbin in order to perfect the details of an agreement between Heilongjiang authorities and Trout Unlimited.

The Garden Villas Hotel was largely reserved for official functions and delegations, and we shared it with representatives of the Communist Party who were in Harbin for a regional meeting. Tom bounded out of the entrance, his bald pate covered, despite it being a sunny June day in the mid-80s, by a cap purchased that morning from a local furrier. Amid effusive accounts of his visits to a day-care center, where the excited children greeted him with songs in English, and his impressions of the daily t'ai chi exercises performed by hundreds of middle-aged early risers in a nearby park, he informed us that there was to be an official ceremony that evening to sign the agreement. So we went on a quick tour of the city.

Over the past century the needle of the political compass has swung wildly in the Manchuria/Siberia region. In the 1890s Russia gained a forced concession from a weakened China that permitted it to build Manchuria's first railroad. This ultimately had the effect of converting Harbin from a fishing village into a major city. After the Bolshevik Revolution many defeated White Russians took refuge there. By the 1920s a quarter of the population was non-Chinese, and Harbin was the largest Russian city outside the Soviet Union. This is evident today in the city's many Western-style buildings and onion-domed churches.

In 1945 the Russian army invaded Manchuria to expel the Japanese. There are two war monuments in Harbin erected to the liberators by a grateful Manchuria. After Mao's victory in 1949, Russian technicians began a decade of intense activity in the city that provided much of its current industrial base. However, Khrushchev's denunciation of Stalin, over Mao's objections, ushered in an Asian cold war. This, more than the triumph of Chinese Communism, frightened Harbin's established Russians. Throughout the 1960s many fled to places like Australia, Canada and San Francisco. Today the city is all but devoid of Russian influence.

Tom's stay in China had been a flurry of meetings with officials in Beijing and Harbin. Armed with a letter of support from President Jimmy Carter, he was both pioneer and point person in the introduction of fly fishing into the country. While the Chinese were obviously interested in the tourism, they were intrigued by the sport itself. Tom had given several slide lectures on stream ecology to forestry and fisheries personnel as well as exhibitions of fly-tying techniques. In September he was to travel to Moscow to pursue a similar initiative in the Soviet Union and was already scheduled to give a fly-casting demonstration in Red Square. He apologized for the panoply of camera gear and 100 rolls of film strewn across both beds of our shared room, noting that he hoped to publish an illustrated book on his experiences in China and Russia, which had the working title *Fishing Forbidden Waters*.

Lapsing into the shop talk of fellow anglers, he raised the temperature of my fishing fever by recounting his conversations with the local experts. Until now, in pursuing my fishing passion in remote corners of the globe, the settings were often exotic but the quarry was not. It consisted of rainbow and brown trout often transplanted from their North American and European native habitats. Such was not the case in China. We were to fish for the lenok, a species of Asian char that is similar in coloration to the rainbow trout but with a slightly humped shoulder and underslung mouth. Large specimens surpass the 24-inch, six-pound range, a nice trophy by any angler's reckoning. There was also the Amur pike, similar to his North American and European cousins in size but said to be a more powerful fighter. The premier attraction, however, was the Siberian taimen, a little-understood salmonid ranging from central Europe to the Pacific. Tom had the translation of a taimen article, published in Czechoslovakian, that reported specimens from the Soviet Union in the 200-pound range! Frontiers International had been unsure as to whether they were indigenous to the Zhan; that morning Tom had been shown a preserved specimen that came from the river. Should one of us catch a taimen it might automatically become the world's fly-fishing record since, so far as we knew, the species had never before been caught on a fly.

Li's admonitions quickly proved prophetic when about two hours into the float one of the supply rafts attempted to negotiate a nasty side channel, capsized and was jammed against the rocks. It was too late for the Scotts' oarsman to change course, and they rammed the half-submerged craft, nearly catapulting Virginia into the water. Charlie and Scott were barely able to avoid disaster as well. Fortunately, no one was injured. We had, however, lost two of our tents and some of our food supply, including most of that night's dinner.

Shortly before lunch, applause rippled through the flotilla as the news went out over our walkie-talkie network that Bob Scott had caught a fish. He had been casting a dry fly and took a small grayling on the surface, a feat that Virginia would duplicate during our streamside lunch break. Meanwhile, Tom and I were experimenting futilely with several combinations of line weights, leader lengths and wet-fly patterns. Our initial speculation that the denizens of this wilderness fishery were unlikely to be wary had given way to growing concern that this would be no easy challenge.

We were also becoming conscious of performance pressure from several directions. Whenever we stopped to cast at a particularly promising riffle, the young oarsmen and camptenders gathered excitedly to watch the "pros from Dover." One can only surmise what must have been going through their minds as they contemplated the spectacle. Bedecked in chest-high waders and ungainly felt-bottomed wading shoes, and wearing fishing vests festooned with such gadgets as tape measure, leader clipper, cutting tool and wool patch ornamented with gaudy flies, we might just as well have been medieval knights or moonmen.

The Chinese organizers of the expedition were becoming increasingly anxious over our lack of success. The fear that poor fishing might abort the U.S.-Chinese initiative was palpable. Statements that we were enjoying ourselves and welcomed the challenge posed by the enigmatic fish were received politely but with obvious disbelief. Our concerned interlocuters suggested we add a frog or worm to our flies, insisting that the Zhan River fish had never seen an artificial fly before! Then there were poor Charlie and Scott, finally floating down the Zhan after undergoing the enormous hassle of sending a thousand pounds of gear halfway around the world to record our triumphs. It had never really occurred to anyone that the fishing might fail to measure up.

After lunch Tom began fishing less frequently and finally stopped altogether. By late afternoon he was plagued with fever, stomach cramps and diarrhea. We reached our first camp shortly before dusk, having floated the river for 12 hours. The four netted sleeping tents and separate dining one were a welcome sight, given that the evening air was filled with hordes of mosquitoes. At first our hosts insisted that there be two Americans to a tent, leaving the remaining 25 Chinese a single one to protect them from the insects and elements. After a hasty caucus, we communicated that Charlie, Scott, Tom and I would prefer to share a tent. Word came back that it was unnecessary, but that our kind offer was accepted.

All in all we were rather bedraggled. The marathon float had left us bone-weary, Tom had retired without supper, and my duffel bag had been soaked through. I scattered my sopped clothing over some willows, knowing that it would dry but little in the moist night air. About midnight we were awakened by flashing lights, shouts and the sound of sloshing legs and hooves beating on river cobbles. Two men forded the stream on magnificent gray horses accompanied by a pack of large dogs. The father and son, deer farmers somewhere in the forest fastness, had found much of our missing equipment (including the tents) strewn along the riverbank and were returning it.

Day 2. After a bad night, Tom was anxious to get off the river even if it meant sending out for horses. The best option, however, was for him to continue on until the morning of the third day. It was then that we were to intersect a narrow-gauge railway trestle where a train would resupply our expedition. Our raft was outfitted with a canopy to shield Tom from the sun. Since he would need to stretch out, I joined our main host, Han Dequan, director of the Planning Division of the Heilongjiang Tourism Bureau. Robert Yu, our 23-year-old interpreter, remained with Tom.

We first met "Rockefeller," as Robert Yu introduced himself, in Beijing. An employee of Harbin's New Trend Travel Agency, he had traveled there to help us through customs and serve as a backup guide while we toured the city and environs. He deferred to our efficient hostess, Chen Li, while quietly assuring me that things would be much better when we got to Manchuria. It seems the women there were prettier and wore brighter clothing, and the beer was better and more plentiful.

I sat with him on the flight north, and he explained his nickname. While his westernized moniker was Robert, he was actually Yu Zai Fu, which translates into "man in happiness." He reasoned that such a person would be a "lucky fellow," who might easily then become "Rockefeller." His best friend and colleague, who would also serve as interpreter on our river trip, was "Churchill," derived from his name Qiu Gang. Qiu comes from the

Chinese character for Confucianism, which represents "religion" or "church," while Gang means "hill."

Rockefeller was reading a book on the thought of Zhuang Zhi, an ancient Chinese philosopher who lived to be a centenarian by eschewing the pursuit of wealth and reputation. Central to his philosophy was the importance of being open and generous with everyone while always looking on the bright side. The sage illustrated how to remain under control in stressful situations with the example of a butcher who never broke or dulled a blade because, whenever he struck bone, he became calm and detached, and the task then completed itself.

Robert showed me how to write several Chinese *han zi* characters, which I promptly forgot while complaining about my shoddy memory. A few days later, as we traveled by train from Harbin to Bei'an, he produced three metal balls from his pocket, a gift from Churchill, and demonstrated how to roll them in sequence between fingers and palm. "Bill, this is very good for your memory; it also brings luck and makes you less nervous before speaking in public."

The fishing seemed to be taking a turn for the better when, after only a few casts, a small lenok took my black Wooly Bugger. It was one of the rare occasions during the trip when we were out of sight of other rafts. Han Dequan was pleased as he photographed my prize; and then perplexed when I released it. No matter, since the ice seemed broken and the joyful news flashed out over the radio. Scott appeared and, balancing bulky television camera precariously on his shoulder, waded out into the stream to film my casts as I tried in vain to duplicate the feat. While we did not know it at the time, I had caught our last fish!

After another marathon float we arrived at camp, once again just before dusk. To my chagrin, my gear had received a second thorough soaking and my clothes were beginning to mildew. I wrung them out and spread them on the bank before squeezing my 6'2" frame into a 5' sleeping bag. As I drifted off, I was aware of the patter of raindrops on canvas, too weary to do anything about my luckless laundry.

Day 3. We met our supply train on schedule. Actually, it was a single, diesel-powered car. Tom, Rockefeller and one of the doctors left the group for the eventful trip out. It seems that the pistons in the engine kept locking up. Only by cooling them for awhile and then banging with a wrench on the casing were they able to continue. At one point several men were spotted lying across the tracks in the distance. The agitated engineer, suspicious of their intentions, fired a rifle in the air to scatter them. It was bandit country.

Despite our first day's experience with the capsized boat, the Zhan was scarcely proving to be a dangerous river to float. Periodically, we encountered a short stretch of rather tame rapids linking together deep, placid runs that were as much as a kilometer in length. Indeed, the most tedious task for our oarsmen was working through the excruciatingly slow-moving stretches. The one exception was the morning of the third day when we entered a series of canyons flanked by sheer bluffs. Here the rapids were longer and closer together, though hardly of the sort to attract white-water enthusiasts.

The countryside was laced with gently rolling hills that were much more reminiscent of Appalachia than the more rugged landscape of the Rockies or Sierra Nevada mountains of the American West. The forest was an appealing blend of stands of conifers interspersed with white birch and willows. A mantle of wildflowers provided relief from the various shades of green. Particularly lovely was a type of yellow day lily that seemed to grow exclusively in the crevices of the otherwise barren 200-foot rock bluffs flanking the river. We were seldom out of earshot of the quizzical coo of wild cuckoos.

That morning our lead raft had spotted two black bears, a sow and cub, crossing the river. The sand bars revealed the tracks of red and roe deer, moose and wild boar. However, with the exception of an occasional raptor and the many families of merganser ducks that scattered in fear before us, we failed to see wildlife.

The tranquility of the Zhan wilderness seemed a curious contrast to the bustle of a nation in evident transformation. From Beijing to the smallest hamlet, China pulsated with activity. The cities were a maze of construction cranes, each nourishing the chrysalis of an emerging, multistory apartment building. Every village was cluttered with ant hills of red brick for the new, one-story houses that were replacing their mud-and-straw-walled, thatched-roof predecessors. Revamping the housing infrastructure of a gigantic population was a national priority.

The housing issue is but a reflection of broader social and economic concerns. Particularly relevant was the quota limiting reproduction that allowed each family to have but one child. The subject recurred in many guises throughout our stay. While all our hosts recognized the need to curb population growth if the nation and its individual families were to prosper, there was concern with the consequences. What would happen two generations hence when inversion of the age pyramid could theoretically give each young adult two aging parents and four elderly grandparents to support? What were the long-term psychological costs of the "little emperor" complex? Proud parents doting upon their sole offspring (preferably male) raised the prospect of one day having to turn the nation over to a generation of spoiled brats. Then there was the problem of enforcement, particularly if a family's first born was female or handicapped—infanticide and abandonment were real issues.

Access to suitable housing, more than employment, was the determining factor in obtaining permission to marry. Rockefeller hoped to wed next fall. Currently, he resided in a dormitory sharing a sleeping room with another single man and taking his meals at the cafeteria operated by New Trend Travel Agency. He was awaiting his employer's success in acquiring one of the 20 percent of the apartments in new government-sponsored housing developments that are made available for purchase by individuals and agencies.

New Trend's foray into the housing market is itself indicative of the growing complexity of China's economy. It is clearly an oversimplification to frame the issue solely in terms of the privatization of some sectors of a previously state-controlled system. To be sure, there is greater emphasis upon private initiative, particularly in the countryside, where farmers can now market their produce directly. Some are said to make as much as 10,000 yuan a year, with a few fabulous success stories in the 100,000-yuan range (versus the average salary of about 150 yuan monthly for urban professionals). China, therefore, may be the only country on a planet beset by rural exodus where there is considerable incentive to remain in agriculture. Indeed, the government recently expressed its exasperation over the fact that in one region as many as 15 million children have been pulled out of school by their parents in order to utilize their labor in farming.

For China's urban masses, the trend toward privatization is more difficult. As Chen Li noted, "You can give a farmer a field, but you cannot give a factory worker his own machine." To be sure, in the cities there is much evidence of small-scale enterprise. A plethora of street vendors, oftentimes flanking government-owned department stores, sell everything imaginable. Restaurants are all but completely individually owned. However, for most urban Chinese, personal advancement is linked to the collective fate of a particular factory or agency.

New Trend Travel Agency falls somewhere between private and public initiative. Ultimately owned by the government, it in turn has its own enterprises such as a hotel and cab company in Harbin. It both cooperates and competes with the other government travel agencies throughout the nation. It maintains a patronal posture with respect to its own employees (witness Rockefeller's housing problem), and provides them with bonus pay for overtime and travel assignments outside the city.

The process of change is, as one might expect, beset with many anomalies. The point is illustrated by Churchill's recent history. A bright young man of 21, he failed the science part of his university entry exam, then went to work on the assembly line in a Harbin ballbearing plant, a factory directed by his father. Using his considerable skills in English, he recently landed a job with New Trend where he earns about 100 yuan per month plus bonuses. By working evenings and weekends whenever other Harbin factories and agencies require English translation, he increases his monthly income to as much as 400 yuan. In contrast, his father's base salary as head of the ballbearing factory is but 160 yuan! It is to such paradoxes that Deng Xiaoping surely referred when he noted that restructuring of the economy would continue despite the risks.

By late afternoon the sunny weather on the Zhan retreated before the ominous thunderheads that lined the horizon. A strong wind began to blow upriver, making the progress of our overly buoyant craft painfully slow. Thunder and lightning coincided with our arrival in camp. The intensifying wind threatened to rip our tents from their moorings. As we huddled in them, whole tree trunks snapped and panicked voices shouted at us to get out. I cleared the flap and was struck by flying pine cones and broken branches. Thirty feet away there was a freshly downed pine tree that had narrowly missed squashing us. Others swayed erratically in the maelstrom, threatening to rectify the error. The crew dismantled camp and moved the tents nearer to the water's edge, completing the task just before a torrential cloudburst. As we lay in the gloom, speculating on our future fate, Charlie shared his survival kit—a small bottle of Scotch brought all the way from North Carolina.

Day 4. The dawn was cool and drizzly. Despite the weather I removed a pair of levis and change of underwear from my soggy bags in the hope of drying at least one change of clothing during the day's float. I continued to share Han's raft sans interpreter. By the second day we had worked out a rudimentary system of communication consisting largely of sign language. When the breeze picked up in early afternoon, I pointed at the sky, blew a puff of air and said, "wind." Han laughed and made a wavy motion with his hand while saying, *feng da*. He then held up a leaf to show me a gaudy creature. I responded to his quizzical expression and soon he was repeating his new English word, "chaterpilla."

I first met Han Dequan at the signing ceremony in Harbin's Garden Villas Hotel. Under the agreement, Heilongjiang province was to admit American fly fishermen to its waters. In return Trout Unlimited would establish a fund financed by a $100 fee paid by each visiting angler to be used to bring Chinese fisheries biologists to the United States to participate in conferences. Trout Unlimited was also committed to providing the Chinese authorities with technical expertise when requested. Both Tom and Han had heralded the agreement as an historic event, while noting that it was but a small beginning.

We had then retired to a banquet room where we enjoyed the first of the many official dinners that awaited us at each stage of our journey. The lazy susan in the center of our round table was loaded with hors d'oeuvres, which were then replaced with a series of hot dishes. I stopped counting at 15. Rice was served only as the penultimate dish, and a wonton soup signaled the end of the meal. The beverages included sweet wine, beer, orange soda, mineral water and a thimble-sized shot of pure alcohol that we Americans quickly labeled "white lightning." Periodically, one of the several Chinese officials stood and made a short speech. He would then raise his shot glass and say *gan bei* or "bottoms up." Courtesy dictated that we respond in kind. It quickly became apparent that the number of potential toasts far exceeded our capacity to survive them. It was then that I noticed that the two young officials flanking me would only wet their lips rather than actually downing the libation. I resorted to the ploy on the next round, only to have them point at my glass while insisting upon gan bei. When I declined with, "I am learning from my neighbors," there was much good-natured laughter.

The next morning Han led our party to the Harbin railway station for the day-long journey northward to the Zhan'he Forestry Bureau, the kickoff point for our foray down the Zhan River. We negotiated the sea of humanity in the main waiting room and were ushered into a quiet, elegant hall with tea service and easy chairs. There was a profusion of apologies over the fact that our train was

10 minutes late, an example of the Chinese fixation, even obsession, with punctuality.

Compared to the average American or European railyard, the Harbin counterpart is a living, pulsating being. China is almost devoid of paved highways, so the rail lines are its arteries and veins. Heilongjiang has been designated the repository of the country's steam engine rolling stock as the national system is upgraded to diesel and electric. Consequently, the province has more than one thousand steam locomotives of various vintages and nationalities, and one is tempted to characterize the Harbin facility as a vast, open-air railroad museum. However conceived, Heilongjiang is a railroad buff's delight, populated by the originators of "huffing and puffing," which are more like antediluvian monsters than machines.

Han Dequan is a wiry, 58-year-old, with strength and stamina far beyond his small stature. A widower, he lives in Harbin with one of his married sons, having relinquished his claim to housing after his wife's death so that the son could marry. He is currently responsible for developing new initiatives for Heilongjiang tourism, hence his presence on our inaugural float trip, after which he was to lead visiting Frenchmen on a ten-day horseback ride through the Greater Khingan Mountains.

At the conclusion of our float, Han and I shared a seat on the train trip back from Bei'an to Harbin. Jin Zhiyong, Deputy Director of New Trend, served as our interpreter while both asked me details about fly-fishing techniques. Jin wanted to write an article about it for local anglers, while Han was concerned about improving the trip for future American guests. We had become much closer than our language handicap should have allowed and had exchanged and accepted mutual invitations. I was to return to China to explore and fish other Heilongjiang waters with them; they were due to travel to the States and would be my guest while in San Francisco and Reno.

Han and I went to the dining car with Churchill as our interpreter. I had been reticent to ask him a question that was foremost on my mind. Earlier in the trip Jin had recounted to me his experiences during the Cultural Revolution. He was a young man at the time and was sent to a rural commune where he had worked for 20 years. While there he had managed to learn much of his superb English by listening secretly to Voice of America radio broadcasts. He noted that the Cultural Revolution cost him the opportunity to go to college, but did not really damage him otherwise, unlike Han Dequan.

With our time together running out, I had finally decided to ask Han about his past. He seemed to welcome the question. Part of the only 4 percent of the Chinese population enrolled in the Communist Party, Han had been a member for 42 years. As a lad he revered Mao Zedong, joined the army, and was assigned to the cultural corps charged with providing entertainment to the troops during the last phase of the war against Chiang Kai-Shek. Discharged in 1951, he returned to his native Harbin. By his late 30s he headed the city's Workers' Palace (a huge cultural and sports complex of theaters, lecture halls, dance studios, and exercise facilities), and also directed Heilongjiang's athletic programs.

At the outset of the Cultural Revolution, he was arrested, along with all officials of his rank, and accused of "many hats" (i.e. crimes). He was asked to denounce others and confess to his own sins of Marxist revisionism, imperialism and capitalism. He was sent to a rural commune 150 miles from Harbin where he was a manual laborer for 18 months, denied all contact with his wife and children. Deemed rehabilitated, Han was allowed to return to Harbin, where he held odd jobs for a short time before being sent back to the countryside for another two-year stint, this time with his family. In a deliberate tone that was surprisingly calm and even gentle, he said,

"I was never afraid of my accusers or the manual labor. What hurt me most was the fact that Chairman Mao believed that we had refuted him. It was not true; we revered Mao and I still love him. But he made an historic mistake. China could not withdraw from the rest of the world. Deng Xiaoping understands this better. I see no real opposition to his program, although some officials find it more difficult to adjust as quickly as others. I do not think that another Cultural Revolution is possible. I am not really bitter about what happened to me, but I prefer not to think about it as the memory is painful. Mostly, I regret having lost time when I should have been improving myself, becoming more skilled in my profession."

Day 5. This was to be our shortest float, since we would reach the village of Xing'e, where we were to leave the river, by early afternoon. The temperature had dropped sharply and the overcast sky periodically spewed sheets of rain. Each day the Zhan had grown in size and volume and was becoming less appealing for fly fishing. There was a consensus that we strike out directly for Xing'e.

We had been scheduled to camp on its outskirts. Given the weather, however, Han had left before breakfast to make arrangements for us to stay with families that evening. I had his oarsman to myself, and the mood was festive as we floated in tandem with four of the camp-gear rafts. The young crew pulsated with the excitement and impatience of young colts who, after an arduous ride, begin to sense their home stable. Jars of pickled meat and smoked fish, chunks of bread, pieces of fruit and cans of beer flew from raft to raft as we depleted the remaining food stores.

They began to sing and urged me to do so. At a loss for more than a few lines of an English song, I sang three verses of a Basque ballad that I had learned years ago while doing anthropological field work in the Pyrenees. As my listeners shouted encouragement, I thought of the story once told to me by a Basque sheepherder in the American West. He had spent his first winter near a town in southern Idaho and decided to learn English by eating all of his dinners in a small local restaurant in order to talk to the proprietor. It took him a few months to realize that it was a Chinese establishment and his teacher knew no English!

Two hundred of Xing'e's 500 inhabitants are Orochen, a hunting people who are more closely related to the Eskimos or Aleuts than to Han Chinese. There are presently 4,900 Orochen in China and an additional 15,000 in the Soviet Union. We had been floating through their traditional hunting territory. Until the Chinese revolution in 1949, they were nomads who lived year round in bark and hide tents. Beginning in the early 1950s, they were settled by the government in communes on the fringes of the forest. Their circumstances today are not unlike those of North American native peoples living on reservations. The Orochen are given special hunting and fishing privileges, and about 30 Xing'e men still spend three or four months a year hunting in the Zhan forest.

The Orochen receive free housing, education and medical care, unlike the wider population, which pays for such services. They are permitted to have three children per family and an effort is being made to preserve their language and customs. A non-Orochen who marries one is thereby subject to the group's traditional law, rather than the Chinese civil code, in some matters. The Orochen language has no written form, and most speakers are now bilingual in Mandarin. They retain great respect for elders, particularly storytellers, who recite in rhyme Orochen tradition. The older generations continue to rely upon shamans for medical care and advice.

We arrived in Xing'e in the midst of a cloudburst and were taken in jeeps to the town hall. There, two attractive young women, dressed in the colorful, full-length smocks that are traditional Orochen costume, served us tea. Once the rain stopped we went outside for a formal welcome. Five horsemen rode into the village dressed in yellow, blue and purple smocks. As they approached each fired a rifle into the air as a greeting. Their saddles were made of wood covered with bearskin, and their heavy stirrups were of bronze.

Charlie, Scott and I were to sleep in the house of Mr. Du, an

Orochen hunter in his mid-fifties. His home was typical of the new brick housing we had encountered everywhere in rural Heilongjiang. It consisted of a small bedroom, a kitchen with pump from a well under the house, and a fairly expansive living room. There was a unit along one wall with several shelves and niches displaying glassware, crockery and family photos. It also held the color television set and huge radio/cassette player that seem to be the ubiquitous status symbols throughout the nation. The most unique feature was the huge sleeping platform that could easily accommodate four or five persons and took up about a third of the living room. It was made of cement, covered with a thin mat, and was hollow so that coals could be shoved under it through holes in the kitchen wall, presumably as protection for sleepers against the area's minus-40-degree winter nights. The entry to the house was guarded by a feisty hen and her brood of chicks. The backyard was a vegetable garden, woodpile and outhouse.

As we unpacked in the early afternoon, Mr. Du answered our questions about Xing'e. He was waiting for the rain to stop so he could go hunting. He planned to spend several months in the forest without returning, although he admitted that he really didn't have to any longer since he lived with his son and daughter-in-law. They made a good living from farming, but he was still a hunter at heart.

Mr. Du had two treasures that he insisted on showing us. He went into the small bedroom and returned with a pan of water, a rock and a set of antlers. He had found the rock (pumice stone) in the forest and demonstrated its miraculous ability to float. No one else in Xing'e had one. He then fondled the roe deer antlers, which were in velvet. He noted that they were very valuable and a rarity (in a country where horn is ground to powder and sold for medicinal purposes).

Later we returned from a walk to find Mr. Du sitting with his antlers. He approached Charlie, our silver-haired elder, and said, "This is my treasure and I want you to show it to your neighbors in North Carolina. It is important that our countries be at peace. We are all just human beings." He was choked with emotion, and they embraced. Mr. Du abruptly left the house. We never saw him again.

That evening we were given a banquet consisting of moose, the stalks of fiddler ferns (tender and tangy) and lenok. When we returned to our residence, the family had gone elsewhere for the evening, but the sleeping platform radiated heat. About two in the morning, as it began to cool, there was stirring in the kitchen. Someone had entered the house to replenish our dying embers.

The next morning we mounted jeeps to begin a lengthy drive to the city of Hei'he on the Amur (Heilongjiang) River, the *de facto* though disputed border between China and the Soviet Union. The puddled potholes of the rural track gradually gave way to a graveled roadway. We were able to transfer to a van whose driver then subjected us to the only fear that we experienced in China. Until we simultaneously erupted in full-fledged mutiny after nearly cracking our heads on the ceiling during a particularly violent jolt, he insisted upon driving about 50 miles an hour on the essentially one-lane, rutted road that was raised six feet above the marshy countryside. He seemed to delight in scattering pedestrians, terrorizing cyclists and challenging the many trucks and buses contesting his supreme right of way. The Friendship Hotel in Hei'he was a most welcome sight.

That afternoon we rested before beginning the long journey back to Beijing. Han and Jin led us to the riverbank where they commandeered a large vessel for a short cruise. Scott was upset when told that he could not take his video camera aboard. It seems that we would be under close scrutiny and could easily become an agenda item in the tense discussions held periodically between the local Chinese and Russian officials.

The two banks viewed through binoculars from our boat deck in the center of the river were a study in contrast. On the Chinese side there was the city of Hei'he, with its 60,000 inhabitants. Its dirt streets, ramshackle hovels and unfinished apartment buildings gave it a frontier air. The Russian city of Blagoveshchensk, with about 200,000 residents, seemed stately and modern by comparison. We could discern the city square with its public buildings and theater, tree-lined walkways in the riverside park where women walked babies in strollers and young girls in bikinis sunned themselves on the beaches. A Russian hydrofoil exploded past us and we exchanged gestured greetings with its passengers. The soldiers manning the guard towers on the picket of vessels anchored along the Russian shore with guns pointed at China were less friendly. Whenever we locked magnified eyes with them through our respective binoculars, they were oblivious to our wave or simply turned away.

Jin noted that there were negotiations afoot to permit an exchange of day-trip tourists. He was hopeful that they might be concluded within the year. However, they were being played out against the backdrop of contention over islands in the Amur/Heilongjiang River and the larger issue of China's historical claim to a part of Siberia as Greater Manchuria.

When we finally arrived back in Beijing, we found Tom Earnhardt, his illness over, waiting for us in the Shangri-La Hotel. His unscheduled efforts to make it all the way home to Raleigh as quickly as possible had foundered to the point that he had reached Beijing just two days before us. The eve of our departure he had concluded the agreement between Trout Unlimited and Chinese national officials.

I filled him in on the details of our fishing failure while vowing that I was determined to return soon to continue my pursuit of the mysterious taimen. He then related a tale that made that quarry pale in significance. Beijing officials had told him, in all seriousness, of a mighty beast in certain Inner Mongolian lakes. Called a "red fish" by the natives, it was greatly feared and had never been caught. Last year one scientist had seen one thrashing about in the shallows and estimated its length at 16 feet and its weight at 2200 pounds. Remember, you read it here first!

Taimen II

We had just finished supper and were slipping into the inevitable round of fishing stories that dominate table talk at any gathering of hard-core anglers. The evening was surprisingly cool and bugless given the setting, a tent camp on the Taperá River in the Rio Branco branch of the Brazilian Amazon. If the magnificent peacock bass was our immediate quarry, all eight of us were suddenly transported to northern climes half a world away. Jeff Vermillion, our trip host, spread before us colored photocopies of an enormous taimen caught the summer before while fishing in Mongolia with his physician father and two other Americans.

"What's a taimen?" was the question on everyone's lips but mine.

Jeff and I were tent mates and as we awaited our fast-impending rendezvous with slumber his voice in the darkness outlined plans to return to northern Mongolia the following summer to further his explorations of the Eg and Uur rivers, part of a drainage that eventually feeds Russia's enormous Lake Baikal. He'd initially heard about the area, and its fabulous taimen, from two friends assigned by the United Nations to assist Mongolia with development of Lake Hubsgol National Park in the northern part of the country. Frontiers International had given him a qualified promise to market his Mongolian program a year later, the conditions being that he solidify his land arrangements and that he take at least two other groups of anglers to the site to further prove up the resource. On that January evening I committed to being part of the first contingent. I would be charged Jeff's cost—to be determined.

Jan was crying as I packed. "Why Mongolia? It's so far! Anything could happen to you!" I fumbled with clichés like "in this day and age no place is very far," but I was harboring my own concerns over flying on probably poorly maintained, dilapidated Russian aircraft. And then, of course, there was the cholera epidemic. I had just heard a news report to the effect that China was considering embargoing flights to Mongolia and quarantining passengers from there. Jan was unaware of it, and I had "forgotten" to tell her.

The trip from Reno to Beijing was not idyllic. From Seattle I had a gruesome red-eye on South China Air that didn't even depart until 3 a.m. Just staying awake in the air terminal was a real challenge. There was no preassigned seating, so I had ended up in the middle of a center row which featured even less leg room for my gangly 6'-2" frame than that afforded in coach by the sadistic larger carriers. It took tranquilizers to keep my claustrophobic panic from converting me into a skyjacker!

Nor was there relief in Beijing. The crush of humanity in its airport made every move reminiscent of rush hour on the New York subway. In-transit passengers were not exempted from the departure tax payable only in yuan. Thus, it was necessary to stand in interminable lines first to buy a few yuan, then to pay the extortion and finally to clear security. During this last exercise a young woman slapped a small padlock onto my bag (without asking) and then demanded 20 yuan (which I didn't have) for it. She refused me the key until I forked over a ten-dollar bill. Even the crowded waiting room for the Ulan Bator flight, though festooned with erect, seated and reposed bodies, was a welcome refuge.

It was there that I met up with my fellow travelers, Jeff's mom and brother. Margaret is a redoubtable New Englander transposed to Billings, Montana, where she taught high-school Spanish until her recent retirement. Dan had just taken his bar exam (he still didn't know the result) after completing his law studies at the University of Montana. Our trip was a graduation present and kind of last hurrah before he was to settle into a professional career.

Dan was 28 years old and Jeff 26. Despite their youth they had a wealth of life and angling experience behind them. Dan had guided for a couple of years at Hubbard's Yellowstone Lodge. Margaret had prepared her brood well for the international encounters. During his secondary schooling he had spent a year as an exchange student in Cochabamba, Bolivia. His fluency in Spanish made it possible for him to guide for Jorge Trucco two years in Argentina. Frontiers International then made him their manager at Manaka Lodge in Venezuela. From there it was off to Russia's Kola Peninsula to guide for two years at the company's Ponoi River operation.

Younger brother Jeff had even more guiding experience. As a high schooler he too spent a year in Latin America as an exchange student in Chile. While a collegian at the University of Kansas, he put in another year abroad at the School for International Training's campus near Belem, Brazil. As a Latin American Studies major, he traveled parts of the Amazon Basin researching his thesis, which dealt with the survival rates of specimens captured for the tropical fish trade. He then began dividing his time as a fishing guide between Alaska in the summer (five seasons) and Latin America in the winter. He worked for Dan at Manaka Lodge one year and then four years for Luis Brown's River Plate Anglers' operation in the Rio Negro branch of the Amazon drainage. It was a destination booked by Frontiers, and Jeff served as its camp host for the largely anglophone clientele. He went on to guide for four years on the Ponoi as well.

Our Ulan Bator flight from Beijing had not been cancelled. Jeff had telephoned Margaret the day before with the information that the cholera epidemic was not a problem in the north—our intended destination. When our plane to Mongolia was called, the scramble (again no seat assignments) resembled preparations of the circus act in which a tiny auto disgorges 10 clowns. We then sat sweltering on the tarmac for half an hour awaiting what turned out to be some kind of mucky muck who was driven in his limousine right up to the idled aircraft. Finally, we were aloft on the wings of Air Mongolia for the three-hour flight.

Ulan Bator should be preserved in amber as a monument to the worst foibles and follies of Sovietism. After deplaning in a half-finished, yet already anachronistic, air terminal, the trip into the city itself was fascinating and depressing, over a vast plain that, to the naked eye, seems to be covered by far more animals (sheep, goats, cows, horses and even the occasional yak) than blades of grass. The fringe of the capital is a grid of unpaved roads stitching together the small animal compounds of the intrepid herders who venture out with their charges onto the devastated pasture. The dwellings were a mix of ramshackle wooden shacks and conical animal-fiber tents or gers. A badly polluted stream, really a trickle, pointed indexically toward a city center that was dominated by a huge coal-fired power plant spewing black gunk from its smokestacks.

After about a day and a half without respite, the prospect of any bed was near irresistible. However, it was only early afternoon so, out of a combination of not wanting to spend a jet-lag-induced sleepless night and great curiosity to explore the exotic city, I resisted temptation and dragged my protesting body out of the hotel. Though one of Ulan Bator's best, our accommodations had the general feel of a military barrack.

My query at the desk about where to change money led me to the hotel's "shopping mall" annex, actually two grossly understocked enterprises that together constituted a kind of gift shop (local crafts—particularly woolens) with the added dimensions of liquor, canned goods and packaged snacks. I was directed upstairs to the money exchange, a small room with two young clerks in Western dress and an elderly woman with bloated features occasionally interrupting her otherwise full-moon face and dressed in colorful traditional garb. After concluding my paperwork, I was directed to her. She extracted a roll of bills from somewhere in the folds of her ample clothing and counted out my Mongolian currency. Then it was back downstairs to buy a guidebook. There were none available in English (kind of refreshing actually!), so I purchased *Mongolia,* a work by Roberto Ive and Aldo Colleoni published in Milano. It made me feel like a modern-day Marco Polo as I prepared to follow his faded footsteps. It was a perfect companion for another tome in my reading matter, Italo Calvino's *Invisible Cities,* a hypothetical dialogue between the Italian explorer and the great Kublai Khan.

I walked downtown past the impressive opera house and civic square lined with imposing ministries that exuded autocracy without even the need for human autocrats. I had agreed to meet our hosts at a particular department store where I hoped to find some sort of unusual souvenir. I managed to purchase two stunning tiny tapestries with a Genghis Khan-cavalry motif for a ridiculous $5 each.

Hurts and Amera were principals in the Hubsgul Travel Agency. Both spoke some English and fluent Czech (having been educated in Czechoslvokia). He was the chairman of the Mongolian Chamber of Commerce and Industry. They were tireless boosters, overflowing with optimism. It seems that the young Turks had just taken over from the old guard communists who had retained power through the transition of Mongolia to full independence during the disintegration of the Soviet Union. While the country was still heavily dependent upon Russian expertise and largesse (Mongolia was greatly in arrears on its fuel bill to Russia and had but a three-day reserve), free enterprise, or at least the promise of it, was in the air. In fact, the only construction underway in the capital of the essentially bankrupt nation was for a private bank and buildings at the Buddhist monastery complex, both telling indicators of the new political climate. The greatest symbol of change, however, had been the conversion of the Marx and Lenin museum into a shopping center.

The next morning the domestic terminal at the Ulan Bator airport did nothing to assuage my flying fears. The virtually windowless, ancient structure felt like a ruin. The crush of humanity was reminiscent of Beijing, but with the added element of assorted domestic animals as the intended travel companions of their strikingly-costumed owners. The back of my seat in our Russian prop plane dangled hopelessly, and the seat belt was broken. I was soon sealed into place by the mound of cargo, some of it alive, placed in the aisle.

Flying at a low elevation we were able to appreciate the evolution of the countryside as we proceeded ever northward. Barren plains gave way to foothills which eventually attained mountainhood. The brown, sparsely-vegetated landscape became greener and lusher. Then we were over the darker verdure of conifer forests. The two-hour flight was uneventful and we were met by Purevdorj, general director of Hubsgul Travel Company's northern operation. Preparations were still underway for our trip, so we were to be given day rooms in Moron's (only) Tourist Hotel, after someone was sent to find a key, of course, since it was locked up tight. Its fetid lavatories, assorted odors, fly-specked dining tables and filthy mattresses made me delighted to be going camping. Unfortunately, they also gave us a glimpse into our future, since we would be overnighting at the appalling establishment on our way out.

Moron itself, administrative capital of the administrative aimag of Hovsgol, has about 30,000 inhabitants. My Italian guidebook in hand, I found myself staring at the impressive statue of the local hero—Davaadorj—who when still a teenager distinguished himself as an underground fighter against the Japanese occupation. In 1948, at only 22 years of age, he died under mysterious circumstances. By then Mongolia was semi-autonomous, but under Soviet rule. As Ive and Colleoni delicately put it, "Certain men were more useful dead under heroical circumstances to the powers that be than alive, given that they might become powerful and dangerous opponents."

Archery has epitomized Mongol culture since at least the days of Genghis Khan's Golden Horde, whose mounted archers swept across most of Asia and into Eastern Europe creating one of history's greatest empires. Archery competitions are still a popular national sport, and Moron's main sports field is flanked by archery murals. I also inspected Hubsgol Travel's half-completed lodging project, a cute complex of individual cottages meant to emulate gers. Unfortunately, like most of everything else in Mongolia, the project was temporarily on hold. It was, however, key to Hubsgol Travel's northern operations, since Moron was the entrée to the Lake Hubsgol National Park, northern Mongolia's main, if still embryonic, tourist attraction. Lord knows that bivouacking clients in the Tourist Hotel as their first (or last) impression was not a slick business strategy.

By mid-afternoon we set off, bouncing over rutted roads in our two Russian jeeps. Given their narrow wheelbase it was most jarring, but we were largely oblivious to the discomfort energized both by relief over escaping Moron and our angler's anticipation. A supply truck of Russian military vintage had been sent ahead to set up our main camp's ger near the confluence of the Eg and Uur rivers. For the next two days we would be camping out in small tents while following the descent of the Eg, fishing its most promising stretches as we went.

For a westerner (as in American West), the immediate noticeable feature was the lack of fences. We were driving through truly open range, the homeland of a few thousand nomads who lived in transportable gers that are moved with the herds as a particular place's pasturage is exhausted. It was much like my home region must have been a century and a half ago. Indeed, the horseback rides of several days' duration, in which the rider is unlikely to encounter a single fence delimiting the Mongolian immensity, are a main local tourist attraction.

We would reach the crest of some low summit and gaze upon a valley floor that was 20 miles or more across, its verdancy interrupted only by the stippling of grazing livestock and one or two white specks—the gers of the only inhabitants who were themselves temporary interlopers. The average household owned about 200 sheep and goats, maybe 20 cows, a dozen or so horses and four or five yaks.

It was late afternoon by the time we wended our way down through a series of canyons to the upper reaches of the Eg. We were to spend the night alongside a beautiful series of deep runs laced together by shallower riffles terminating in a broad tailout. The water could not have been clearer. We guests were to rig up and go fishing while staff set up camp. Margaret would fish the tailout, I was to begin at the promising-looking headwaters, and Dan planned to work the middle stretch.

He was the first in the water, wading straight out in front of us to where he began casting and skittering his floating Mouse fly on the surface. His shout jerked my attention away from the six-inch long, black Bunny Leach that I was tying onto my tippet. His rod was bent to the breaking point, which failed to even move the taimen. It then rose to the surface, creating a huge boil. After about 10 minutes the five-foot fish showed itself, moving leisurely towards us into the shallows. However, as Jeff tried to beach it, the taimen swam casually away, seemingly oblivious to the intense pressure that Dan was exerting. He was powerless to even slow, let alone stop, its progress.

For an agonizing moment, it seemed that our quarry would gain the rapids and be gone. But Jeff was running downstream and reached the tailout just before the leviathan. He waded out into the current and spooked the taimen back into our run. Fifteen minutes later it was time for the photo op. But there was a problem. Dan could not pick up the weary, now practically inert, fish by himself. So as he lifted the head, Jeff raised the tail and I snapped the pictures. It was about 60 inches and, given its chunky bulk, probably weighed that many pounds or more. While we didn't realize it at the time, Dan had just caught the week's largest fish on our first collective cast.

At that point, I was almost too shaken to rig my rod. The proof was that I promptly tied on my own Mouse fly without first stringing the line through the rod guides. After adjusting for that bit of buck fever, I began working my water. About 20 minutes later a fish swirled at my surface offering. My disappointment evaporated when, on the next cast, I had an aggressive take. The 37-inch taimen was far more acrobatic than Dan's, treating us all to four magnificent jumps.

About an hour later Margaret caught a 31-incher, and by then we had company. Two men perched on a small motorbike had arrived at the other side of the river. They were fishing with handlines. First they caught a 12-inch lenok that they used as bait, chucking it out into the current of a deep run snubbed against their bank. As the dusk deepened into darkness, they were rewarded with a 40-inch fish. After cleaning their catch they putt-putted away to God knows where.

A taimen virgin no longer, that night I lay in my tent taking stock. I felt that one mystery had been solved. The tail section of the taimen was rust-colored, indeed so much so that we would use it to our advantage over the next several days. Except for when fishing the deeper pools, we would walk the banks hoping to sight the telltale band of color that revealed a large fish in a holding pattern. It had probably also given rise to China's red-fish legend.

There was another conundrum. The Eg is not a large river and is ice-bound much of the year. Nor is there an obvious food source to sustain its considerable numbers of enormous taimen. Were they migratory? The answer seemed to lie in some combination of preying upon lenok, waterfowl and other taimen, as well as simple longevity. It was likely that we were fishing for quite elderly specimens.

By noon of the third day we were at our more permanent camp-site. Our truck had broken down, and Purevdorj had had to rent a ger in some distant town. This also meant that we would not have our full store of intended supplies. That afternoon the camp staff began fishing for food. At dusk Purevdorj shot a deer.

The ger was more than ample for the four westerners; the Mongolians slept in the smaller tents. In addition to Purevdorj, there were two jeep drivers, Odchun and Renchin, and our comely young cook, Chimgee. We each brought along a sleeping bag and were provided a cot, all four of which laid end on end didn't begin to exhaust the interior perimeter.

It takes the better part of a day to assemble a ger, which is sort of like an elaborate tepee. The wooden skeleton is crafted of basic supports erected vertically and arranged in a circle to about the height of a standing person. Next comes a second tier ascending at a gentle angle. A small opening is preserved for venting smoke. The ger is covered with felt blankets of varying weights and layers depending upon the season.

The result is amazingly flexible and comfortable. It was August and with cloudless skies. So our daytime temperature ascended into the high seventies and low eighties, yet given our latitude and streamside location we awoke each morning to a dense river fog and hoarfrost. We appreciated the cool of the ger's interior in the late afternoon and the warmth of its wooden stove in the evening and early morning.

This was to be home for the remainder of our trip. In addition to fresh fish, Chimgee gave us a daily reminder of where Marco Polo had borrowed the concept of pasta for Italy. Our main fare was delicious venison spaghetti and raviolis. The general conviviality of the Mongolian people did have its downside. As news of our presence spread throughout the district, we attracted an ever-growing evening contingent of horsemen. It seemed that every male Mongolian is horse-trained from about age five. Our visitors were dressed like cavalry men in the Golden Horde, with flowing

brown robes, finely decorated felt footwear and traditional conical head gear—excepting the baseball cap of one cosmopolite proclaiming his loyalty to the Chicago Bulls! Our visitors were bent
on a single mission, a drunken spree on us.

Purevdorj was well fortified with cases of vodka. The first night
the Vermillion brothers waded into the fray while older-and-wiser
Margaret and Bill cowered in the ger. The Yanks held up their end
miserably, retreating to our refuge after about an hour of imbibing
straight pulls on the rapidly circulating bottle and then paying
dearly for their audacity with a bleary next day. Their stand proved
to be of the one-night variety, and for the remainder of the trip the
background noise as we all drifted into slumber was that of an
embryonic saturnalia seeking its sealegs.

Jeff had brought along four inflatable rubber kayaks meant for
river transportation only. The routine was to put in at some point
on the Eg, Uur or downstream from both on the river now known
logically as the Eguur. Roads were sparse, but much of the streamside was open pasture easily traversed by our jeeps. The staff could
meet us at midday a couple of miles downstream with the welcome offering of cold drinks, a hot meal and short nap. After the
afternoon's float, our jeeps again awaited to transport us back to
camp.

Floating the slow-moving rivers and occasional gentle rapid in
an undulating, rubbery cocoon was a somnolent experience, almost
akin to a body massage. We were each pretty much on our own
to select a likely looking stretch of water to fish, and we'd spend
each day lazily leapfrogging one another from one magnificent run
to the next. The fishing was good, if not spectacular. We all caught
taimen, the experienced Dan excelling with several three-or-more
fish days. Jeff fished but little, attending to our whims and generally keeping the flotilla together. Margaret and I averaged a taimen
or two daily, if we don't count her spectacular five-landed, four-
lost extravagance. Actually, after a tiring stretch of casting my ten-
weight rod and heavy flies, I became fond of switching to lenok

fishing with lighter tackle. It was much like angling for brook trout. If not spooked, they were wary but willing takers of a dry fly. My catches ranged from 14 to 20 inches in size.

We were just feeling our way regarding fly fishing for taimen. They were in deep pools and shallow runs alike, lurking around structure but also in featureless slack water. Where possible we sight-fished, where not we found basic steelheading techniques to be productive, whether fishing wet with large black Bunny Leaches or skittering Mouse-imitation flies on the surface.

The strikes ranged from vicious surface ones to the subsurface variety that were so subtle as to defy detection. At times a fish might ingest the fly without any reaction, simulating a snag rather than a hook-up. Once hooked their behavior was again erratic. Some taimen exploded, leaping wildly in desperation or anger, others simply dogged it and came to hand without much of a fight. It seemed evident that they were territorial since they didn't seek refuge in the rapids below the tailout of their particular run. Taimen are hard-mouthed and therefore a challenge to hook under any circumstance. Particularly difficult were the ones that took the fly and then swam towards you, making it all but impossible to hand strip line quickly enough to maintain tension, let alone to get them on the reel. We landed only about half of our takes.

The fish seemed fearless, particularly the large ones. Rather than dashing to safety once aware of our presence, a taimen would hold its position or ease off only a few feet, usually in the direction of deeper water. It would also become lock-jawed, ignoring the fly no matter how well presented. At that point you might as well move on.

In my memories of this most memorable of trips, one day stands out, our last at the main camp. By preference I had been fishing on my own up to that point, and Jeff suggested that we spend the morning together. He wanted to start at a deep run just below the convergence of the Eg and Uur where, a few days earlier, we had taken fish. That particular day Jeff had ascended the steep ridge along the right bank and, despite poor light, spotted an enormous fish. Our matinal sun now promised to provide optimal sighting conditions.I began fishing the slow-moving headwaters of the right bank and had four strikes and a fish landed within half an hour. They were all in the 30-inch range, nothing to get too excited about. Meanwhile, Jeff returned after having climbed the bank with the news that there were at least five taimen below me, four of which were in the 60-inch plus range! Since they were impossible to see from my stream-level vantage point, he would direct me. I was using a black Bunny Leach on a floating line. The plan was to cast it into the main current, which would then drift my fly downstream until Jeff indicated it was abreast of a waiting fish. I would stop feeding line, causing my rig to swing out of the flow towards the bank, hopefully past the taimen's lie.

My first effort came up about six feet short, the length of line that I then stripped off the reel before making my retrieval in preparation for the next cast. Just as my fly floated into the taimen's zone it snagged on a sunken branch only about a foot above the fish. "Break it off as gently as you can and put on another," Jeff said. I tightened my line and broke the tippet. But then the fly floated free and the enormous taimen ate it! I changed to a Mouse fly that I skittered past its nose, and the taimen made a false grab, before moving off into the main current.

The fish further downstream posed a bigger logistical problem. The water depth along the bank there was over my head and the shore itself overgrown with vegetation. I joined Jeff in his observatory, and we contemplated the monsters. None would be easy to approach. For the next hour I worked a large single and two smaller ones. The fishing was extremely awkward since there was no way to back cast, and my weighty Leach made rollcasting speculative. Nevertheless, I did manage to get several drifts to the general vicinity of a fish and had one follow the fly for about 30 feet before turning away.

I rejoined Jeff, and we moved further downstream. It was then that we spotted a true behemoth from our aerie. The taimen had to be over 70 inches. It was in the toughest lie of all, close to the bank where the vegetation seemed impenetrable. There was one small slot in the thicket, but only about 25 feet upstream from the fish's lie. It seemed doubtful that I could ease down to it without alerting the quarry, but there was no alternative.

I was unsure if I had been detected as I feebly rollcast a Mouse fly as far out into the current as possible. Although its drift was off line, the fish moved to the fly and made a false strike. It then eased upstream and even closer into the bank, stopping no more than 15 feet below me and the same distance out in the current. There was no way that I could rollcast undetected. Jeff joined me, and we devised a plan. We first rested the taimen for about five minutes. He then stood behind me holding the fly so that I could load the rod slightly. On the whispered count of three, he let go as I forward cast. This slingshot technique produced about a 20-foot result that was sufficient, given the fish's cozy proximity to both angler and shore. It twitched a few times, but without offering. Again we changed the fly pattern, but no luck. After maybe 40 tries, I stopped casting.

At that moment two armed horsemen approached on the other side of the river and began shouting and gesturing wildly at us. Jeff used his few Mongolian words to greet them, and they responded by prodding their steeds into the river, holding their rifles aloft as their mounts swam to our shore. They disappeared, and we spent a nervous five minutes speculating about their intentions. But then here they came on foot and just slightly upstream from us, chattering away and, to our great relief, smiling. Plop! A plume of water shot skyward where they had cast their spinning rod, baited with some kind of foot-long prairie rodent skewered on a treble hook.

Our solitude and tranquility shattered, Jeff told me to wait while he worked his way back upstream through the tangled thicket to retrieve both of our kayaks. My new companions kept up a constant banter to which I nodded and smiled, clueless as to the content of our conversation. I whiled away the time by making one lousy roll-cast after another at the disinterested taimen. At times the streamer seemed to actually bump its nose, but to no effect. I was on autopilot when one of my efforts provoked a totally unexpected strike. The fly disappeared momentarily into a dinner-plate-sized maw. I was too dumbstruck to set the hook properly. I did so only as the taimen spit out the impostured tidbit. It was over.

Jeff and I floated down to our luncheon rendezvous, where the staff feted us with warm soup and yet another variety of Mongolian pasta. In the afternoon we were to fish another couple of miles of river, down to the visible point where a low ridge intercepted the left bank, pinching off any further jeep access. The midday fishing proved slow and, after the morning's excitement, my efforts were halfhearted. I even floated through the occasional promising run without stopping. The siren song of the jeeps (with their beer cooler) was louder than any taimen call. So I was the first to reach our crew, all of whom were flailing away with spinning gear. I lingered on the opposite bank awaiting the others. Jeff arrived and we had a chat, sprawled out on a gravel bar.

When Dan and Margaret proved tardy, I decided to try a few casts into the rather unpromising side channel through which we had just floated. The enormous taimen shattered the surface, arched two feet into the air and took my Mouse fly upon reentry. It was on! The fish reached the main current, and I was well into my backing. Fifteen minutes later, and after having been privileged with the display of five acrobatic leaps, I had my trip maker measuring just over 50 inches. We released it to a chorus of protests from the other side of the river. So far the catch-and-release learning curve was proving to be a bit steep for our Mongolian hosts.

The next morning we broke camp. Fuel had become a concern, and we headed for the town of Erdenebulgan, scarcely more than a wide spot in a dirt road. The "service station" was a cement hut with above ground storage of fuel dispensed by a hand-operated pump. The frail woman had her hand full since we had the misfortune of arriving right after a Mongolian Army transport truck. After watching her methodical efforts for an hour, and with little end in sight, Purevdorj decided that we should wait in a local acquaintance's house. The concrete structure itself was cramped both spatially and aesthetically, but the interior was a delightful panoply of oriental rugs and wall hangings. As the women of the household prepared tea and cookies, the husband showed us his photo albums. He was a wrestler of national prominence and had toured Western Europe putting on exhibitions of the sport's Mongolian style. He'd been to Copenhagen and was particularly proud of having been photographed with Danish royalty.

That afternoon we proceeded to one of our earlier campsites on the Eg where I had sight-fished for a sizable taimen. Jeff and Margaret decided to see if it was still there. I spent the late afternoon reading, preferring to savor my previous day's magical moment and memory. As it turned out, they found the taimen holding in precisely the lie that I'd fished earlier. This confirmed our growing suspicion that taimen are highly territorial, a fact that would have considerable implications for Jeff's future approach to the resource. Clearly, this was a fishery that required careful rest and rotation, which also meant that he would have to expand his scope considerably. Margaret celebrated her dénouement by landing the 50-inch fish.

Next morning we headed towards Moron and the dreaded one-night sentence in the Tourist-Hotel jail. Like the Chinese rafters of my first taimen trip, scenting home base our jeep drivers put the pedal to the metal. As we topped one mountain pass, I convinced our driver to stop on the excuse that I wanted to examine the *ovoo* (cairn) that Mongolians build at virtually all lofty topographic transitions. Steeped as they are, though but lightly, in animistic religious tradition, leaving some kind of offering at an ovoo is said to bring luck—as does circling it thrice. I placed my coin and carried out the circumambulatory ritual in the belief that we needed all the help we could get to survive this ride.

I had a day-long layover in UB before departing for home. Amera was to be my hostess. That morning we toured the local Buddhist monastery—Mongolia's finest. During the Soviet era the religion was banned. The older monks had been executed and buried in mass graves. Now signs of renewal were everywhere. There were many visitors ambling through the grounds, and we joined them in spinning the prayer wheels. Two new buildings were under construction and the sound of young male voices intoning sacred chants emanated from another. It was rumored that the Dalai Lama might be paying a visit shortly.

I purchased stale copies of the three local English language newspapers, but should not have. The headline of the *UB Post* (August 13, 1996) trumpeted "Cholera Epidemic Hits Mongolia." Several parts of the country, including Ulan Bator, were under quarantine. More than 500 people were ill. The article ended with the news that,

> "All kiosks in Mongolia have been officially instructed to close, shops have been allowed to remain open but are being checked by medical personnel. Street vendors have been ordered to close their businesses until further notice and restaurants and cafes have been temporarily shutting down across the capital. Precautions have been taken when burying the six people who have died of cholera. Few people have been allowed to attend the funerals."

Lest I should worry, however, Mongolia's intrepid medical community was clearly on the cutting edge. According to another article, three of its cancer specialists had just perfected a technique of removing the malignant part of esophageal cancers and then stitching the remainder of the organ to the stomach that is then moved up into the chest cavity. The bad news was that should I need such a procedure I was a poor candidate since, "Mongolians are fortunate in that their stomachs are usually very elastic due to the amount of tea and airag they drink."

The *Mongol Messenger* (August 28, 1996) bantered that "Tourists Flounder as Death Toll Rises." Aside from providing quaint usage of my native tongue, it also informed me that new restrictions were in effect due to an outbreak of bubonic plague in Gobi Altai Aimag which had killed three people.

As a further contribution to my English education, the *Mongolian Independent Business Times* stated, "Mongol TV and Radio Beheaded." To my relief, reference was to the sacking of their director—no Mr. Smith he, but rather Ulziisaikan Enkhtuvshin. I was simply too dense to fathom other tidbits. Apparently one B. Gansukh and his "eight accomplishes" had just been "evicted" by the Sukhbataar District Court for embezzlement by hoodwinking the president of the Trade and Industry Bank. Not only was Gansukh an embezzler, he had "managed to sell his three-room apartment to 12 different persons separately." The lesson for all was clear,

"An American dream of a young person did not materialize into life as he chose illegal means and this case serves as a strong reminder for others wishing to make quick "dough" not to cheat, especially the President."

Indeed!

On a more somber note, the *UB Post* reported that the government intended to compensate political prisoners "wrongly detained" prior to 1989 with free apartments. The Mongolian embassy in Moscow had also just filed a formal request with the Russians for information regarding "the burial ground of 38 Mongolians, including prominent politicians A. Amar and D. Dogson, who were executed in Russia in 1941." A monument was to be built in UB for Mongolian Prime Minister P. Gender, executed in the 1940s. I thought of that solitary statue of Davaadorj bearing solitary witness in Moron to what was obviously a national tragedy that is yet to be fully transcended.

Over lunch Hurts pressed me for my impressions of our trip

(totally favorable excepting the Tourist Hotel) and regaled me with statistics regarding Lake Hubsgol National Park. It seems that it had 15,000 visitors annually. He wanted to know if I would consider opening a casino there. I passed on this obvious business opportunity as politely as possible.

Departure from Ulan Bator day dawned cold and gray. The biting wind and snow flurries augering the late August storm underscored my good fortune. I was to overnight in sultry Beijing, which was in the midst of a heat wave, while the incoming anglers for Jeff's second probational week were about to endure arctic conditions.

Mission accomplished.

On Naughty Bears
and Noddy Terns

"Black noddy tern—Ánoüs tenuiróstris—In U.S. seen only at Dry Tortugas, Fla., where it is rare but regular visitor."
— *Golden Guide to Field Identification:*
Birds of North America

Gotanybearsaroundhere? Snakes? Crocs? Sharks? Wherever the intrepid globetrotting angler alights, the critter question is quickly posed. Indeed, it is the fauna more than the fishing that provides both fear and fascination to the angling adventure. The fear, of course, flows from the possibility of close encounters with potentially dangerous animals, from the viral to the venomous, not to mention the monstrous—and on their terms and playing fields. There is something irresistible in the opportunity to see magnificent creatures in the wild, whether of the dangerous variety or the simply exotic.

My mind is a Noah's ark. Sighting a plethora of tropical butterflies, monkeys (howler, squirrel, and spider), tree sloths, river otters (Asian, South- and North-American), foxes, coyotes, manatees, moose, black and grizzly bears, porpoises (marine and South-American riverine), guanacos, macaws, toucans, parrots, cockatoos, eagles (harpie, golden, bald, white-tail, sea and Steller), jabirus, flamingoes, roseate spoonbills, egrets, emus, rheas, sharks (bull, lemon, blacktip, nurse and hammerhead) and many kinds of rays are all an integral part of my fishing memories. Were I a dedicated birder my species' list would range well into the hundreds, the legacy of casual sightings while angling on five continents and numerous islands. Non-anglers will listen to critter tales attentively, while descriptions of stalking and fighting trophy fish produce glazed eyes and mumbled excuses for suddenly remembered urgent obligations. We need only consider the prime-time slotting of *Nature* on public television, much of the programming on the Discovery Channel, not to mention the celebrity of the *Crocodile Hunter,* versus the pre-dawn scheduling (at least in my viewing area) of fly-fishing shows on ESPN.

If microbes were of concern in Mongolia, when first faced with the prospect of fishing the Amazon my thoughts naturally turned to piranhas. Who cannot remember some Hollywood scene of victims disappearing in a matter of seconds into the maelstrom of a piranha-frothed surface? So I was perplexed to see small children diving into the Rio Branco as I prepared to embark on my maiden voyage upon Amazonian waters. In the ensuing days our camp staff was in and out of the drink with a nonchalance that soon had me wading the Taperá in pursuit of tucunaré (peacock bass), with thoughts of piranhas, if not obliterated, at least relegated to the back burner of my mind.

Sometimes sandy and hard, but more often muddy and forgiving, the bottom of tropical South American streams that I have waded is uniformly perfect for camouflaging a reposing freshwater sting ray. The rule is to always drag your feet (some anglers carry a stick for probing the unknown). The only occasion on which I have retreated was once on the Apa River near the Pantanal. I was chest deep in murky water when I felt gentle bumps against my pant legs, as if some of the truant pupils in a school of fish had inadvertently run into me. When I then caught piranhas on my next two casts, and something cut my fly line in two on a third, I decided that it was a good time for a shoreside beer.

But in all my ventures the only real damage done to my person has been that inflicted by the omnipresent no-see-ums. Is there a part of the planet unafflicted by them? Wherever I go, they seem to provide me with dependable déjà-(sans)-vu. They have many aliases—sand flea, midge, *jején* (Spanish), *piún* (Portuguese) and *mokrets* (Russian). I sometimes think that I am the culprit, a kind of entomological Johnny Appleseed whose mission is to populate the world with the little bastards by transporting them as his persona's penumbra.

There are times on a fishing trip when a particular glory of Mother Nature becomes so intrusive as to preclude angling. I am always distracted in June by the copulatory ritual of 10-foot nurse sharks frothing and spewing a dozen feet into the air the waters of the shallows off some remote key. I am mesmerized by an eagle ray's aquatic ballet. I always leave the dock in anticipation of watching the soaring adults, the tentative juveniles and the ungainly white frigate bird chicks of one particular nesting tree in Abaco's Marls and another in Yucatan's Ascencion Bay. The latter also holds out the prospect of a showstopping encounter with its resident flock of flamingoes. Then there was the year the mangroves in the lagoon behind Boca Paila Lodge were festooned with tens of thousands of mating butterflies, not to mention the day that the rain-soaked terrain of the Uruguayan pampas was alive with tarantulas. It is this ever-present, yet largely unpredictable, possibility of sighting the next jabberwock or unicorn that adds much of the spice to an angler's gruel.

Every experienced fisherman is likely to have had a close encounter with some critter, in the water or out of it, worth telling. Indeed, such tales tend to improve with each recounting. The following are but some of the tastier chocolates in Bill Angler's sampler.

In 1969 the saltwater crocodile was placed on Australia's endangered species list. The beleaguered saurian had been pursued relentlessly for its skin by professional hunters, pressure that had eliminated them entirely from much of their former range and reduced numbers drastically in the most favorable rivers of Australia's tropical north. All that remained was a core population of wizened old crocs that had learned to evade their enemy. Much like the American alligator, once protected the salties made a remarkable recovery. Larger than its American cousin, the saltwater crocodile is predisposed to becoming a man-eater. So the trouble began.

The barramundi, akin to the Atlantic snook, is the main game fish in the northern Australian river estuaries that are prime crocodile habitat. For the barramundi fisherman, the sinister presence is never out of mind, as anyone who has seen the film *Crocodile Dundee* can appreciate.

Since 1992, in the Northern Territory alone there have been at least six fatal and 13 non-fatal crocodile attacks, not counting probable additional unreported ones on the Aboriginal reserves. The tales are gruesome. On March 17, 1987, Kerry McLoughlin was fishing for barramundi on the South Alligator River in Kakadu National Park. In northern Australia's usually dry climate it is common to cement the river bottom in lieu of constructing expensive highway bridges. For most of the year the dry or barely damp causeways are easily passable. On this particular day McLoughlin was wading across the river when the tidal flow raised its level. He slipped off the causeway into the river channel and began splashing his way toward the bank through waist-deep water. Hard of hearing, he was oblivious to the shouts of several horrified spectators, including his son. The huge crocodile approached from upstream and then disappeared beneath the surface. As the hapless man reached the far bank the croc lunged from out of the murky water, decapitated him and swam away with the twitching torso.

Then there was the show and tell of my Australian fishing buddy. While fishing the Daly River, Geoff Hawkins and I were anchored in a deep run when our small aluminum boat was rocked suddenly by a sharp blow from below. He scrambled to the fish finder and observed an enormous mass on the screen, so we moved immediately. Geoff then pointed out the adjacent 50-foot knoll along the shoreline where, in 1990, Lena Pan Quee and her son had pitched their tent believing themselves to be well above possible harm. In the middle of the night the crocodile left the water considerably upstream of the sleeping campers. It entered the tent and grabbed Mrs. Pan Quee, crushing her chest. Her son leapt upon its back and dug his fingers into the croc's eyes, and it released her. Much the worse for wear, she did manage to survive the attack.

One day, about a quarter of a mile out to sea off the Cobourg Peninsula, Geoff and I were blind casting for trevally and queenfish. He was perplexed by the wave action over a small, misplaced reef that he had never noticed before. We motored over to get a better look, and it slowly sank out of sight. The croc was easily more than 18 feet long. We were in about 50 feet of crystal clear water, so I urged Geoff to take us closer to see if we could spot the beast. It was then that he told me a sweetheart tale, and our aluminum skiff shrunk to insignificance.

Regarded as prime barramundi water, at one time the Finniss River was among the Northern Territory's most popular angling destinations. That is, until the legendary "Sweetheart" came along. Today there is a stuffed 15-foot-long saltie on display in the Darwin Museum, captured by the authorities after several croc attacks on fishing skiffs plying the Finniss. The cranky animal was given to ripping outboards off of transoms, sinking several craft. Curiously, it ignored their desperate occupants, all of whom managed to swim to safety. Today few fish the Finniss since, according to the local Aborigines, the croc in the Darwin display is an imposter. The genuine and much larger Sweetheart still lurks in the wilds.

Given the option of wading with sharks, waltzing with bears or swimming with crocodiles, there is no question which not to choose. Proximity to sharks and bears may make the pulse beat faster and the adrenalin flow, but the prospect of an actual attack remains quite low. Not so with crocodiles. I doubt seriously that a person could attempt to swim crocodile-infested waters, like Australia's Mary River, with much chance of survival. One need only observe the "boneyard," the appropriate nickname for the water-buffalo crossing on the Mary. Low tide in that estuarial stream exposes hundreds of skeletal remains of what were once massive animals.

After a week of barramundi fishing, there is relief in simply being off the water, a sense of release from the undercurrent of tension inherent in being the quarry.

Jay Trainor is a large man, hence his nickname "Bear." It was appropriate that it was Jay who found the abandoned Minolta 5000 on the bank of the Lower Gibraltar River in Alaska's Lake Iliamna region. The camera was in mint condition, except for a few teeth marks.

Practically a year later to the day, I scrambled out of a float plane on the Brooks River, one of Alaska's premier bear-viewing spots. There were signs that warned the visitor to exercise extreme caution, and particularly not to leave *anything* along the shore that might attract curious bears. Whenever walking trails in bear country, it is advisable to make as much noise as possible so as not to trigger a spontaneous ursine encounter. My personal ploy in such circumstances is to chant the mantra "Ho bear, Yo bear," thereby providing Jan with additional prima facie evidence of my angler's dementia.

Lewis Little and I began fishing egg patterns for the five-pound rainbow that were gorging themselves on roe while lying behind spawning sockeyes. The bears had their own agenda as they scavenged and fished for the spent spawners. The sun came out and I began to cook inside my waders and down parka. So I decided to strip off the coat, which I placed on the bank along with my wool hat and new Minolta 5000 camera.

Actually it was my third and last fancy camera, before I finally got the message from the deity that I am not destined to be a Minolta owner. The first, and its set of expansive (and expensive) lenses, had been stolen from a rental car in Portugal when Jan and I stopped off to attend a conference in Braga on our way to Kenya for a photo safari. My second Minolta disappeared after I had carelessly left it on the back of a restaurant chair in Santiago while on a trout-fishing trip to Chile.

Lewis and I became completely absorbed in the catching, so we failed to monitor carefully the movements of a sow bear and her two large cubs. They entered the river about a hundred yards below us and gradually began working their way upstream. Suddenly they decided to take possession of our run, and it was too late for us to retreat or for me to retrieve my belongings. We were forced into a swampy back channel and pinned against a sheer gravel bank that was impossible to climb.

We shouted and whistled until it became obvious that the bears both knew that we were there and didn't care. At that point we were transported to the set of some Disney nature film. The two cubs (a misnomer for critters weighing several hundred pounds) were in a playful mood. Each grabbed an end of my jacket and made a wish. Mom chewed on the Minolta for awhile (déjà vu) before dropping it into the stream and frying its electronics. She stuck her nose into the camera case, doing a brief imitation of Jimmy Durante, and then chomped on my Irish wool hat. By then the cubs had discovered a log drift from which they could leap into the water together and cuff each other playfully while floating downstream.

Showtime lasted for about half an hour as Lewis and I stood helplessly and forlornly, waist deep in our marshy haven. When the bears finally moved off, I retrieved the remnants of my coat and camera, which I sheepishly deposited in the trash bin at the ranger station. I retreated to the float plane where I sat pensively until it was time to leave. I have two mementos of the day. I still wear the wool hat, which suffered no apparent damage. I also have a framed bear picture, the last taken with my star-crossed Minolta before the bears decided to photograph Lewis and me.

I did not go to Tierra del Fuego expecting to see much in the way of wildlife—possibly a few Magellan geese. *Au contraire*. Not only was there more afoot and aloft, the natural order was itself reversed as if in some kind of antipodean, magic-lantern-illusory fashion. It was not just that the lion lay down with the lamb, rather the lion was lamblike and the lamb leonine.

My first surprise in this windswept landscape that makes my native, dessicated Nevada seem positively Edenic was the flight of nine Piper Cubs appearing on the horizon that gradually transmogrified into nine condors. Watching the wayward escapees, seasonally down from the Andes for God-only-knows what purpose, took a considerable bite out of my first afternoon's angling for the Río Grande's fabled sea-run brown trout.

Over the next several days curious grey foxes came within casting distance. Fearless beavers shared my runs, sometimes coming out of the current to sit within arm's length while munching some tuber or choice piece of grass. Their very presence was itself anomalous since there wasn't a tree within miles. They had been introduced to the area from Canada back in the 1930s or 1940s as a valuable furbearer but were no longer trapped given the depressed world market for furs. They had adapted marvelously to their treeless circumstance, substituting grass and tubers for saplings. As if this were not contrarian and counterintuitive enough, the so-called "domestic" animals—horses, cattle and sheep—bolted like herds of startled antelope at first sight, no doubt mistaking us for their gaucho persecutors.

The companion to my condor bookend was a guanaco morning. I first discerned their presence as a single, unnatural protuberance seemingly perched upon a distant hillock of the slightly wrinkled terrain. When the bump multiplied fivefold, I realized that I was vastly outnumbered as observer. I became absorbed in my casting for the next 15 minutes, landing and releasing a 10-pounder. It was then that I noticed my newfound companions. A large male and his harem of several adult females (seemingly betraying his Middle Eastern connections to his camel cousin), a couple of juvenile males loitering respectfully on the fringes and a collections of little guys—maybe a herd of 15 in all—had closed the distance between us and were fully visible, heads still and erect and with 30 eyes fixed firmly on my every move. I exchanged rod for camera (inexpensive!) and worked my way slowly across the current to their side of the river. To my delight, rather than flee, they continued their approach before halting approximately a hundred yards away, well within range of my modest telephoto lens.

With the pictures in the can, it was back to fishing. A few minutes later I raised my eyes once again to what was now my gallery, a herd of rapt guanacos standing at attention lined the far bank. Feeling a bit like St. Francis of Assisi, I slipped out of my angler's role and into that of the photographer once again, exhausting my film supply. Occasionally, one of the adults would take a few hesitant steps, eyeing me all the while as if requesting my permission. Eventually they wandered off in the general direction from which they had come under the mistaken delusion that they were still free to roam the steppes when, in fact, they were now frozen on film and imprisoned within my memory.

Lago Refugio (Lake Refuge) was created but a few years ago when Bolivia's Rio Marmoré changed course and flooded both a major pasture of the Rancho Refugio and adjacent forest. To access the lake our 30-foot dugout canoe had to negotiate the water-hyacinth-choked narrows flowing through a ghostly canopy of dead trees that now served as the vast nesting ground of literally thousands of tropical birds. The raucous calls of dozens of mated pairs of both red and blue macaws heralded our progress, while bands of curious squirrel and howler monkeys were the jungle's self-appointed sentinels. At one point we could have reached out and touched the immobile head of a large black cayman, its two eyes fixed upon us out of a camouflaging mat of aquatic vegetation.

After a morning of relatively slow action provided by the occasional solitary peacock bass teased out of a likely-looking patch of shoreline cover, suddenly Mike Coe and I were in the midst of a tucunaré convention. Hundreds of burly fish, all weighing better than five pounds and some in double digits cruised around our boat oblivious to its presence. Our first few casts triggered a feeding frenzy that made it impossible to retrieve one's fly without a strike. We switched to poppers and other improbable offerings and challenged each other to make a fishless cast, but it was to no avail. Within an hour between two anglers we released more than 50 fish.

It was then that our party was crashed. A family of pink freshwater porpoises began cavorting around our perimeter. Gradually the surface became littered with fish that were still alive but with severed tails. We realized that our catch-and-release efforts were futile since the dolphins were easily running down our exhausted playmates. The wily mammals were seizing the moment's opportunity to stock their open-air refrigerator with disabled, but not yet defunct, peacocks to be consumed at some later dinner hour. We collected a few for our own repast.

A few days later Rob Stewart and I were again at Lake Refugio but undergoing a very different angling experience. It seemed like all of the tucunaré in the lake had joined the vast school that had then disappeared. After a couple of utterly futile angling hours under the scorching sun, our attention strayed easily to the hundred or so zebu cows that were trotting towards corrals ahead of dogs and mounted men. At our urging, our guide "Mister" beached the boat and we entered the ranch compound. Overcoming the initial timidity of the manager and his two shy, if unabashedly-curious, children, we were given a detailed description of hardscrabble life in this particular bush. As we were about to take our leave, the little

Casting About in the Reel World

boy and girl were sent to the main house and reemerged each carrying a set of front paws. Would we like to buy such treasures? The male and female jaguars had been hunted down with a dog pack three weeks earlier after killing cattle.

"Don't move!" Captain Billy Sydnor, my Florida fishing guide was beside himself. We were staked out at Pie Key on a falling tide hoping to ambush passing tarpon as they vacated Loggerhead Basin. I was maintaining my vigil on the bow while Billy scanned the water from his elevated perch on the poling platform over the stern.

The dynamic between client and guide on a Florida flats skiff is unique in the world of angling. When you fish out of a lodge, your guide is usually its employee. If you float a Western river, he may well own his boat and equipment, but there is considerable democracy in the experience. You may be expected to help with the launch and drive a vehicle as part of the take-out. The scrambling in and out of the boat for periods of wading and the guide's manual rowing somehow create the illusion that you are two guys going fishing together. Not so on a flats skiff. When you step aboard, you enter your captain's dominion. When you speak to him, you look up at an imperious figure that is the most prominent relief on an otherwise simmering 360-degree horizon. The annals of Florida flats fishing are replete with stories of misunderstandings. I have never heard of a marriage being performed on a flats skiff, but divorces between angler and guide are common. More than one angler has been "taken back to the dock" and summarily thrown off the boat after a shouting match. My buddy Bob Morgart calls his favorite Keys guide "the boat nazi." If you doubt the accuracy and seriousness of all this, read Tom McGuane's black-comedic novel *Ninety-Two in the Shade*.

So when Billy said "don't move," I didn't. He then told me his tale about the only other time he had seen a black noddy tern. He and another guide had a day off and went tarpon fishing, each in his own skiff so they could fish simultaneously. A bird landed on

Billy's poling tower, and his ornithologically oriented friend declared it to be a black noddy tern, a web-footed denizen of the Gulf Stream that rarely comes ashore. There had only been a handful of sightings in the Florida Keys. So Billy and the black noddy tern visited while the companion fired up his engine, ran into the dock, retrieved the camera in his car, and returned to photograph the unusual visitor from the high seas. "Well, Billy, I have a camera in my tackle bag. Why don't you get it out and take our picture." I had never seen a black noddy tern, but I could feel the one that was walking around on top of my hat. Apparently the exhausted wayward traveler had spotted me standing in the bow and decided to use my head for a rest stop!

Billy began shooting from the stern and then moved forward expecting to spook the bird with each new invasion. But the tern seemingly had no experience with people and hence no fear. The last shot was as close up as my camera would focus. It was time to go back to fishing, so I clasped the bill of my hat and transcribed an arc in the air designed to send the bird on its way. Instead it apparently fluttered in place for a moment and then simply landed in my hair, prompting a whole new round of photography by an ecstatic Billy. Finally, I gently swept the intruder from my head and it landed at my feet, giving me my first glimpse of a black noddy tern.

The three of us fished in the same spot for the next half hour as my new friend helped me look for tarpon. I offered it a cookie, but its hooked and pointed bill bespoke different dietary preferences. Billy decided to move, and we both assumed the tern would spook once he fired up the engine. No way. Rather it flew up onto the poling platform and, as we gained speed, its webbed feet began to slide around on the slippery surface. But then the bird managed to strike an aerodynamically sound stance and was converted into a living maritime version of a hood ornament, a pose that it maintained for the next few miles. Suddenly it lifted off in flight and headed out to sea, no doubt to recount its version of the implausible encounter to incredulous companions.

Casting About in the Reel World

* * *

To my knowledge, I have only been mortally endangered on one occasion by an animal encounter. It was during my near debut as a toreador while camped on the Paraguayan bank of the Apa River. It is difficult to exaggerate the size of zebu cattle, the breed that populated this particular ranch. Suffice it to say that it would be hard to mount a heifer without benefit of stirrup. But then the gentler distaff side of the race pales by comparison to the odd range bull.

Our tent camp was not entirely without amenities, including a portable crapper, an aluminum-frame, canvas-chair sort of contraption. One fine morning I strolled away from our little imitation of civilization intent on a daily constitutional. Enthroned and engrossed in my novel, I was startled by the appearance of four surly cows and a bull who were equally unamused by my presence. Fortunately, a barbed-wire fence separated us into distinct jurisdictions, if, of course, one discounts the open gate that escaped my notice. I went back to my reading.

The four cows went past me without incident, albeit with evident irritation and quickened pace. His excellency was far less conciliatory. With lowered head and flared nostrils, he snorted and pawed at the ground, filling the air behind him with trailing dust plumes. I froze in place, partly out of fear but also out of options. With pant legs rearranged effectively into an anklet, flight was impossible. Some minutes in life are much longer than others. After an interminable 60 seconds or so, King Zebu raised his head in growing disinterest and mercifully trotted after his concubines. The stars were back in their firmament; thankfully I had just avoided becoming an angling legend of the most ignominious variety.

Bikini Bombing

I should remember to thank Yvon," I mused, having just tried on my new Patagonia Marlwalkers. Yvon Chinard, owner-founder of Patagonia, fishes the upper Dean the same week that I fish the lower camp. So, while we aren't fishing partners, we travel out together and sometimes chat on the connecting flights and at the Vancouver airport. For at least 20 years I had been waiting for the ideal saltwater-flats wading shoe. All of the previous prototypes were wanting. They were too thin-soled (causing stone bruises), archless (foot fatigue) or made of rubber or neoprene (too hot). I have therefore relied on Converse high-top tennis shoes and athletic socks lo these many years. But that approach was far from perfect since it admits sand and small bits of coral rubble that must be removed frequently to avoid blisters and cuts. I had finally worn out my latest pair of Converse tennies and, with the passing of the years, these old standbys were becoming more difficult to replace in a world that panders shamelessly to the Air Jordan concept. It was time to "get with it."

I was off to Bikini Atoll and its challenging coral-endowed flats for a week of fishing for trevally, bonefish and exotic reef species. The side benefit was to trade Reno's mid-December winter gloom for Bikini's radiant (hopefully not radiating) warmth. The logistics of getting there are daunting. From Reno it means flying to Los Angeles, overnighting in Honolulu, six hours on Continental Micronesia Airline to Majuro in the Marshall Islands for another in-transit night and finally the weekly Air Marshall flight to Kwajalein and Bikini Atoll. On the island of Eneu, we were to be met by a boat and then proceed to a diving lodge on Bikini Island. In all, a 2½-day odyssey.

I should have recognized the first signs of trouble at Reno airport's American Airlines' counter. The check-in agent seemed just a bit befuddled by the exotic connections listed on my ticket. I explained that Honolulu was my first day's destination. After several false starts, she returned my ticket with a mumbled explanation that she had pulled the Los Angeles-to-Honolulu portion by mistake and had stapled it back into my packet. It didn't occur to me to check my baggage claim.

I was to meet Gary Aka, my frequent fishing companion, in Honolulu. The trip was Gary's idea, a sort of Arthurian search for the holy grail of Pacific reef and flats fishing that once characterized his natal Hawaiian waters, but then passed into the realm of legend by the time he fashioned his boyhood's fishing imaginary exploring Oahu's diminished possibilities.

Bikini Atoll, site of America's major nuclear tests in the '40s and '50s, had long been off line as acceptable human habitat. Only recently was it possible to sample the area's fabulous diving and fishing. Over the previous two years a few Bikini fishing articles had cropped up in the outdoor magazine, and Kaufmann's, an outfitter in Portland, was promoting the place. We were told that there hadn't been a party of anglers on Bikini for the last six months, so off we were to sample a prime, nearly pristine, fishery. The dive operation had closed for the season in early November, so we were to meet our guide in Majuro. It would just be the three of us fending for ourselves at the lodge. It sounded sort of like camping out indoors, which was fine with us.

With considerable chagrin and no small sense of panic, I reviewed my limited options as I filled out the claim with Hawaiian Airlines for my errant bag. We had been warned of piece and weight limitations, so I had packed everything into a single, medium-size North Face (rubberized) grip. Fortunately, I had hand-carried my gear bag and rod case. With the exception of my Patagonia Marlwalkers, hat and two changes of Tarponwear, I had all the basics for fishing with me. Given the weak link, the once-weekly flight from Majuro to Bikini, there was no way that my bag (checked through only as far as LA!) could possibly catch up with me.

Actually, if a bit desperate, the situation seemed not entirely hopeless. I was macabrely assured by the recollection of an article that I had just read in some stale issue of an outdoor magazine while waiting to see my physician. It described minimalist approaches to camping, including that of a paleontologist who regularly traveled from New York to his expeditions in the Gobi Desert with little more than the clothes on his back and a light tarp.

It was 9:30 p.m. as I pleaded with the clerk in the gift shop of the Honolulu Airport Hotel to stay open a few more minutes. I managed to buy a pair of shorts, a passable floppy sun-hat, and two garish shirts. She had no footgear. Upstairs in our room, Gary's size 34 spare pair of long-legged fishing pants just managed to cover my 38 waist if I didn't secure the fly, and his extra long-sleeved Patagonia shirt was tight, if more forgiving. I was dressed for fishing, if not for mixed company. Gary had no backup footwear. It was then off to the convenience store at a nearby Exxon service station under the Nimitz Freeway to pick up some toiletries. About midnight I was ready for a few hours of sleep before our 4:30 a.m. departure to the airport. After check-in I was able to pick up three pair of socks, but still no shoes, in an airport shop.

In Majuro we were to stay at the RRE hotel, as in Robert Reimers Enterprises. I asked the RRE driver about shoes, and he told me I could buy anything that I needed in the RRE store, Majuro's finest. Given the sorry, rundown aspect of the town, that wasn't entirely encouraging. The several-mile drive from the airport was along a natural causeway, a highway traversing a sand spit between open sea and inner lagoon that was seldom wide enough to accommodate more than a single row of flanking structures. We seemed to be driving through an interminable Third World version of an outdated strip mall, constituted largely by dilapidated buildings and boarded up storefronts. Instead of cruising teenagers, however, Majuro Mall was populated mainly by toddlers and tots.

The lobby of the RRE hotel was on the second floor of a structure that looked more like a bunker than a building and was accessed by a stairway reminiscently as steep as the standard issue on a Mayan temple. We hauled our luggage heavenward only to be informed that we were staying in the garden bungalows. So it was back down the concrete ladder and off to our assigned quarters, both of which proved to be occupied, or at least untouched since the departure of their previous occupants. That detail was sorted out quickly and we found ourselves each with a surprisingly pleasant and modern room. They were obviously nearly new, quite clean and boasted space age air conditioning equipped with its own remote control and cable television that provided an electronic umbilical cord (ESPN and CNN) to the familiar world we'd left behind. Though mid-afternoon in Majuro, it was time for the live telecast of NFL Monday Night Football, just the right pacifier for the anxieties of a luggageless traveler perched on the edge of the unknown. As I watched the Tampa Bay Buccaneers prevail over the Minnesota Vikings, there was little to suggest that I had left home, excepting the periodic message on the screen advising me to pay my cable bill by the 15th of the month in order to avoid the $30 reconnect charge.

The RRE store, conveniently across the street from the RRE hotel, was surprisingly large and its inventory varied. Its size bespoke more prosperous times when the money flowed from the American subsidy to facilitate the new nation's (1986) transition to independence. A combination of the programmed decrease in such cash infusions and local mismanagement had dampened at least some spirits, not to mention the economy. In the RRE store there were about three clerks for every customer. Near the checkout lanes Western Union maintained a large presence touting itself as the world's fastest transferer of funds, modern facilitation for the playing out of a traditional Marshallese communalistic ethos. The Marshall Islands, like so many other overpopulated island nations, had developed a far-reaching capture economy based on the emigration of members of extended families who were expected to help out the folks back home.

The RRE emporium had shoes, but not in my size. I struggled to no avail to convince my suddenly ungainly 11D feet to accept 10Bs. But then the clouds parted and a single pair of size 12s appeared priced at a ridiculously low $25 US. To my uneducated, Converse-biased eye they appeared to be proper attire for a discriminating teenager engaged in a pick-up basketball game—at least on a Majuro playground. My new shoes were actually comfortable and seemed to put a slight bounce in my step. Even better, when laced tightly they seemed far more impervious to sand than Converse high-tops.

As my guardian angel nudged me towards the checkout, I picked out a knapsack to carry my new wardrobe and paused briefly at the briefs' counter where the only three pair in my size came in psychedelic orange, green and yellow. I bought one of each. I was now fully outfitted, ready to take on the nucleated world of Bikini Atoll, a minimalist camper no longer.

Rod Bourke, our guide-to-be, dropped by in late afternoon. He was a 29-year-old Aussie with a degree from the University of Tasmania in aquaculture. Rod had worked on a shrimp farm in North Queensland before coming out to the Marshall Islands. His first employment was with RRE's Bikini Atoll diving and fishing lodge, but he was now the general manager of its Majuro clam farm (supplying the aquariums of tropical fish fanciers). They were spawned and raised in large tanks under close supervision. According to Rod, when he took over the farm was poorly managed and a money loser. However, this year he'd tripled its sales.

Micronesia's Marshall Islands are a combination of a mid-Pacific backwater and crossroads. Historically, they were "discovered" by the Spaniards (1529) and then subsequently entered into the belated colonial enterprises of first the Germans in the 19th century (1885) and then the Japanese in the 20th (World War I). Conquest of the Marshalls, fortified by Japan, was a strategic part of America's Pacific Campaign during World War II. After the conflict the Marshalls were administered as a trust territory (1947) for about four decades by the U.S. until attaining independent nation status (1986), but firmly within the American political and military orbit. According to Rod, the ancestral Reimers in RRE Enterprises was part of the German colonial baseline, but was a family-line that had been thoroughly "Marshallesed" by the beginning of American hegemony. Robert Reimers was a merchant with stores on Majuro and some outer islands. He gained the confidence and custom of the American authorities, creating his own little commercial empire during the heyday.

Rod was somewhat harried since two days after our trip he was scheduled to be married. He had wedding arrangements to finalize and honeymoon tickets to purchase. He apologized for being unable to hang out with us. His parting shot was that we had to depart the hotel the next morning at 4:30 a.m. to make our 7 a.m. flight on Air Marshall. "I know it doesn't make much sense, but they are sticklers about it."

Gary and I ate a reasonably good meal in the RRE (of course!) restaurant. We tried to sample the local Taka beer listed on the menu, but were informed that the brewery had failed. It was probably for the best, since later, according to Rod, "at first it gives everyone the runs but then your system gets used to it." So we washed down our repast with the Dos Equis featured on special for $1.50, as tonight was "Mexican Night" at the good old RRE. On Rod's advice we ordered box lunches for the morning.

Wednesday—At the cruel appointed hour the hotel van departed for the airport, stopping briefly at the clam farm to pick up Rod. He had several cartons for our week but noted that we lacked any fresh green vegetables since the supply plane had failed to show. We had four loaves of bread, some cheese, lunchmeat, several pounds of potatoes and a few onions and carrots. This was meant to round out the basics, since the lodge was well provisioned with canned goods, eggs and frozen meats and poultry. We arrived at the airport by 5 a.m. and had it entirely to ourselves. I went to sleep on a concrete bench, and it wasn't until an hour later that the place began to stir. Our supposedly exacting taskmasters from Air Marshall were among the last to arrive.

We boarded our German Dornier aircraft and made a single stop at Kwajalein. There we proceeded through rather stiff U.S.-manned controls, since the island is primarily an American military base. While we awaited the final leg of our flight, two American matrons arrived to work as volunteers restocking the airport's Pacific Islander handicrafts store, operated by their Hospitality Club in benefit for the improved education of Marshallese children. Normally it isn't open on Wednesdays (the Bikini flight day), but they agreed to meet us there on our return. They displayed fine woven basketry and wall hangings, as well as interesting woodcarvings from as far away as Truk, Palau and Ponepe.

We arrived at Eneu without incident some three hours after departing Majuro, having flown with some American Department of Energy replacement staff for their research facility at Bikini where they monitor radioactivity levels in the environment. We were met by a Philippine crew employed by IBC, or International Bridge Corporation, a Guam-based firm with a maintenance contract on the atoll's infrastructure. They were to transport us by boat the seven miles to Bikini Island itself. Rod asked their chief mechanic if he'd serviced the other boat, the one that we were to use for fishing, and the chief mechanic asked Rod if he'd brought along the spark plugs! A week of such finger pointing had commenced.

Bikini Island is one of 20 forming Bikini Atoll, arranged around Bikini Lagoon as a roughly circular, highly discontinuous landmass. Bikini Island is presently the only inhabited one with, counting us, in December 1999 a population of 11 people. Three of the atoll's original 23 islands were completely vaporized by the nuclear tests.

The native Bikinians were resettled in the late 1940s by the U.S. government, which then converted their home area into America's major nuclear testing site. Captured German and Japanese warships, as well as antiquated American ones, were assembled for what came to be known as Operation Crossroads, a series of tests lasting for more than a decade and designed, among other things, to ascertain the capacity of naval vessels to withstand nuclear attack. More than 20 vessels now litter the sea floor, a magnet for the world's scuba-diving community.

The history of U.S.-Bikinian relations is inglorious. At the time of the population removal, the effects and staying power of radioactive contamination were unclear, so it seemed that the natives might be allowed to return within a reasonable period of time. They were first resettled, in 1946, on Rongerik Atoll (1/6 the size of their home islands), and were then pretty much left to their own devices. They nearly starved before the American government became sensitive to their plight. So, after they constituted a kind of refugee camp settlement on Kwajalein for awhile, in 1948 the Bikinians were relocated onto tiny Kili Island, sustained by a U.S. government subsidy and food shipments.

By the late 1960s and early 1970s, some Bikinians were agitating to return to their homeland. After years of monitoring and cleanup efforts, scientists believed Bikini and Eneu Islands to be habitable. More than 100 islanders returned to pursue their traditional way of life. However, by the late 1970s it was apparent that the water supply and coconut crops at Bikini Atoll were still unsafe. In 1978 the inhabitants were again relocated by the U.S. government, some back to Kili, some to Majuro, others to the United States. At that time a $6 million trust fund was established for them, augmented in 1982 by a significantly larger ($20 million) fund, as well as a damages' settlement of $75 million in 1986. The Bikinians currently receive quarterly payments from these sources that will cease in 2002, although a part of the corpus is designed to remain in trust in perpetuity so that some form of distribution from earned income should continue indefinitely. The arrangement, of course, preserves the present status of the Bikinians as wards of the U.S. government. Their future, and that of Bikini Atoll, is far from clear. Meanwhile, the DOE continues to monitor radiation levels on Bikini Island, particularly testing such items as the coconut crop, consumption of which is felt to be the prime source of transmission of radiation to humans at the site.

As a Nevadan I can relate to this history of radiation and its posed dilemmas. When I was but a school boy, my mother bundled my brother John and me into the car in the pre-dawn darkness of a wintry morn to drive to Reno's outskirts in order to escape the city's neon penumbra. There we awaited the announced celebration (or was it a cataclysm?) of 20th century mankind's most spectacular monument to itself. Suddenly, the sky was incandescent as if by the triggering of a gigantic flashbulb. We were bathed in the brief artificial sunlight of the atomic explosion several hundreds of miles to the south at the Nevada Test Site.

When a teenager, I was once caught in a summer thunderstorm while collecting reptiles at Pyramid Lake. On the drive home with my business partner in our Sierra Reptile Farm, we listened to the radio's warning. After that morning's atomic detonation, the winds had shifted suddenly, directing the fallout northward rather than eastward. Anyone soaked by the afternoon's radioactive rainfall was instructed to take a shower immediately.

Residing in Nevada I am regularly "bombarded" with our state's anti-nuclear campaign, and particularly the opposition to storage of America's nuclear waste at Yucca Mountain. The rhetoric is laced with apocryphal description of the near imperviousness of radioactive materials to decomposition over time. Presumably, its deterioration is to be measured in terms of half-lives each lasting for thousands of years.

I could empathize with the Bikinians and their wanderings. I could feel the rush of optimism over their homecoming and the subsequent devastation of their second exodus. Yet here I was standing on Bikini Island, the very caldera of America's nuclear-testing volcano (and not that long ago) with supposed impunity. We were not to eat locally grown food or drink the water—otherwise the radiation danger was presumably less than occurs naturally at some other places on our planet. Then, too, there is Hiroshima and Nagasaki, cities obliterated by atomic bombs yet both inhabited today, as is the countryside around Chernobyl. I am sure there is a sound scientific explanation, but such surface evidence makes it elusive for this Nevada boy.

Bikini, like its sister islands, is flat and has surprisingly little rain. The island's most notable vegetative feature is an extensive coconut plantation that stretches for more than a mile beside the five-mile-long dirt road that encircles the island. RRE's diving lodge was a pleasant surprise. We were to stay in a comfortable complex with several rooms giving out onto a veranda that faced the lagoon but a few feet away. The rooms were named after sunken warships. Mine was the Nagato, flagship for Admiral Yamamoto from which he ordered the attack on Pearl Harbor. Our *nachtmusik* would be the gentle lapping of an indefatigable surf. It was even possible to spot cruising giant trevally while seated on the veranda, an event that caused us more than one frantic fire drill during the coming days.

We were also blessed by a main lodge building complete with reading library, large pantries and an enormous walk-in fridge and freezer system. It was then that we discovered somehow the power had gone out long enough to defrost everything. We bleakly contemplated thousands of dollars of thawing steaks, chops, ground meat, turkeys, chickens and four cases (about 40 dozen) eggs. Rod plaintively opened a package of steak, sliced off an odiferous piece and tossed it to one of the half-starved, half-feral cats that plague the place. It pounced upon the offering and then rejected it, turning away in disgust. We inventoried the pantry and found a large supply of pasta and rice (it wasn't too bad once you picked out the insectival black specks), canned veggies and Spam. Along with the fish that we might catch, we wouldn't starve. But we had definitely taken a step backwards towards minimalist camping.

With our boat unfit, Rod decided we should fish Bikini Island the rest of the first day, supposedly while our craft was being serviced for the next one. It was unclear how this was to transpire without spark plugs. Ideally, we were to fish Eneu, site of the unmanned airport, Aomen, about eight miles distant, and Nam, another eight miles or so beyond Aomen. If the weather was propitious, we might even venture to Shark Pass and its neighboring keys more than 20 miles away. The main attraction there was to view the hundreds of gray reef sharks in the passage that had recently been brought to the world's attention by a television program filmed and aired in 1999 by the Discovery Channel. However, under the best of circumstances the journey was reputed to be of the rock-'n'-sock-'em, shiver-your-timbers variety, particularly in our oversized, unwieldy, flat-bottomed aluminum boat, a vessel better designed for storming a beach than skimming the waves, let alone fishing a flat.

So we whiled away the afternoon on one of the more difficult flats I have waded. In places the bottom was ankle-deep soft. Other stretches were littered with slippery rock shelves and coral heads where prudence demanded that you watch your feet rather than watch out for fish. I worked the shallow slick on the inside of the surf crashing over the reef. At times the water was only a few inches deep, but could swell to thigh depth with a surge capable of knocking you off your feet. So we fished with one eye cocked on the bottom and the other on the surf—as it would turn out, a common posture at Aomen and Nam as well.

I was primarily looking for bonefish. They were few and far

between and, inexplicably, amongst the wariest that I have ever sampled. Gary was in deeper water concentrating on blue trevally. He caught a small one while I endured total bonefish humiliation. The tide was rising, and Rod asked in all seriousness if we wanted to head in, the alternative being to swim across two or three channels on the way back. This confirmed my growing sense of "you better watch out for yourself, Bill." We headed in. Along the way I tried blindcasting into a not inconsiderable surf on the lagoon side and hooked several small swallowtail darts. If the first afternoon was an omen, fishing Bikini Atoll promised to be anything but easy.

Closer inspection of our fate back at our caravansary revealed that the Marshallese staff's idea of shutting down the place for the season was to walk away. The soft ice-cream machine was coated with goo; the deep-fat fryers, breadmaker, ovens and stovetop all bore the evidence of the Last Supper. Rod impugned at length Marshallese character. We mucked the place out for about an hour before cooking up our dinner of rice, canned succotash and fried Spam, washed down with a cheap California Chardonnay in plastic cups. Dessert was soft ice cream, Rod's passion and priority.

We were going to make it.

As I dressed the next morning for our first full day at Bikini Atoll, I congratulated myself on yesterday's performance of my ersatz fishing outfit. My only concern was the footgear, comfortable and better than Converse at excluding grit, yet after less than a day the toe of my left shoe had been shredded by the rock and coral heads. I found a large roll of duct tape and encased the damage in a silver shroud.

To no great surprise, our boat motor was still broken. After lingering at the dock in fruitless anticipation for most of the morning, it was off to fish yesterday's flat. Our repeat performance produced a similar result. As we scurried back to the shore to avoid the incoming tidal surge, my bonefisherman's pride was definitely bruised. I couldn't recall back-to-back shutouts in 20 years of fishing for the gray ghosts. Again blindcasting into the lagoon surf produced a few tugs, several juvenile bluefin and golden-barred trevally, as well as a "giant" one, all weighing under a pound.

Our boat remained injured and our island-hopping plans on hold, though there were assurances that all would be ready in the morn. Late afternoon I accompanied Rod in our single-engine fishing boat for some bottom fishing within a mile of the dock. He brought along water and our uneaten lunch sandwiches "just in case," explaining that it could become dicey were we to lose power. If, perchance, we drifted out of the lagoon and into the Pacific, there were thousands of square miles of solitary open water.

We put out a drift anchor, and Rod explained to me the jigging techniques of a bottom fisherman. I took the short, stout rod in hand and tried a few cranks on the reel. It promptly fell to the deck leaving me to stare at the rotted reelseating. My bottom-fishing career was over before it began. I watched Rod catch two red snapper, two small grouper and a Coronado trout. We limped back in on our increasingly cranky motor. That night I steamed some of our Majuro potatoes and carrots while Rod prepared the fresh fish.

On Friday there was joyous news. Our second motor was repaired! We sailed off to Aomen Island like confident corsairs under a cerulean sky, arriving without incident. There we walked a huge flat that held a few more fish than its Bikini counterpart. While we didn't see any bones, the bluefin trevally were larger and more prevalent. Rod and I each hooked and promptly broke off one in the 10-pound class. We stalked and cast (unsuccessfully) to a 20-plus bruiser. In the surge through a cleft in a small reef it was like fishing in an aquarium. We landed queenfish (three pounds) and several small outrageously colored peacock grouper and Moses perch. The highlight of the day was a heart-stopping opportunity to cast at two cruising giant trevally that were easily over 50 pounds. One rushed my streamer (and my heart), but then turned away.

On the trip back we trolled and each caught a red snapper. I also hooked and landed a nice bluefin in the 10-pound range. It was and would be our best day, topped off by a sumptuous meal of years-old Chef Boyardee Beefaroni, canned peas and some wretched canned roast beef.

The plan for Saturday was to fish Eneu Island. By now the toes of both of my shoes were tattered. Selective duct taping had proved ineffectual and short-lived; I encased both feet in yards of the stuff. The overall sartorial effect of a partner bedecked in Honolulu gew-gaws, fly agape and with the feet of an Egyptian mummy appealed greatly to the sadistic streak in Gary Photographer!

We set out for Eneu and within two miles heard the warning alarm of a disabled motor. By 11 we were back at the dock for another undetermined wait as the imperturbable IBC crew fiddled with our latest snarl.

"I'll bet you thought I was a racist," Rod opined. Since our arrival he had peppered his abundant oratory with critical comments regarding the work ethic and attention span of the Marshallese. He was also prone to refer to the "Japs," even in Gary's presence, which made me wince. However, far from being some Aussie okker (which rhymes with Rocker as in John), Rod was betrothed to a local girl of considerable ethnic hybridity. Her ancestry was a cultural map of the region—Japanese, Marshallese, Gilbertese, Vietnamese and Filipino. After the ceremony they planned to honeymoon in Tasmania, a wedding gift from his parents and a surprise for the rest of the family. It seems that everyone was to gather at his parents' house on Christmas Eve, ostensibly for a conference call to wish the newlyweds well. In fact the plan was for them to appear as a living Christmas present to all.

"Where do you plan to live?" I asked.

"When I came out here, a veteran Australian bloke told me that I shouldn't stay for more than two years. Otherwise you go native. It really affects your personality. Well, I've been here for 3½. I'll come back for one more, to see what I can do with the clam farm, but then we're off to Australia. We've discussed it, and she wants to give it a go. I never appreciated how really good we've got it in Australia until I came out here."

On balance, Rod was an enjoyable and fascinating guy. I appreciated his candor and enjoyed our reciprocal slanging (no doubt a reflection of our mutual Celtic heritage). We exchanged incessant "Yank" and "Aussie" aspersions. My only discomfort with Rod was a kind of "hurry-up-and-wait" quality to his approach. Clearly, our string of mini-disasters weighed far more on him than it did on us. Actually, for Gary and me it was becoming like a game in which we awaited the next pratfall inevitably taking shape on the horizon like some dark cloud formation. If the promised squall might soak our bodies, we were determined that it not dampen the spirit. We knew that it would be brief and transitory, possibly even exhilarating. Then, too, I was well appointed with reading matter. Each delay was another excuse to further penetrate my *Essential Rousseau,* take a *Turn* with V.S. Naipaul in his American South or guffaw at David Lodge's lampooning of my academic profession's *Small World.* It was clear, however, that Rod only half-believed the constant assurances that we were actually enjoying ourselves.

Finally, we headed to Eneu in the transport boat for an afternoon's fishing while IBC continued its motor surgery. The angling at Eneu was mighty like that at Bikini and Aomen in style and results. At the point of the island where ocean and lagoon surfs mingled in a watery moment of indecision, I had several satisfying shots at decent bluefins, but the fishing was better than the catching.

At Eneu I was also hobbled by a new foot problem. The interior soles had collapsed, exposing a kind of waffle-iron grid of hard plastic. Instead of providing support, the effect was to divide the bottoms of my tender feet among corrugated peaks and valleys. Consequently, while Rod and Gary completed circling the entire island, I took a shortcut across the gravel air strip in deep slumber between its weekly, Wednesday-morning burst of activity, and past the "Welcome to Bikini" sign, rusted and faded to the brink of illegibility.

While awaiting my companions, I surveyed the deep waters of the mooring area. I spied a nice bluefin and cast my streamer, which it ingested on the surface almost like a dry fly before I could make my first retrieval strip. I stood helplessly while the awesome beast ripped out a couple of hundred yards of backing, and then wrapped the fly line around a coral head before breaking off. It was all over in about 30 seconds.

That evening Rod "borrowed" some steaks from the IBC boys, probably their conciliatory offering in lieu of a functioning motor—and we feasted.

The plan Sunday was for us to go to Nam. Dockside the IBC crew proudly put the finishing touches on our motor. Gary and I fished off the end of the dock while anticipating the latest launching. I caught several Sierra mackerel, and Gary decided to try blindcasting with a crank-bait outfit. It was then that a giant trevally smashed his surface lure and was on but briefly. Gary held up the shattered remains of mangled plastic and treble hooks twisted beyond recognition as wordless testimony to the improbability of our subduing such a creature with our suddenly inconsequential fly-fishing gear.

At that moment our intended transportation was backing down the steep boat ramp. However, before reaching the water it suddenly reared up, driving the propeller and drive shafts of the twin engines into sand and cement. There was a rending metallic scream as the lift operator, oblivious to the disaster, proceeded with the launching. He finally heard our frantic shouts. It seems that the IBC crew had removed the pin on the tilt-up trailer bed as some sort of convenience before, rather than after, securing the boat in the water.

Once again we were becalmed in Bikini. It was obviously too risky to leave the dock with suspect props and drive shafts on both motors. At the very least, a time-consuming precautionary inspection was in order. So it was off for another session of bonefishing frustration on our boring Bikini Island flat. I saw about five in three hours but then pulled the plug. My morning's improvisation with extra socks was woefully inadequate. My feet were throbbing and threatening to blister or maybe burst.

Rod and Gary decided to fish a different part of Bikini Island while I declared an afternoon's reading holiday. They had no luck, but Gary returned with an assorted collection of flip-flop soles, in various states of decay, that he had beachcombed on my behalf. The most useful and touching gifts in life sometimes come in the strangest of forms. Dinner was canned tuna casserole improvised by yours truly.

The next day our boat was rumored to be in the water, motors repaired. It was just as well because we were beginning to get Bikini Island rock fever. We were to proceed to Aomen to retrieve the anchor, which we had cleverly lost earlier in the week but would need today, and then proceed to Nam. Anchor retrieval came off without a hitch as we easily spotted the trailing rope in the pellucid waters. Halfway between Aomen and Nam the sandy, coral-head bespeckeled shallows ended abruptly at the brink of the seemingly bottomless, purplish depths of the Romeo Test's mile-wide crater. As we proceeded across it, there was again the all-too-familiar sound of an engine alarm.

Midstream we were forced to abort our Nam expedition. Limping back to Aomen on one motor at cautious speed took the better part of an hour. Rod decided that we might as well fish the place's low-tide cycle, since later the rising one would produce calmer seas for our tenuous crossing to our home base. The fishing was about par for the week, with occasional shots at decent trevally. The wading was difficult, and we also walked a couple of miles of shoreline studded with jagged volcanic rock formations. I seemed, finally, to have made my peace with the shoe gods. The converted flip-flops provided comfortable inner soles, and the several layers of duct tape were sufficient for a day's fishing in my makeshift silver brogans.

Unlike Bikini, where cats and rats had all but obliterated the ground-nesting sea bird population, Aomen was like a scene out of Hitchcock's ornithological film. Hundreds of terns and the odd frigate bird arose before us as we walked the shoreline. They circled overhead in raucous protest, gaining altitude for near-miss dive bombing reminiscent of the Marshall Islands' aerial combat more than half a century ago. The confusion and cacophony made our fishing futile as multiple shadows flitted across the water's surface, spooking every fish in sight. Ungainly chicks, unable to fly or even scale the low sand bluff that separated seashore from vegetation, formed a cadre of infantry retreating before our advance, effecting a wobble that resembled my own.

Back at Bikini, Rod asked if we would like to accompany him in some bottomfishing. It seemed that he had promised to bring back 200 pounds for his upcoming wedding and our departure day loomed. Gary suffers from seasickness in anchored craft, and I preferred to pursue my reading, so we declined. Rod decided to take the IBC crew with him in our stead. He dismissed the precarious motor situation, noting that they would be within sight of the dock.

I read obliviously until well after dusk before realizing the hour. It was nearly 9 at night and the gang was still absent. Gary and I decided to inform the DOE crew, the only other inhabitants of the place. Judy, the lady in charge, peppered us with questions and we recounted our week's circumstances as she tried unsuccessfully to raise Rod on the radio. She told us to wait while she and her assistant headed for the dock, determined to set out in the DOE boat (equipped with searchlight) to hunt for our companions. She returned shortly with the glorious news that the missing crew was dockside and that Rod would be along shortly. Before he arrived we were the recipients of a care package of fried chicken, a chicken salad and a pot full of beef curry. Hallelujah!

Rod recounted, sheepishly, that they'd had a flat tire on the van that took them until nearly nightfall to repair and then spent considerable time in the dark trying to extricate a snagged anchor from a possessive coral head. He displayed his meager catch of reef fish; far less than the 200 pounds promised to the presumably ravenous assemblage. In some marriages the problems begin even before the wedding.

Our last day dawned glorious. Getting to Nam had become a

cause. We piled into the van and piled out. It seems that yesterday Rod and the boys left the doors open while they walked back to the settlement to repair the flat tire, since they had no spare, and when they returned the vehicle was crawling with feral cats. The dominant tom had marked odiferously his territory.

We drove slowly to the dock with sliding doors open. There we found the IBC surgeons forcing a Johnson part onto a Honda shaft. It was a close, if imperfect, fit. As we left the dock, the hybrid engine was clearly running roughly while emitting a pathetically weak stream of water from its cooling system. Rod opined that Nam was out of the question, but we might try for Aomen. Gary and I seconded his caution, but with obvious disappointment. Limping to Aomen took time but brought on no new disasters. So Rod decided that we might as well continue on to Nam, which we did.

At one time Nam was as similarly elongated as the other islands making up Bikini Atoll. It was now more rounded, a mile of the island having been obliterated by the Bravo shot, the most powerful (at 15 megatons) of all the Operation Crossroads' tests. In the distance was an enormous cement bunker, its top half neatly sheered off and hurled considerable distance where it stood like some wayward piece of a nucleated jigsaw puzzle. Actually, one of the fascinations of the visit had been the opportunity to observe the outcome of the titanic clash of mankind's most powerful force and an even greater one—Nature. It was no contest. The islands we visited were littered with the debris of the test period, but after fewer than 50 years the pipe, cables and concrete had become but a slightly exotic part of an uninhabited wilderness landscape. Somehow, the U.S. Navy's installations seemed neither more impressive nor permanent than the errant flip-flops that Gary had collected. Everything blended together in cairns along with broken seashells and coral fragments—nature's own detritus.

At Nam I caught two five-pound bluefins in the whooshing surge of expended surf adjacent to the reef. The most memorable part of the day was the gladiatorial contest between juvenile moray eels and shore crabs. If a crab ventured too close to the water's edge or perched on a waterside formation, a two-foot eel would launch itself into the air, oftentimes ending up draped across a rock or fully a foot or more up on dry land. It was a spectacle truly worthy of a Discovery Channel cameraman's attention.

Given our week, the trip home was surprisingly uneventful. There was no motor trouble on the way to the airstrip at Eneu. The plane was on time. The lovely ladies of the Kwajalein Hospitality Club met us as promised and opened their treasure trove. We bought our Pacific Islander souvenirs. At Majuro we were met by a representative of RRE who had my wayward red bag. It was an anticlimactic ending to a most fascinating misadventure, a trip that with and for all its warts has a special place in my memory.

Camp Hell

I write these words on a Manaus-Miami Varig flight. Below me in the dense Amazon forests linger the recent memories of a week spent fishing for peacock bass. It was my second trip into this netherworld where my fly fishing experience overlaps with that of a different angling fraternity, the "crank baiters." We are, in many ways, like two immiscible New Guinea tribes inhabiting adjacent valleys but speaking unrelated tongues, worshipping different gods, sharing mutual disdain and engaging periodically in largely symbolic combat. While there is considerable overlap (some unsavory Benedict Arnolds are crossovers who slink back and forth between the camps) and extension of both techniques to other species, we are defined and segregated by our totemic animals. Fly fishermen belong to the Trout Clan; crank baiters are of the Bass Clan.

Fly fishermen are the few, spincasters the many. Trout clansmen sip Chivas and Chardonnay, Bass clansmen swill Jim Beam and beer. The Trout clansman's fly is avian, subtle and spun out of feathers and thread tied upon a single hook so tiny as to defy lynx-eyed scrutiny; the Bass clansman's lure is earth-bound, weighty, gaudy and bristling with treble hooks.

The Trout clansman casts his carefully weighted and tapered line with precise timing and dexterity designed to "turn over" his wispy fly and present it on the surface with the delicacy of an alighting (or emerging) insect. He seeks to make his presentation as close to the lurking fish as possible so as to avoid unnatural "drag" to his "drift." Reference is to the possible tug of several micro-currents upon the 10 or 12 feet of leader and the gossamer terminal tippet that are the camouflaged extensions of the otherwise heavy, visible fly line. Drag causes the fly to skitter across the surface, a sure tip-off to a wary trout.

Conversely, the crank baiter, or "theadliner" as he is aptly called in New Zealand, depends upon the weight of his lure to pull a near-invisible and uniform monofilament line off the reel. Since there is no way to avoid the entry-agitation of the plopping lure, the Bass clansman either targets species that are attracted by the bedlam or cast well beyond the fish's lie and then retrieves the offering through the critical strike zone.

The fly rod is lengthy, willowy and almost weightless, a sheer delight to hold and in the hands of the skilled practitioner a baton for conducting one's own *Water Music Suite*. Learning to cast a fly rod well is a lifetime's undertaking that is as open to improvement as perfecting the golf swing. The short, stocky crank-baiting rod is more accessible to everyone; the instrument itself well-suited for knocking Tantalus's fruit from furtive trees.

The Trout clansman's gear is an extension of his persona, his relationship with it tactile. He may tie his own flies and build tapered leaders. By wading he blurs the distinction between the terrestrial and aquatic realms. His vest is an amazing labyrinth of pouches and pockets bulging with the secreted gear (including possibly raincoat and lunch) that makes him as self sufficient as an orbiting astronaut. The Bass clansman is far more removed. He transports his gear in a plastic or metal box, its imprisoned lead and lures rattling about in grating protest. He fishes from shore or boat, physically unencumbered by any of his angling accoutrements.

Even our philosophies seem to differ. Fly-fishing scribes pen works like Ernest Schwiebert's *Remembrances of Rivers Past,* Nick Lyons' *Bright Rivers,* Thomas McGuane's *The Longest Silence* and A.A. Luce's *Fishing and Thinking.* Crank-baiting authors are more into hype. As I prepared for my first tucunaré encounter, all that I could find to read was Larry Larsen's *Peacock Bass Explosions!* (his exclamation point and one of his subtler uses of superlatives).

My first encounter with the cretinous enemy, however, had proved disconcerting. Armed with my arguably effete, and certainly elite, prejudices that stereotyped crank baiters as beer-swilling, loud, oafish good old boys, the plug-casting Taperá River companions during my maiden incursion into Amazonia proved to be anything but. In fact, we hit it off so well that some of us have maintained loose contact since.

For many a crank baiter, the peacock bass (actually a cichlid despite its name) is the quintessential quarry. While the species has been introduced into the waters of southern Florida and Hawaii, outside their native range their growth rate is disappointing. To catch a double-digit peacock, you must head out for the jungle camps of South America (Colombia, Venezuela, Bolivia, Brazil, the Guianas). Frontiers International had provided us with an excellent poop sheet that put me in touch with Don Daughenbaugh, purveyor of improbable flies. Don had developed several peacock bass offerings, particularly one that he called the "Brycon" for whatever reason. I gave him a $150 budget, leaving the selection to his discretion. Since Don deemed his efforts to be still in the experimental stage, he committed me to calling him upon my return. He wanted both a reading on my results and any suggestions. He was also working out successful patterns for tiger fishing in Africa's Okavango Delta, one of my intended future destination, so Don was a particularly promising contact.

Of course, there is a certain fraternal tie at work. We crank baiters and fly fishermen are, after all, at base sporting anglers jointly opposed to the real Darth Vaders, the "commercial fishermen." Nor do most of us fly fishermen start out as such. In my youth we kids were of the cane-pole, baited-hook angler variety. My first fish, a bluegill extracted by an ecstatic 5-year old out of Southern California's Big Bear Lake, scarfed down a kernel of canned corn. My first trout, caught out of the Truckee River off the Sierra Street bridge in downtown Reno and launched in reactive epiphany over my shoulder and out into the moving traffic, had succumbed to a red salmon egg.

My introduction to fly fishing (or its caricature) was more accidental than intentional. As a lad of 10 I was shipped off to a YMCA summer camp by my relieved parents. I was to spend a week, along with several other inmates, supposedly enjoying a horseback pack trip in the headwaters of the Sierra Nevada mountains' West Walker River. We were camped at some small lake, its waters filled with cruising brook trout that were pretty much better at spotting us than we them. In the crystalline waters my salmon-egg offering looked like a basketball attached to a rope. I couldn't actually hear the fish laughing scornfully, but they definitely seemed bemused. My fellow pimple-faced privates in the angling brigade were suffering a similar lack of success, save one.

Billy Cantlon, son of a dedicated fly fisherman physician father, was decked out like some sort of extraterrestrial. His stocking-feet waders, suspended by suspenders and cinched tightly at the waist with wading belt, felt hat, and, most of all, the amazing vest whose wool patches were festooned with fanciful, feathered creations, made Billy a prime candidate for our adolescent derision. One small detail saved him from being the skewered wiener at that evening's roast. *Billy was catching fish.*

I shadowed him for much of the afternoon and, probably to get rid of me, he gave me a couple of flies. This was, however, but one component in solving the riddle. At first I couldn't cast them with my short spinning rod without adding sinkers to my leader. The unnatural sinking action that they imparted to my presentation was just as off-putting to the brookies as were my previous efforts. I then hit upon using a tree twig as a bobber (I had none of the plastic variety). It gave me just enough weight to be able to chuck out about 15 feet of line. The unweighted fly then took several minutes to sink to the full depth of my six-foot leader. By that time initially spooked fish were back cruising the neighborhood. *I was catching fish!*

After losing my two flies, still faced with a couple of more days of incarceration and my pleas for further largesse politely dismissed by Billy, I had recourse to the child's ingenious ingenuity. I shredded one of my socks for the wispy threads that I then tied into an unlovely tangle on a bare single hook, further securing the abomination with a dab of candle wax. It was only good for a few casts, but, miraculously, it caught fish. If my fly-fishing persona was not actually birthed by that experience, clearly sperm had met egg and gestation was underway. For my next birthday I nagged my bewildered parents into making a $20 oblation toward the $40 cost of the bamboo rod that I purchased out of the proceeds from my newspaper route.

To prepare to fly fish for tucunaré, I first read "Flyfishing Excitement," Larsen's sparse (eight page) chapter 13 (some subliminal numerical hex?), which, despite its hyperbolic lead, is actually replete with useful tips. Then, too, fly fishing is not the most efficient mode for catching some species. It took me one trip to Costa Rica, another to Belize and four to Florida to boat my first tarpon, when it is common for first-time anglers to catch a sizable trophy while bait fishing shrimp-chummed waters under a bridge of the Keys. It has taken me 20 years to land five permit, that wariest of the saltwater species to fool with a fly, whereas lobbing a live crab in their general direction is an almost sure-fire method. The peacock bass is not quite that disdainful of the fly fisherman's art, but it certainly ranks somewhere in the hierarchy of difficulty. It is clearly more efficacious to kerplunk a Woodchopper plug, with its three treble hooks and noisy propeller, in the middle of a likely lagoon. The more racket the better, since big peacocks are ravenous and will cruise a considerable distance to check out the commotion—at least until they become the disabled veterans of the woodchopper wars.

There is a certain tyranny of distance entailed in traveling nonstop from Reno to a jungle camp well up a tributary of the Amazon. You arise in the dark, dress ludicrously in light clothing despite the single-digit temperature and icy roads, and drive through the pre-dawn while praying that your cabbie doesn't have car trouble on the way to the airport. In Dallas you change planes for Miami and then while away five hours in the airport before boarding your 9 p.m. red-eye flight to Belem and Manaus. After clearing customs, it's off to the smaller satellite terminal for the hour-and-a-half charter flight upcountry to Barcelo. There your outfitter transfers his catatonic guests into small boats for the 2½-hour trip to the lower camp on a feeder of the Rio Negro. What follows is my version of Camp Hell. I will be vague about places and change the name of persons in order to protect the guilty. As Dave Barry might note, *I did not make this up.*

There was to be no rest for the weary. After a quick snack, we were taken out fishing. I expected to be far too whipped from the trip to enjoy it but found that I did. I was beyond exhaustion, "in a zone" as my kids would say. For the first half hour my guide, João, contemplated my vain efforts to cast as closely as possible to the structure afforded by fallen trees and shoreline indentations. He was polite but transparent when he asked if I intended to fly fish exclusively or would I be casting lures as well? His concern was palpable as he contemplated a long and barren week together. However, part-way through our second lagoon, I caught a small peacock and then a huge fish took my streamer and headed for cover. I had little choice but to bear down on it by palming my reel, fearing that the 25-pound-test leader would break. It didn't. The trophy peacock simply straightened out my hook and was gone. We managed to catch several more smaller fish and a photo-op 10-pounder that, as it turned out, was the second largest that I was to land on the trip.

Curiously, since he'd had scant exposure to fly fishermen, João was an excellent guide for my purposes. He knew instinctively how to position the boat to keep me within range while not interfering with my back cast. He knew by reading my body language when to move. João's task was made more difficult since Narcissus, our American translator/camp host, fished with me on all but the last day. Narcissus is an expert fly fisherman, so we could fish simultaneously, I from the bow and he from midship.

During the week we caught more than 200 peacocks, mostly under five pounds, as well as the occasional jacunda and arowana. By fly fishing rather than woodchopping, we had managed to catch many butterfly and spotted peacocks as well, the smaller cousins of our targeted prey that, at a couple of pounds, were simply too small to consider the lures of our lunker-seeking camp mates. The most memorable fishing moment was when a school, or rather marauding pack, of monster peacocks suddenly appeared alongside, hammering baitfish on the surface and launching the survivors into the air and right up onto the bank. Narcissus and I cast in the general direction of the melée, and I was rewarded with an immediate savage strike. Ten minutes later we landed a majestic 15-pounder and took the obligatory photos, truly perfunctory record-keeping since its awesome electric beauty and bizarre shape were already emblazoned forever in my memory.

At one point we ascended for hours a hitherto unfished river, glimpsing the mountains of Venezuela and British Guiana. Then we nearly paid for our miscalculation by almost running out of fuel before fortuitously coming across one of our camp's boats. There was the day a pair of blue and yellow macaws perched above us on the same limb of a tall tree like two lovebirds while the jungle's stomach grumbled with the sounds of an invisible band of howler monkeys. João told a harrowing story as he indicated where, the previous year, he had been attacked by an anaconda. That day the river had come up quickly, swollen by upstream storms, and the staff was breaking down the flooded camp. As he waded waist deep across a side channel, the snake grabbed João's pant leg, wrapped him up and pulled him under. He bit its head, but to no avail. Fortunately, he was able to grasp a tree limb and pull himself back to the surface. He yelled for help, and one of his companions came running. The rescuer whacked the assailant with his machete, and the huge anaconda released his shaken prey and disappeared. João no longer wades.

In short, I had a most enjoyable week on the water. The same was not true of the land. We were eight anglers in camp. When we sat down to our first dinner, Sol announced,

"Gentlemen, I am the luckiest man in the world. I have done everything that I ever wanted to do since I was 16. When the house limit in Vegas was $500, mine was $5,000!"

Since we weren't even past the strangers-feeling-each-other-out stage, the rest of us were left pretty much speechless. Sol's companion, Sy, saved the day, or at least broke the silence.

"Sol's a great guy once you get used to him. The best thing is that when I tell him to shut the fuck up, he does!"

Sol and Sy were neighbors in the same retirement community in Florida. They were two spry dudes in their 70s who loved to fish together. Sol had been in the wholesale liquor business in New England, and Sy was retired from a major Northeastern accounting firm.

After hearing Sol's opening speech, I dove into my mental foxhole as far as my Nevada casino connections were concerned, running up the colors of my academic credentials instead. About midweek, however, my professional (im)posturing was exposed. As feared, once Sol learned of my business life, he took every opportunity to talk casinos. He was on intimate terms with all the bad guys, once saved Lucky Luciano's life and personally knew where the bodies were buried in the Nevada desert.

I grew to be quite fond of them. Sy, in particular, had an understated sense of humor, a capacity to laugh at himself and the verbal skills of a genuine raconteur. His questions were often personal and pointed, but somehow you didn't mind since he would cool his mark with an impish grin and ingenuous "People will tell you so much about themselves in a fishing camp! It's all so interesting." Above all Sy was a truly gentle man.

Then there was the crew-cut, ex-military Rambo, in his 60s. His favorite expression was "That's bullshit!" The first time I heard it was when we ran into him on the river, and he asked how we were doing. We told him that we had caught several fish. After listening to his expletive, we added that they were all small, prompting him to say that that was about the only true statement he expected to hear from a couple of fly fishermen. Rambo traveled with a collection of photos of prostitutes doing vile things to their genitalia and with his (presumably taken with a timer). He eagerly shared his treasure trove, along with his advice on how best to go whoring in San José, Costa Rica. It wasn't clear whether this was a display of Rambo's machismo or an attempt at male bonding with the rest of the guys. Probably both.

Rambo was fishing with the camp's best guide. Before week's end he was deferring to Antonio's superior casting skills. Whenever his guide hooked a fish, Rambo would reel it in. Most days theirs was the top boat as far as big fish were concerned. Nevertheless, each night at dinner Rambo declared the fishing to be lousy and too far to travel for. He had pretty much the same to say for Venezuela where, enigmatically, he was headed after this sojourn.

Fric and Frac were two longstanding fishing buddies from the Midwest. They were wizened veterans of that most difficult of freshwater angling pursuits, muskie fishing. Every summer for nearly 30 years they had pursued their sport in the north woods. They spoke reverentially of the challenge posed by an extremely difficult and rare quarry, only half-jokingly reporting a success ratio of one fish per 10,000 casts. Fric married for the first time at age 47, and Frac was his best man. Many of the 400 guests wept at the truly poignant fisherman's toast that Frac wrote for the wedding banquet. He repeated it from memory at our dinner table. Frac, Fric and Fric's Sue were now an angling threesome, though not on grueling jungle trips.

Their muskellunge masochism notwithstanding, Fric and Frac expected to catch many and large peacocks. They had been to South America four or five times and were heavily into invidious comparisons with other rivers, particularly after they had boated only two or three large fish each of the first few days. So Narcissus sent them to a small branch stream with excellent small lagoons. He told them to motor upstream for half an hour and then begin fishing. Narcissus' plan was that they would hit five or six lagoons intensively, but it was not to be. Rather, they had jawboned their guide into entering every likely spot, taken a few casts, cherry-picked a couple of large fish and then moved on. At day's end it had taken Fric and Frac two hours' travel time to return to the main river.

The problem was that each of the lagoons contained a spawning pair of large fish guarding their bed. Given the territorial instincts and spawning behavior of large peacocks, Fric and Frac had essentially fried a whole river that Narcissus planned to dole out carefully to 10 or 12 anglers over the course of the season. They hadn't a clue nor were they even overly impressed with their own day. Frac answered my polite query about the fishing with, "I guess it was O.K."

Finally, there were Big Bob and Little Bob, father and son from Tennessee. Bob is a graying, seriously overweight man in his late forties. His bearded, round face reminded me of Burl Ives, as did his melodious speech. But Bob was no folksinger; rather he was an international arms dealer. He was also a big-game hunter, having made numerous trips to Africa. He initiated vain attempts to network with me by asking if I belonged to the Safari Club (it holds its annual convention in Reno) or if I knew his favorite taxidermist (a resident of my hometown). I drew two blanks.

Bob and Bobby were obviously close. In my experience there is a special bond between Southern fathers and their sons that is a genuine American phenomenon. If one of my angling friends from California calls to cancel a trip, it is usually for a business reason or possibly because of gathering clouds on his domestic horizon. I have had a Southern father cancel a trip on me because he had to drive his son to boarding school and another because he was too nervous to leave home during the first week of his son's summer employment. I have also had Southern fathers condition the pleasure of their company upon including their sons. I am envious of the intimacy evident when a Southerner speaks of his boy or begins a story with

"My daddy once said...." The quality of their relationships with wives and daughters is a different matter, perhaps best captured in the drama *Steel Magnolias,* but then that's another subject.

Anyway, Big Bob was clearly our 800-pound gorilla. His peacock bass fishing experience was extensive and seemed to encompass every important river and significant angler. He and Bobby were down for three straight weeks. They were to fish with us for the first and then fly by floatplane directly to their second camp located on the Taperá. Bob was our outfitter's major client, and it showed. There was a supply of his favorite brand of soda pop in camp, off limits to us plebes. He ignored the schedule, arising at his leisure and fishing pretty much when and where he wanted. If Bob spoke at dinner, it was as the expert angler and historian. Two years earlier, during an 18-day stint (according to his daily ledger), he had boated over 600 peacocks, more than a hundred in the double-digit range.

All was not well in Bob's world. When he arrived in Manaus, he had learned that he would face severe competition on the Taperá. It seems that our outfitter and his former partner had had a falling out and there was now a houseboat of alien anglers anchored smack in the middle of "Bob's" waters. To make matters worse there was a third outfitter who kept turning up unexpectedly with his boatload of clients. The vast jungle suddenly seemed crowded with sharp-elbowed fishing entrepreneurs practicing on each other's ribs. Bob was caught in the crossfire and was indignant that he hadn't been informed earlier so that he could have considered his options. He had been assured that our outfitter had an exclusive on certain rivers, which turned out simply not to be the case.

As the week progressed, Bob declared our fishing to be passable if not spectacular. Bobby, our least jaded angler, was having a great time. He caught several large fish and was unabashedly enthusiastic. It was also evident that father and son were savoring the opportunity to spend such quality time together.

After dinner on the third evening, Bob tapped his finger for emphasis on the cover of *Primary Colors,* his reading material for this trip.

"If half of the allegations in this book are true, it is a national embarrassment that we elected Clinton president," he opined. Rambo chipped in, "It's a mystery to me how he ever got elected. Who voted for him?" Silence. Obviously, no one at our table had (I voted for Ralph Nader). In fact, no one seemed to even *know* anyone who had voted for Clinton (well, maybe except for me). There was the genuine befuddlement that flows from the evident disparity between the outcome and one's personal electoral mathematics. Sy excused himself by declaring that his mother taught him to never discuss politics or religion. Others followed his example and retired for the evening, leaving Bob, Bobby, Narcissus and me to carry on. Bob began,

> "Last year I read *The Hot Zone* while I was down here. I believe
> that if ebola ever gets a foothold in the United States it's going
> to kill 90 percent of the population. I've got my 800 acres
> and I plan to protect myself. You know people are going to flee
> the cities. It's going to be everyone for himself. I'm ready."

Bobby added that they lived in redneck country, and it was difficult to defend your property even without an ebola scare. It had taken years to run off the locals who thought they had a right to hunt the 800-acre farm because they always had. Now they stayed on the perimeter, but with an eye on their old stomping grounds in case the opportunity to bust a buck presented itself. Bob said he was considering fencing the property with a deer-proof enclosure that would allow him to farm whitetails. Given the siege climate, however, he added that it would be necessary to put in a perimeter road and patrol it regularly. Such is the high price of acting out one's bucolic fantasies in rural Tennessee!

Unlike Rambo, who was also an African hunter, Bob seemed reluctant to talk much about the Dark Continent. He had been seriously injured in the crash of an overloaded bush plane that failed to take off and was also frightened of African disease. In addition to ebola, there was AIDS which, conventional medical wisdom notwithstanding, in Bob's estimation was likely mosquito-borne.

Bob had about exhausted the list of worthy African trophies and was currently engaged in pursuing the world's "top 10 game fish" as calculated by *In Fishing* magazine, the most influential organ of the crank-baiter world. Narcissus had sent him the article in the fantasy that his client might pay him $100,000 to be guided to all 10 trophies. Bob had already caught his pike in Sweden and his muskie in Quebec. The object was to land the quarry irrespective of the technique. So, unlike Fric and Frac's 10,000-cast, self-flagellation ritual, Bob had caught several muskies by trolling.

He was fixated, even obsessed, with the challenge of catching a pirarucú, Brazil's enormous (several hundred pounds) and elusive river fish. I have only seen one, or more accurately, the surface swirl created by one. Bob announced that last year he had made a pact to exchange a rifle for a pirarucú, thereby elevating the art of guide-bribing to a whole new plane. On this trip he had a disassembled firearm with its parts scattered through his ample luggage, the better to smuggle it into Brazil. The new revelation punctuated his earlier comment that they could put him in the middle of the interloping anglers on his second river and he'd "stake out his territory, by God!" Bob listened with great interest while Narcissus described the pirarucú aquaculture project that was providing the dear and delicious fish to the Manaus market. Bob then asked, in all seriousness, if the fish farmers might let an angler into their ponds?

Bob was also the only one of us outfitted to take on another of South America's angling challenges. Our rivers were inhabited by several species of enormous catfish that could weigh up to hundreds of pounds. Bob had a sturdy sea rod, heavy line and leader and a collection of enormous hooks. He also put out six trot lines, each attached to one of the large buoys that he had brought along. He had devised a program whereby, once a fish was hooked on the rig, the buoy could be freed and the line attached to his rod. Clearly, Bob was into technology, if not sport.

Indeed, he finished his extraordinary jungle disquisitions with descriptions of the present and next generation of smart weapons.

He spoke in awe of the 75 percent kill ratio of the night-scoped arms used to fire from helicopters at targets (peasants standing in doorways and looking up) in the Central American conflicts and opined that within 25 years the average dogface would have a totally integrated system that would give him the same honing-in powers that were evidenced by American rockets during the Gulf War. Such nirvana was possible, of course, only assuming that our present president didn't screw things up by cutting the defense budget. As I lay on my cot listening to pleasanter nocturnal jungle sounds, I decided that it was all right to pray for Clinton even if I couldn't vote for him.

Another evening's tabletalk was a discussion about the relative merits of debarbing hooks. Not surprisingly, Rambo allowed as how debarbing was "bullshit." Sol and Sy either harbored no opinion or had decided to again sit one out. Bob agreed with Fric and Frac that debarbing hooks is a sure way to lose fish. Since Fric was wearing a T-shirt that proclaimed commitment to "Catch and Release," I struggled to make the logical connections, particularly after having witnessed the streamside surgery in which pliers are used on a woodchopped-peacock's face full of barbed treble hooks. By comparison the scene in the Western film when they extract the bullet without anesthesia is downright soothing.

The week ended pretty much on the note where it began. My fellow anglers had only landed a couple of plus 15-pound fish per day, per boat. In short, the fishing stunk. In the Manaus airport we commingled with a stream of anglers coming out of other jungle camps. The conversation was dominated by weights and numbers, with only the occasional flashes of enthusiasm in a long litany of disappointment.

In Search of El Dorado

An oft-told tale in my native Nevada is the 1900 bank robbery in Winnemucca, a caper supposedly perpetrated by Butch Cassidy and the Sundance Kid. While it adds zest to our particular version of the West, unfortunately it never happened—the undisputed protagonism of the two legendary figures, that is. If we can believe the classic film of their lives (and who can doubt the veracity of Robert Redford and Paul Newman?), once circumstances became too hot for the notorious pair in the American West, they split for South America. Their austral crime spree, not to mention their earthly existence, ended in the ambush set by the Bolivian army. However, life is never quite as neat as the flicks. In Cassidy's case, at least, there are books suggesting that he survived, slipped back into the United States and lived out the rest of his considerable days in uneventful obscurity.

Such thoughts crowded through my mind as I listened to Justo's story about the gringo gang, led by two famous outlaws, that became the scourge of his district before slipping over the border just ahead of a posse. It seems that, among other nefarious deeds, they had murdered a reputedly wealthy Welsh immigrant and his family by laying siege to their ranch near the Arroyo Pescado ranch that we were to fish later in the week, at which time I saw the plaque memorializing the staunch settler's bravery in holding out (until burned out) for a couple of days.

The only problem was that we were camped on the banks of the Río Pico, which is in Patagonian Argentina, several miles south of Esquel and light years away from Bolivia. Yet Justo was the proprietor of this particular estancia, located in the foothills of the Andes, and his account, if not exactly first hand, was handed down from his father. His grandfather was a witness to the events when both the pursued and their pursuers passed through the family property headed towards Chile.

Justo was in his early 20s and a brash young man to be sure. Each evening he would ride into camp, accompanied by another young dandy or two, to smoke some of Earl Cohen's cigars and drink our whisky. They were quite a sight in their gaucho array. Justo was half-Basque, and disclosure of my own, albeit academic, Basque credentials earned me a visit to the nearby rustic ranch house where his widowed mother and little sister treated me to maté and stale cookies.

While the family was a fairly big frog in the local pond, the district itself was quite peripheral to Argentina's elaborated ranching world. It seems that the forested foothills had been calculated to be simply too marginal and recalcitrant for potential pastureland during the initial dividing up of the pie. Subsequently, landless gauchos, including Justo's grandfather, moved into the vacuum, homesteading or squatting as the case might be.

Theirs was a hardscrabble existence, one that was largely incapable of retaining the loyalties of the young. The district was in the throes of a major rural exodus. Justo had a couple of hundred head of cattle, a band of sheep and a few horses, a modest operation by Argentine standards. The main house was little more than a shack.

While showing me the stable and corrals, he noted that winter was particularly tough. The snow often reached a horse's belly, and after a day's ride of caring for the stock, your sheepskin chaps were encased in ice. Bronchitis, bordering on pneumonia, became a constant companion. So I gave him a pair of slightly tattered stocking-feet waders and then downplayed his effusive gratitude, privately bemused by the mental image of his pending wintry sartorial performance.

It was on the Río Pico trip that Raúl San Martín, our outfitter, told Mike Michalak and me about a fish in Argentina's subtropical north called the dorado. Mainly a denizen of the Río-Paraná system, in the massive lower reaches of the main river it is pursued by plug fishermen as their preferred quarry. Catches in the 30-40 pound range are not uncommon. Of more interest to a flyrodder, the dorado migrates upstream to spawn, and virtually all of the tributaries of the Paraná have a run. Raúl thought it possible to catch them in the skinnier headwaters on large streamer flies and surface poppers.

The dorado takes its name from its golden-hued coloration. Once hooked they are strong fighters, acrobatic, and excellent to eat, an all-around fine gamefish. Curiously, according to Raúl, locals paid them scant attention. Several years earlier he had lived in the north and knew some first-class dorado waters. He was prepared to set up a trip for the following September. Mike and I were in.

Raúl and his brother Puma met our by-now overly swollen group at the Tucumán airport. We had been scheduled to float his special stream, but the news was not good. The entire region was in the throes of a major drought. Raúl and an assistant had just completed a trial run on the Río Popayán that had taken roughly twice as long as calculated. It wasn't until the third evening of a scheduled two-day float that they appeared at the take-out rendezvous where an anxious Puma awaited with the van. By then he had progressed from panic to preliminary mourning. There was simply no flow in the river, and they had had to drag their enormous rubber raft most of the way through a few inches of water. They were beaten and eaten (as in mosquito-bitten).

Plan B was Termas de Río Hondo, the very antithesis of our intended "jungle" experience. It is a resort town (*termas* means "hot springs") with an extensive tourism infrastructure ranging from luxury hotels to campgrounds. The area's appeal had been enhanced recently by construction of a dam on the adjacent river. We were to fish the reliable releases from the impoundment's storage.

Our second illusion was dispelled almost immediately, since we were to share the waters with both vacationing spin casters and bait casting locals. Argentina was mired in an economic crisis with stratospheric unemployment, hence no shortage of subsistence fishermen with time on their hands.

I began fishing within a couple of hundred yards of the dam. Just as I had about exhausted that particular stretch, a dorado was on and carving out a series of near-vertical, matched jumps. I eased it into the shallows and missed my photo op when the approximately eight-pounder got off. At the time I gave the matter little thought, but should have. I had just lost the largest fish that I was to see on this particular trip.

For the next three days the high point of my angling was the conversation with my guide Juan. One day as we drove back to our hotel he pointed out the local casino while issuing a warning, "We call it the *desplumadora*" (feather picker), thereby instantly providing my delighted companions with yet another of my several unflattering nicknames—*El desplumador.*

The fishing was slow and the catching worse. We all landed a few one or two-pounders, appearing like traces of color in a placer miner's pan, but it was definitely anticlimactic after a several-thousand-mile, two-day odyssey to get here. Nor was our discomfort diminished by our surroundings. Both sides of the river were laced with shantytowns lacking even a minimum of services. The shoreline was strewn with garbage and laced with little feeders of raw sewage. It was only by repressing thoughts of the obvious that we were able to wade the river at all. It was time to move.

Raúl was clearly making it up as we went along. He discounted the possibility of fishing the substantial waters of the Río Bermejo, which forms the border with Bolivia, since the daily papers trumpeted the ominous progress of a budding international confrontation. Bolivian commercial fishermen were using dynamite to stun migrating dorado, and both countries' armies were on alert. There were worse alternatives than sewer fishing!

Our backup was the Río Juramento, a stream that Raúl had never fished before, so we stopped along the way to pick up a local dorado veteran. Our headquarters was the dusty agricultural town of Joaquín V. González, and it was on edge. A few days earlier the federal police had killed three men in a shootout in a local bar. The details were murky and the civic mood sullen.

Our fishing was to transpire on a nearby ranch owned by Ricardo Sariguietta. As it turned out, he was Basque on his mother's side. Once again my academic credentials allowed me to pass through the looking glass of formality and into a more private inner circle. He invited us to the estancia's headquarters and proudly displayed his many stuffed hunting trophies, which included a remarkable and rare giant armadillo and a weird creature that the locals called a "catdog" because of its combined feline and canine features. He also warned us to be careful of the extremely aggressive yarará snake, a relatively small viper. One had bitten and killed a young boy on the ranch the year before.

We were into another tailout situation, since about 12 miles upstream there was a largely completed dam on line, and it was already controlling stream flows. The plan was to float the river in Raúl's raft, which was of a size that could have almost landed an entire division of Argentine troops on some Falklands' beach during that recent bout of international unpleasantries. There were several problems. With six anglers and their gear aboard, the raft was all but unresponsive to the oarsmanship of the slightly built Raúl. This meant that we were not always able to alight where intended, nor were we always successful in avoiding assorted hazards (rocks, logs, etc.) along the way. At one point we were helplessly skewed upon a channel diverter constructed out of dead brush bearing two-inch long thorns. Fortunately, the raft's hide was thick enough to withstand them, because had it popped, the swift current would have swept us collectively under the man-made barrier.

The second problem was our inability to move upstream given the pathless, thick and thorny understory. That, combined with our limited capacity to navigate, meant that we were often into, and then past, a promising run before there was time to react. In short, compared to us, the three men in the tub of the nursery rhyme were positively a streamlined operation.

Compounding problems one and two, there were simply too many of us along. We would stop and then try to fish downstream, but there was seldom enough water for more than two or three rods.

There was also the mystery of water clarity. One moment the stream was clear and the next totally roily and unfishable. It would then take an hour or so for it to clear again. We guessed that there must be upstream construction in progress, maybe on the dam. As it turned out, this was not the case. Rather, it had to do with water releases. It seemed that, given the drought, our local ranchers had held back the flow, but were then sued successfully by downstream Corrientes Province for doing so. Released under court order, there was now a substantial amount of compensatory water surging in pulses down a river course that was defined by sandy banks.

One morning as I was working a run, there was a rushing sound. I looked at the opposite bank only to observe about two hundred yards of it, including several trees of reasonable size, simply disappear. I was then accosted by a riverine tsunami as the stream threatened to leap my bank. For the next hour the river digested its new channel, its waters roiled by its work.

The penultimate day of our angling schedule we did a float on the beautifully clear upper reaches of the river, putting in just below the dam. While this was far and away the aesthetically most appealing experience of the trip, the fishing remained disappointing. A powerboat with local bait casters preceded us downstream. Their delicate technique entailed stringing several-inch long strips of rotten sábalo (a herbivorous native fish) meat onto a treble hook and then using several-ounce lead sinkers to bounce it along the bottom. At our mutual take-out point they showed us their catch, three dorado in the 10- to 15-pound range. For our part all six of us had been skunked.

With tails and spirits dragging, we mutinied, insisting on proceeding to Salta, our air departure city, the next morning rather than further anger or amuse the dorado deity. It was a wise choice. Salta, delightfully situated in the Andean foothills, has a moderate climate and wonderful colonial architecture. It is also the home of chacarena music, an Argentine genre reminiscent of Mexican rancherías. Our timing was fortunate, since that evening there was a chacarena street festival.

Salta also has an anthropology museum. Its display of artifacts and induments of the region's several Indian tribes was standard. What was decidedly not is the mural adorning one whole wall that depicted human migrations from the Old World to the New. I was, of course, aware of the Bering Strait land-bridge hypothesis and the somewhat less plausible trans-Pacific (a la Thor Heyerdahl) one, but that just demonstrates the narrowness of my professional training. For it seems that the Americas were actually populated by wanderers from Antarctica whose ancestors had first gone from Southeast Asia to Australia and then on to what I had previously thought to be the planet's only uninhabited continent. According to the Argentine anthropologist upon whose work the mural was based, Tierra del Fuego was the first New World landfall of the progenitors of Native American peoples.

I met Jan in Buenos Aires for a side trip to Iguasu Falls. Just below the main cataract there is an enormous pool of frothed water, where the considerable Rio Iguaçu seems to be regaining its composure after the vertiginous plunge before proceeding on to its rendezvous with the nearby Paraná. As I contemplated the scene from the walking trail, suspended a couple of hundred yards above the river, I noticed a massive form rising slowly in the clear waters of a back eddy. I queried a passing park ranger and was told that it was a dorado, obviously in the 40-plus pound range. "Fishing is prohibited here in the park, so they get very large, Senhor." For the next half hour I watched for the fish, which would lazily appear and then disappear into the foam. Occasionally, it was joined by other dorado, smaller yet all in the trophy range. I studied their behavior and vowed to return.

Later that week I visited the Museum of Natural History in Rio de Janeiro. Despite the dusty and dilapidated condition of its stuffed and bottled specimens, to enter the several rooms of the fish display was akin to an intergalactic journey. The Amazon basin has no fewer than 3,000 species, many of which defy the human imagination. Contemplating this enchanted bestiary, I realized just how narrowly we anglers define and then canonize our "game fish." For a fly fishermen, and even when including marine species, the list scarcely makes it into the double digits.

The literature from Jorge Xifra regarding the Apa River, a feeder of the Paraná that configures the border between Paraguay and Brazil, promised sight-fishing for dorado—the fly fisherman's dream. I was at an Andros Island bonefish camp, a layover on my way south, when I got the phone call from Mike Michalak. A freak storm had blown out the Apa. Our impending trip was cancelled until the next September. So it was back to Reno with dorado again on the back burner.

By the following year we were up to five anglers, a possible cause for concern since the fishable waters on the Apa were supposedly limited to maybe a half mile of river. After a red-eye flight to Asunción, Bob Morgart and I changed to a charter and were in Valle Mí, a river port town on the mighty Paraná, by noon. Mike and his two clients from Virginia had arrived a day earlier and were already at the Apa.

For the next couple of hours we endured a bone-crunching ride on the hubcap-deep ruts of the only dirt road on this 500,000-acre estancia owned by International Packers Limited. During one stop at a line cabin, where a dozen or so employees were gathered to drink their midday maté, I asked how many head of cattle were on the property. No one knew since they were semi-wild and had never been rounded up on one occasion.

The countryside was a far cry from the "jungle" that we had been led to anticipate, rather it was open savannah interspersed with the occasional grove of trees. The Apa itself was bracketed by a vegetative corridor that was about a hundred yards wide before conceding to scrubland and rough pasturage. Our tent camp, which was definitely of the dusty variety, was in the fringe where forest met field.

As Bob and I rigged up for the late afternoon's fishing, our three companions trudged back into camp somewhat sobered by their day. They had caught but two small dorado among them. The water was chocolate and the fishable stretch scant, little more than a hundred yards of rapids. What's more we had considerable competition. There was a semi-permanent fishing camp on the Brazilian side. Its owner, Celso, the *fazendeiro,* or proprietor, of the enormous contiguous ranch, was a delightfully exuberant fellow who was given to extending his hospitality to the multitude, including us as it turned out. The downside was that this introduced several spin casters at any one time into the already crowded waters. The good news was that this did not necessarily translate into overfishing, since the dorado were migrating through and presumably renewing our fish population.

After a few futile hours of casting, and thoroughly scorched by the unrelenting sun, I was an easy mark for Celso's shouted invitation to join him. He escorted me across the river in a small skiff, and I was soon seated under his shaded canopy, deliciously cold Brazilian beer in hand and treated to stories of giant dorado taken on this very spot. Celso claimed that he and his guests had hooked

200 fish over the past few days and he had five impressive ones in an ice chest, two over 20 pounds, to prove it. It is never truly consoling to contemplate another angler's catch, but it can certainly be encouraging!

For the next several days we flailed the murky waters with spotty success. Lanier was the only member of our party to score in double digits, taking a 15- and 20-pounder. We all caught dorado in the two- to five-pound range, and my largest was an eight-pounder. The best time was had when we took our modest quarry on surface poppers (Dahlberg's and Bob's Bangers).

The place was not without its enchantment. Downstream on a sand bar there were three large, basking caymans. Parrots, parakeets and the occasional toucan or pair of macaws provided stellar bird watching. The monkey sightings during the pleasant walk from camp to stream were infrequent enough to be special.

On the other hand, there was something quite illusory about our camping venture. Celso lived but a couple of miles away in a thoroughly modern ranch house complete with the twin symbols of contemporary life—a television and computer. He kept inviting us to move in, but we demurred, preferring to spend our few thousand dollars on the privileged rustic life—as in sharing our evening meal with the nightly mosquito swarm. It was not to worry, since Celso wanted Mike and me to come back next year as his guests. And, by the way, if we entered via Brazil our charter flight could land on his private strip.

Partway through the week, and to Jorge's chagrin, I mutinied. That is to say, despite strict orders not to leave our little patch of rapids, I did. My curiosity had been whetted by the sudden appearance of two boats whose anglers anchored above us and began casting lures into our midst. This had prodded Jorge and his assistant, José, into action. Jorge shouted to the interlopers that this was a specially designated, catch-and-release section of the river that was definitely off limits to spin casters. While a total bluff, he brandished a rifle and José a pistol to underscore the point. Their amazingly unperturbed interlocutors shrugged, made a few more casts that were seemingly more related to machismo than angling, and then motored off casually to disappear around the bend that I was determined to explore.

My upstream foray was scarcely encouraging since it disclosed a veritable flotilla of fishing craft. I asked Celso about it, and he remarked that there was a major public campground about a mile upstream that was easily accessible over a good road. For the remainder of our week, we sighted the odd boatload of local anglers peeking at us from afar, seemingly deliberating whether or not to test our (armed) defenses. This particular "game" did not exactly contribute to a Waldenian or Waltonian mood. Nor did Celso's disclosure that in Brazil (though not in Paraguay) it was illegal to fish rapids such as ours. However, as their owner he considered himself exempt, further insulated by an occasional case of beer given to the local warden. Actually, I was learning quickly that such piscatorial *droit de seigneur* is standard, and even expected, within South American game-law enforcement.

The week was not a total bust, since it led ultimately to my debut on Paraguayan national television. Jorge had a fishing show in Asunción and was recording our modest efforts on video for it. I was knee deep in swift current when I hooked a two-pound dorado. It was a considerable distance to shore over a slippery bottom stippled with invisible freshwater rays, so the idea of beaching the fish was unappealing. I therefore put my rod between my knees and handhauled in the dorado. As I fumbled to extract the debarbed hook with long-nose pliers, ever mindful of even this little guy's formidable choppers, it slipped out of my grasp. During the ensuing Gong Show, I managed to end up holding nothing more than my line. My rod and reel were embarked on their own journey downstream, bouncing over three small waterfalls before coming to rest at the feet of the ecstatic Mike. "It's okay, Bill, you can release him now." I let go of the thread binding me to angler's ignominy, and Mike reeled in a considerable amount of backing, then the fly line and finally a dorado! Lest I forget, he later sent me a copy of the video aired by Jorge on Paraguayan national television.

In January 1998 I needed refuge. Two months earlier my partner and I had been forced to close our Riverboat Hotel and Casino. Dealing with the drama of 400 loyal employees cut suddenly adrift and dueling with banks and creditors while skating on the thin ice of possible bankruptcy had definitely frayed both mind and spirit. I headed south.

Mike Michalak was touting his newest destination, sea-run brown-trout fishing in the Rio Grande of Argentina's Tierra del Fuego. Jeff Vermillion was exploring British Guiana in search of a tucunaré possibility for his Sweetwater Travel Company. There was a hiatus of about 10 days between the two trips, and it obviously made no sense to return home to Reno for such a short interim. Not to worry. A year earlier I had toured southern South America with a team of academics from the University of the Basque Country. Sponsored by the Basque government, we gave a series of lectures in Santiago, Buenos Aires and Montevideo on various topics—it being my particular assignment to describe to South American Basques the experiences of their fellow ethnics in the American West. In Montevideo I was asked to repeat my lecture for the Basque club Eusko Etxea in the small, deliciously named country town of Durazno ("Peach" in Latin-American Spanish) by its president, Alberto Irigoyen.

Alberto was the administrator of the two estancias owned by his wife, Adriana Patrón's, absentee family. I stayed with them at the Santa Margarita and fell in love with the pampas. We became the fastest of friends, and they had been urging me to return with enough frequency so as to underscore the invitation's sincerity. The prospect of complete repose with no other challenge than the long-standing personal one of finally reading Joyce's *Ulysses* seemed sheer lotus to this particular eater. There was, however, one little fly in that ointment; Alberto and Adriana knew that I was an angler (they aren't). "We have fish, too, on the estancia—mojarra and tararira. You will be very happy."

I had never heard of tararira but knew that a mojarra was akin to panfish found in some Midwestern farm pond. Jeff Vermillion thought he knew of tararira and proclaimed his disinterest in pursuing "a carp with teeth." Adroitly I tried to communicate to my friends that even Bill Angler could find worldly bliss without perpetual angling. That was all before I underwent my lobotomy, of course.

On the ride from Río Grande's airport to the hotel, and making small talk with my Argentine guide-to-be, I described my pending itinerary. "Tararira! You are going fishing for tararira in Uruguay? How I envy you. It is my favorite fish and there is no better place."

He went on to describe a dark-gray, torpedo-shaped prehistoric predator with a vicious set of teeth. My angler-curiosity gland began exuding its hormone.

The leaden skies, cool temperature and swollen rivers of what should have been the Uruguayan summer underscored the universal discourse on how the weather had suddenly somehow gone awry since mankind tampered with Mother Nature or, at the very least, some celestial matchmaker introduced *El Niño* to *La Niña*. It was touch and go to even reach Santa Margarita, given that many of the low-lying causeways were awash. My hosts had scheduled me to fish in one of their arroyos (streams) and on the Rio Yi with a local hunting and sometimes fishing guide.

The trip to the arroyo was a total bust. Within half an hour Alberto had stripped the gears of our transport tractor and I had managed to wade chest-deep into frigid rainwater while forgetting I was carrying my pocket watch, and then proceeded to ping my rod tip with a heavy streamer fly on about the third cast. Tractorless, timeless and rodless, we cellular-phoned back to headquarters for a ride from a *mayordomo* who could scarcely suppress his disdainful merriment over our dreadful performance. Taking our show on the road to the Río Yi was only marginally better. It poured that particular day and the river was positively sinister. *El Gallego* ("The

Galician" nickname of our guide Enrique Reyes) wended his small boat skillfully through the torrent and past a particularly Dantesque whirlpool (a week later two brothers were drowned there despite wearing life vests) before anchoring in a back channel whose level was swollen several feet beyond normal. The water and presumably the fish extended yards into the enveloping brush. In short, it was another of the many days chalked up in the "experience" column of Bill Angler's scorecard.

It would be two years before I would again tempt the gods of Yi. We were now no longer talking about a mere skirmish targeting a single foe, but a larger multi-front campaign. Uruguay has a dorado fishery, albeit a modest and castigated one by, say, Río Apa standards. It is concentrated in the mighty Río Uruguay and its tributaries. I would fish for tararira with *El Gallego* for a few days on the Yi before we pursued dorado out of the town of Mercedes on the Río Negro.

Regarding the dorado fishing, my angling expectations were quite low. We would be fishing heavy, turbid, structureless waters, the very antithesis of the fly-fishing ideal. However, my environmentalist curiosity was piqued. I wanted to experience and understand the complexity of angling on highly accessible waters of a South American country. The Yi and the Negro form part of the same drainage but are now separated by a massive hydroelectric dam that created Lake Palmar about 20 years ago. Thanks to it, Uruguay is now self-sufficient in energy and exports power to Argentina.

I was particularly fascinated by the impact of dams on nature, convinced that they are the single biggest threat to any environment. I came by this prejudice naturally. Twenty miles downstream from my hometown on the Truckee River, which links alpine Lake Tahoe with Pyramid Lake (after the Great Salt Lake the Great Basin's largest body of water), exists one of the world's least auspicious and America's most important river barriers—Derby Dam. Scarcely taller than a man, it is the first nefarious consequence of the National

Reclamation Act (1902), fathered by Nevada's Senator Newlands, which diverted much of the lower Truckee to the Carson River drainage and into the Lahontan Dam impoundment. Its waters are the lifeblood of the Fallon agricultural district which, while arid Nevada's finest, remains modest by almost anyone else's standards. More significantly, the act has served as the foundational enabling legislation for most of the 20th century's considerable dam building throughout the American West.

The impact of Derby Dam on the local environment was devastating. With their source choked, Winnemucca Lake dried up entirely and is now a salt flat, while Pyramid, home of unique fish such as the cui-ui and Lahontan cutthroat trout and a major pelican rookery, dropped 80 feet and threatened to become too saline to support most of its biota.

During my boyhood, as a casual angler and serious fur trapper on the Truckee, I learned all too well the pernicious effects of damming. Below Derby the river was practically too sluggish, warm and polluted to support life. Upstream, the river's flow through Reno was minimized by diversion dams for the ditches irrigating the few ranches and farms of the Truckee Meadows. Between the California state line and town of Truckee, the Sierra Pacific Power Company installed three small generating plants, each powered by waters diverted into flumes a couple of miles upstream, thereby creating hiatuses in the main channel where torrent becomes the trickle through an otherwise degraded riverine habitat.

On the drive to Santa Margarita, Alberto updated me on the country's profound and deepening economic crisis. Both Brazil and Argentina, Uruguay's behemoth partners in Mercosur, were mired in recession and the world price of wool had dropped from about $3.50 to $1.15 a kilo, scarcely worth the shearing. Australia was slaughtering millions of animals to avoid total collapse of the wool market, and Uruguay's sheep numbers were in free fall. To make matters worse, the beef cattle alternative was recently clouded by an outbreak of hoof-and-mouth disease in the north of the country, effectively interdicting most meat exports. The price of beef had tumbled from 73 to 58 cents a kilo, or below production costs. The quarantine period would last for at least a couple of months, assuming there were no further outbreaks. Unemployment was well into the double digits and petty crime on the rise. Durazno's biggest employer, a flour mill, had just closed—loss of its hundred jobs triggering a negative ripple effect throughout the local economy.

"The big question is whether we've hit bottom. I don't think so," Alberto opined.

The initial plan was for him to deliver me to Enrique's tiny sporting goods store (he is also a gunsmith) each morning and then collect me in the evening for the 10-mile drive back to Santa Margarita. We were to fish on La Cueva del Tigre ("The Tiger's Cave Estancia," a name taken from a natural formation that was once the lair of the now-extinct Uruguayan puma). The sign at its entry offered *agroturismo* (rural tourism), and the owner's pantomimed disgust as *El Gallego* took him aside to communicate that I planned to stay with my friends at Santa Margarita convinced me to spend the next night here.

Wilson Mendez awaited us at the river. A powerfully built man, Wilson was a fencer by trade, a worker in one of the many gangs that normally contract out their services to estancia owners. With economic times hard, they had no work; however, Wilson was *El Gallego's* jack-of-all-trades. Enrique and his new spouse, Adriana, a notary public, administered rentals in Durazno as a part of their frenetic household strategy, and there were always repairs to be made. Throughout our trip Wilson was to camp nearby to protect our equipment from theft. He had several baited hand lines in the water but had caught nothing.

The weather was cloudy, breezy and cool, infusing an inauspicious chill into the water since tarariras prefer it warm. Nor did the moon favor us. *El Gallego* informed,

"The tararira is active during the waning moon. We have a rising one, nearly full. They will eat during the night, not the day. The best times to catch them are the hottest months—December through February—during the new moon. In October they spawn and can be caught easily because they guard their redds and attack anything that comes close—even other tararira. Some die defending their young and most of the fish receive wounds. They are not good to eat at that time; their flesh becomes soft and almost rotten."

By noon the sky cleared, and we were soon sweltering. But the fishing remained practically non-existent. I hooked a six-inch *cabeza amarga* ("bitter head"), scarcely longer than my steamer fly, which looked somewhat like a perch. Enrique killed it for Wilson to use as bait.

We made our way through a series of lazy pools, frequently striking rocks barely concealed beneath the surface of the *café-au-lait* waters. If a bit jarring, the massive rebar cage surrounding our propeller averted disaster. The true delights of the day were vegetative and avian. Unlike the forbiddingly thorny brush of the banks of the Río Juramento, the verge of the Yi was gentle and penetrable. The crowning species was the native weeping willow. Flocks of green parakeets, punctuating the silence with raucous cries, appeared and then disappeared all in an instant. Cardinals, herons, kingfishers, woodpeckers and a plethora of finches flitted about unnerved by our progress. My favorite bird was the tero tero, which rummaged about the shore in pairs.

"It is our friendliest bird because it always nods and says hello."

Watching their stiff-legged gait, halted in mid-step for a bobbing of the head, became the sideshow of the day's amusement. The main event was the sighting of 13 roseate spoonbills arrayed on a distant sand bar, the object of an hour-long stalk that rewarded our patience with close-up photos before the flock burst into a pink blur smudged against the chartreuse of the willowy backdrop.

"They are just passing through; they came here from Africa and will leave the Yi in a week or two."

The next morning Alberto delivered me dutifully to Durazno, stopping along the way to let me photograph two flocks of ñan-duses (rheas) flanking our dirt road like soldiers assigned to guard duty. The sky was clear and yesterday's blow now an intermittent breeze. The water temperature persisted with the chill from the recent weather, but was clearly rising. There was no morning fishing, but spirits were high for the afternoon as we fingered the succulent lamb ribs cooked by Wilson over his campfire, downing our meat with a local kind of hardtack or country cookie as it is called.

Despite the warming of our waters, the tararira remained elusive. Enrique complained that the day before my arrival, when he and Wilson had launched the boat and set up camp, several local anglers left his favorite hole carrying a gunnysack filled with juvenile tarariras,

"They were probably netted. It is unlawful, but no one pays any attention. You can scarcely eat such small fish; they were the future spawners."

Later Enrique would cut and discard a trot line festooned with about 50 hooks. Clearly, the castigation of the resource was of the 24-hour variety. In the late afternoon Enrique had a strike on a spinner, but the fish escaped before we could even glimpse it.

This venture was indeed becoming full-fledged agrotourism rather than angling. As we bounced along a rutted track towards the ranch house, two gauchos astride their sheepskin saddles and with flounced pantlegs, high boots, and sashed waists drove a band of heifers towards the corrals. There, amid a dust cloud from which emanated shouting and the barks of two dogs, the hapless cows were crammed together in a narrow chute. Immobilized, they endured invasion by a stocky young man, his slickened rubber-gloved arm glisteningly green with manure. He was Santiago Bordaberry, a local vet and son-in-law of José Tesoriero, owner of the estancia and seated calmly amidst the melée recording the results of the examination that was intended to select the candidates for artificial insemination.

To stay out of the way I headed for the main house, carrying my overnight things in a plastic sack and chided by the terrified baby parakeet peering out of a saddlebag. It had fallen from its nest and was destined to receive Spanish lessons from its new master. Rita, the housekeeper, showed me to my room and prepared me a cup of coffee served with the flair of English high tea in an elegant dining room. I began to regret not having brought more proper attire than my tarpon wear. Fortunately, the lady of the house, who was a moderately well-known landscape and still-life artist schooled in Paris, was away in Montevideo.

For the next hour I explored the house and grounds, which were reminiscent of a modest English country estate but with a tiled roof and floor Spanish flair. The impression was amplified by the many little touches of hunting scenes, English-language coffee table books on gardening and country crafts, exposed ceiling beams and antique furniture. I imagined the place to be a hundred or more years old, a relic of the eclipsed elegance of the fin-de-siècle Río-de-la-Platan prosperity when Argentina and Uruguay were the world's wealthiest countries. It was then that the South American was the stereotypical playboy for Parisians and Londoners alike, and wealthy estancieros made the obligatory European Grand Tour, hauling back vast amounts of furniture, crockery and art to adorn their properties as the easy antidote to their sense of social inferiority deriving from the rusticity and remoteness of their everyday existence. The place exuded elegance eclipsed, the decline bespoken by split silk seat coverings, dinged-up tables and chairs, cracked tiles, peeling wallpaper and the odd water stain on plastered surfaces.

I was, however, wrong in my assessment of the age of this particular property, built as it was by a German owner in the 1950s. Twenty-one years ago José Tesoriero, an Argentine, purchased the estancia but was forced to sell off parts of its land to satisfy his creditors. La Cueva del Tigre was down to about 1,000 hectares (or about 2,500 acres) and little more than 400 head of cattle—barely viable in today's ranching scene.

After dark, Julio Tesoriero, José's 26-year-old son, offered me a whisky that I drank while Santiago Bordaberry practiced his English with and on me. Santiago had been an exchange student in veterinary medicine for a year at the University of Minnesota and spoke highly of the States. On his father's side he is descended from French Basques and on his mother's from Navarrese, so he was fascinated by my work. When I answered his query about the fishing, he gave me his card and offered to take me to his father's estancia the following weekend. There both the tararira and the capybaras were plentiful since few anglers and hunters were granted access.

Santiago left and Julio and I chatted while he barbecued tripe, beef fillets and pork sausage. He had studied agriculture in Montevideo and then tried selling cars there for a year before realizing that he was not cut out for city life. His two sisters were studying in the capitol, and he was heir apparent here—if, of course, there was still a here to inherit one day. He was off to Europe in a few months to visit a chum from Valencia and then knock around for a month or two. Rita brought out a mound of lettuce and tomatoes, and José appeared. The three of us ate together in a covered patio, washing down our repast with red wine while fending off the persistent advances of the two cattle dogs.

Next morning I found José in his office off the living room doing paper work. I went in to pay him and be motioned toward a chair, "Santiago is ex-President Bordaberry's son, you know [which I did]. He was no democrat," José added jocularly.

In fact, Bordaberry had a checkered political career. Originally a member of the *Blanco* (white) party (rural and conservative), he ended up being elected as vice president on the *Colorado* (red, liberal and urban) ticket. Once in office, through a series of maneuvers and events, he assumed the presidency and shortly thereafter, suspended parliament. That in turn provoked a *golpe* or *coup d'etat* by the army in 1972, which brought Uruguay 13 years of military dictatorship. José remarked,

> "When I was still in Argentina, in the Toay Department of La Pampa province, there was a *golpe,* and I felt like shooting off rockets in celebration. Under the Peronists everything went to hell. The army lacked politicians, and there were many posts to fill. One day an officer came to me and said 'we need you to be the *intendente* of Toay.' I agreed on the condition that it didn't interfere with my private affairs—I was very busy. I didn't like it much, and it was too time consuming, so I quit after just two years. I am proud to say that I never abused my office. I had a credit card and never charged a tank of gas, although it was expected. I was outraged by some things. Once they brought for my approval the new driver's licenses—little booklets with the necessary information about the driver. There was an envelope pasted to the back cover. 'What's this for?' I asked, 'It's for the driver to put some money in for the policeman who stops him' they said. I had them all destroyed."

José opined that the next election here in three years would most certainly be won by the leftist *Frente Amplio* (Broad Front) party. A year ago it had received more votes than any other, prompting the traditional adversaries of the Blanco and Colorado parties to forge a ruling coalition. Given the crisis, its stock was quite low. José could smell the waft of impending Uruguayan *Peronismo.* Before Perón he had worked as a gameskeeper on an Argentine estancia owned by Germans and operated as a hunting preserve. Perón outlawed hunting preserves and soon after the Germans sold out,

> "Today most of the owners of big estancias in Uruguay are foreigners—French, Italians, Argentines, Brazilians, Americans. Several of them have told me that if Frente Amplio wins they will pull out."

The morning was warm and clear, our spirits high. The water was tepid to the touch. I snagged a small fish that looked like something that might have crawled out of primal slime and so ugly as to be indescribable. It was a *vieja del agua* (old lady of the water). Then on my first cast to a rocky shoreline, and before I had full control of my line, a tararira smashed my streamer, dashed 10 feet, frothed the surface in anger and was gone. *El Gallego* stripped off his pants to drag our craft through a particularly shallow stretch and said,

> "If this was a time of the waning moon, I would never enter the water. It is then that the tararira are voracious and even attack people. My stepson almost had his heel shorn off while swimming in this river. It is a bad wound. It festers because tararira have some kind of poison in their mouth."

The next stretch was a 200-yard-long, deep pool. While blind-casting, I had my second strike. A dark tube hurtled itself out of the water and then came fairly meekly to hand. It was only about a two-pounder, but, after the drought, I was anxious for a photo. Enrique lifted the fish into the boat, where it flailed the air furiously and was then suddenly free and cartwheeling overboard. Fortunately, a few minutes later, I caught another small tararira while casting from the shore. It was the perfect twin of my escapee, and I used up the last of my film on its impressive denture and elongated dorsal fin. I shouldn't have, since Enrique soon caught a 10-pounder while trolling a lure. His impulsive reaction at its first leap was to keep the fish. "It is the right size for eating." When I demurred, he quickly relapsed into his catch-and-release mode. As it turned out, the fish had ingested the plug and was bleeding profusely from slashed gills, so we did kill it. He then cautiously recounted his best day on the Yi three years earlier when he caught more than 30 tararira, killing 16 between four and seven kilos. He'd given them away to his neighbors,

> "I seldom keep fish, Bill. Adriana has never eaten one of mine to this day. But I like to play with them more than you do. I fight them until their bellies point to the sky."

I struggled to avoid becoming too patronizing or pedantic while commenting that reducing a fish to such a point of exhaustion diminishes its chances of survival.

After another of Wilson's shoreside barbecues, we went further afield down river. It was there that we found the shredded half-eaten remains of one of the roseate spoonbills. The rest of the flock was gone. The ground was too hard to reveal tracks, but Enrique surmised that the prey had been taken by one of the few remaining wild cats that remained in the forest fringe of the Yi. He salvaged the improbable bill and a wing while I took a feather.

On the way back to La Cueva del Tigre, there was an encounter of the reptilian kind that filled me with *déjà vu*. When listing the local wildlife, both Alberto and Enrique had mentioned *yacarés* (dwarf caymans) and *lagartos* or lizards, which I also took to mean of the small variety. But here lumbering across the road in front of us was a four-foot long, chunky black tegu lizard. More than four decades earlier, in my Sierra Reptile Farm days, I had owned one. Instinctively, I was out of the truck and running after the startled creature without the faintest idea of what I might do had I caught up with it. Luckily for both of us I didn't, and the uncorked spirit of a vanished youth returned to its bottle.

Irigoyen was far more bemused than amused by my report of the Bordaberry invitation. Alberto had been scheduled to fish with us the following Sunday, the day we intended to try the ex-president's estancia,

"As a matter of principle, I won't be coming along."

It wasn't entirely clear why.

Next day Enrique, Wilson and I were off to Mercedes through a Uruguayan countryside of wheat fields and pastures rolling as gently as the folds of a philosopher's furrowed brow. Enrique spoke,

"Before they built the dam there were many more fish in the Yi—more species too. We had dorado, sábalo, surubí and bogas right here in Durazno. My father took me to see them where they schooled below a natural dam. It was magnificent to watch a dorado gather its strength and then ascend the flow over it. Now there are no dorado, no surubí and but a few boga and sábalo left in the Yi. Only the tararira still survive, and they are very castigated. Last year we circulated a petition asking for the authorities to build a fish ladder at the dam, but it will never happen until a fisherman is president."

The local tourism authorities were intent upon turning the Yi into an attraction, complete with "I love the Río Yi" bumper stickers. Camping, kayaking and, above all, sport fishing were on the rise. A month earlier Durazno had hosted the "National Tararira Fishing Championship." The sponsoring local fishing club obtained permission to net tararira in a nature reserve and then release them into a 3-mile stretch of river bounded by two natural barriers. Thirty boats, each with two anglers, signed up for the competition.

Enrique was not Galician by ancestry, rather he was descended from an Andalusian (Sevillian) grandfather who emigrated to Uruguay in 1912. There were so many Galicians among the Spanish immigrants, however, that "gallego" is an identity extended in Uruguay to all Old World Spaniards other than Basques. It was conferred upon Durazno-born Enrique because of his accent after living in Spain from 1978 to 1985. His real, as in original, profession was musician—a trumpet player. He'd gone to Spain for a six-month gig with a Spanish band that he met touring Uruguay and stayed for seven years.

In 1985 he came back after the collapse of the dictatorship because it looked like Uruguay would pass a law subsidizing musicians—which came to nothing. So he turned his boyhood passion for hunting and fishing into a profession. Along with his younger brother he hunted in the winter months for furs and meat, spotlighting animals at night and dispatching them with a .22-caliber rifle. Hares, introduced from Europe, were abundant. They were worth about $1.50 undressed and in their best year the brothers killed 2,000. In a winter you might also kill 50 five-dollar foxes and 100 three-dollar nutrias. There were even a few river otters to be had ($3-$4). Until protected recently, rheas were also hunted for their feathers and meat; their eggs are still collected and, while illegal, it is easy to buy them in Durazno. In summer the brothers killed a few tegu lizards and received $10 a skin for their trouble.

There was bigger game as well. In the early 20th century a wealthy Basque estanciero, Anchorena, released European axis deer and wild boar on his estate. They are now present in much of the country. The lamb-killing boar are particularly numerous and are viewed as a scourge by all but the hunting fraternity. Last winter the two brothers killed more than 50 boars, some dispatched by their guided clients. They now belong to a boar-hunting circle in Durazno that has 15 dogs.

If the hunters are welcome when pursuing boar, the landowners are more reticent regarding the native capybaras. Increasingly rare and now protected, they are still poached relentlessly. Alberto had complained to me about hunters who sneak on to his property at night to spotlight a capybara and, if unsuccessful, blast a sheep instead. Even if you catch them, the judge will likely let them go since people have to eat. It is a problem for the landowner, poacher and quarry alike.

Enrique and I were to share a hotel room in Mercedes while Wilson camped with our gear in a city park. We launched our boat at a government dock, and Enrique tried to extract information about the dorado fishing from an evasive official. It was only after he explained that we were into catch-and-release that his interlocutor lightened up,

"Try going up the Bequelo tributary. You may find something. But it is still early. The dorado haven't really arrived yet."

The Río Negro was enormous and the Bequelo still too large for my taste. At times Enrique's depth finder proclaimed us to be in as much as 30 feet of water. He found some underwater structure, and I blind cast until casted out, after which I resignedly acquiesced in equally fruitless trolling.

At the boat ramp the next morning, I chatted with a knowledge-able young man, a local fishing guide awaiting a party of Argentines,

"Since the dam, the fishing has gone down. There are still dorado, but they are now much smaller. Poachers string nets across the mouth from bank to bank. They kill everything that enters no matter the size. The lower river is now com-pletely unpredictable. If they release dam water it might be too high and too cold for a couple of days. Then they turn off the flow and, well, you just never know. The river is fill-ing up with sand. You have to be very careful. It is nothing to hit a sandbar right in mid-stream."

The year before he had guided 12 Americans, eight of whom fly fished. They had caught a few dorado, not many. He generously told us about a series of lagoons 7 miles downstream where there was both structure and shallows. He thought we might catch some *tangueros* (tango dancers) there. Enrique later speculated that "tanguero," the local word for baby dorado, might derive from their habit of thrashing or "dancing" on the surface, but he wasn't certain.

We checked out the lagoons without success. I was fast losing interest in the angling. Strenuous mechanical and mindless chuck-ing of a very heavy streamer on a relatively heavy rod under an austral summer sun was wearing me down. As we headed back to another Wilson lunch, I pronounced myself through for the day. Since I planned to wander the streets of colonial Mercedes, Enrique observed that I might as well begin right now with the Castillo of the Baron of Mauá. He pulled up to the dock of a parkland alive with picnicking school children. While I walked up the hill to the house, he stayed with the boat.

The estate, which now belongs to the city of Mercedes, was built by Irineu Evangelista de Souza in the 1850s, or when Uruguay was Rio Grande do Sul province under Brazilian rule. De Souza was a self-made man, who began as a store clerk and ended up founding a bank and steamship company, as well as constructing the area's first railroad. Along the way he was made a baron and then a viscount, his extraordinary escutcheon emblazoned with a locomotive and steamship and bordered by four gas street lamps. Its motto proclaimed that "anything is possible through hard work."

Housed in one wing of the manse was the fossil collection of local amateur paleontologist Alejandro C. Berro. The metamessage of the little museum's exhibits was the importance of conservation if the country was to maintain its floral and faunal heritage. The femur of an extinct giant armadillo pointed towards the precarious plight of today's smaller representative. Given the several hundred kids crawling all over the grounds, hopefully there was an abundant youthful audience for such sorely-needed attitudinal adjustment. One caption proclaimed that Berro had created a controversy in his time (the 1920s) by claiming that man was present in the Americas much earlier than previously thought, since he'd found human evidence in association with Pleistocene faunal remains. In light of recently uncovered prehistorical evidence, and unlike the bizarre human-migratory claims made by the Salta Anthropology Museum, Berro may well have been on to something.

I had hoped that we would head straight for Durazno the next morning, but Enrique was set on one more try for dorado. So we again launched our craft at Paso Correntino on the Rio Negro, 25 miles upstream from Mercedes. After another stint of blind man's bluff, at noon I put my foot down when informed by some local anglers that we should fish underneath the nearby high tension lines where they cross the river since eloctrocuted morning doves attract both dorado and tararira there.

That evening back at Estancia Santa Margarita and during the afterglow of dinner, I asked Alberto and Adriana about current President Batlle. He was rumored to have received death threats from contrabandists and might even be wearing a bulletproof jacket. Batlle is the son and grandson of former Uruguayan presidents and, through a fluke, finally became president himself a year ago, thereby claiming his "birthright". Within the Colorados he leads a minority faction, and his own party is the greatest opponent and critic of his present policies. An elderly man in his late 70s, Batlle seems more concerned with legacy than reelection. He has taken head on what are, arguably, Uruguay's two gravest issues—contraband and "the disappeared ones."

During my stay there were daily press reports of seizures of smuggled goods (mainly in the false bottom of trucks entering from Brazil). Contraband in practically everything is totally ingrained in the country, seemingly implicating politicians and bureaucrats of every level of government. If a pervasive corrupting influence within Uruguayan life, it is also one of its mainstays. Batlle's campaign had thus far been unrelenting and incorruptible. No one was quite sure where it might lead next.

To underscore his reformist zeal, in his inaugural address Batlle verbalized the unmentionable. Namely, he vowed to initiate investigations into the torture and disappearance of dissidents during the military dictatorship. Along with Argentina, Chile, Paraguay and Brazil, Uruguay had formed part of the infamous Operation Condor which linked together the security services and military commands of the five nations which, along with CIA collaboration and the training imparted at the anti-terrorist School of the Americas (founded in Panama by the United States), was the response of the five military dictatorships to leftist revolutionary challenges articulated in such movement as Argentina's Monteneros and Uruguay's Tupamaros.

As a condition of the transition to civil government, the military dictators had exacted guarantees of immunity from subsequent investigation of, and possible prosecution for, their actions while "defending the country." Pinochet's legal problems and the current siege mentality of Argentina's military underscore the fragility of such arrangements. Nevertheless, in Uruguay Presidents Sanguinetti and La Calle had both doggedly observed the truce while arguing that there would be no trace found of the 100-200 disappeared ones anyway. Batlle launched investigations that were uncovering many leads. Again, no one knew where it would all lead.

Finally, the president was opening up the general Pandora's box of social equity in a country where the destinies of 3 million people are essentially controlled by 300 families, their interests protected by a bloated and totally perfunctory army (by one recent study Uruguay's armed forces could resist an invasion from Argentina for three hours and one from Brazil for six). Batlle had published the statistic that the average working wage was $90 per month while that of a legislator was $5,000. In sum, the president does not seem a shoo-in candidate for a gold watch at some future retirement banquet.

Adriana noted,

"The Tupamaros were intellectuals and they started out as Robin Hoods, taking from the rich and giving to the poor. They were also good at public relations. One time they kidnapped a politician who had claimed publicly that the average Uruguayan made a living wage. They gave him a budget in captivity, the going wage, and let him spend it on a daily order for his food. When he was released several months later, he was a broken man, half-starved. The Tupamaros had made their point, and it got everyone's attention."

It seems that the Tupamaros were heavily into symbolic irony, including of the deadly variety. At one point they kidnapped, tortured and killed Dan Mitrione, an American specialist in torture techniques working as an adviser to Uruguayan security forces.

Had I been told all of this by a student radical it might have been different. But my commentators were the daughter of one of the 300 families and the son of Colonel Irigoyen—as in Juan Alcides Irigoyen Ulhij. Alberto himself had attended the military academy, intending to follow in his genitor's footsteps. Colonel Irigoyen was the consummate soldier, a true military loyalist. When it became apparent that the police and civil authorities could no longer cope with the Tupamaro threat, the army agreed to take them on. When much of the high brass was reticent to assume the point, it was

Colonel Irigoyen who agreed to address the nation with the decision as the military's spokesman. Subsequently, when the *golpe* was proclaimed but his commander refused to go along, Colonel Irigoyen convinced his general to let the troops leave their surrounded garrison as they were political innocents while the two officers would remain behind. It could have cost him his life; it did cost him his career. The new military dictatorship decreed Law G, under which the ranks of the military were purged of dissident officers, communists and homosexuals. To be rifted accordingly was the ultimate infamy for a proud soldier who had refused to rebel against his commander-in-chief, President Bordaberry. Although subsequently reinstated, the blow proved fatal. It also cost his son a military career. It was unthinkable to admit to the ranks Colonel Irigoyen's son; Alberto was suspended.

Adriana opined,

"Today it is very difficult to teach history to our children. In the classrooms the descendants of the torturers sit side by side with those of the tortured. What do you tell them? What do you not tell them?"

It is the same story whether talking to Juan on the Rio Dulce or Alberto and Adriana in their kitchen on the Estancia Santa Margarita. It was America's dirty war that allied North American anti-communism with Latin American oligarquism in a holy crusade against the "left." The problem, of course, was that the social inequities in the battleground, whether Guatemala, El Salvador, Nicaragua, Chile, Argentina, Peru, Paraguay, Brazil or Uruguay, were so egregious as to make any crusade in their defense ultimately indefensible. The social and political legacy of the campaign is little understood by my fellow countrymen, who, to the extent that they have historical sensibility, equate anti-communism with the defense of liberty and democracy. The legacy in Latin America is of an entirely different order. It is a war that pitted one segment of Uruguay's 300 families against another, the edge cutting in many cases right through households. It was a civil conflict in the truest sense of the word, but within the privileged class—a campaign conducted more in defense of proletarians than by them. Such wounds almost defy scarification, at least during the lives of the generation that experienced them. It is small wonder that Latin America tried denial, but ultimately unsuccessfully.

I had a welcome Sunday morning off as we had been put off by Bordaberry, who then promised to call at midday. He didn't, so after lunch we set out for the lower Yi with both Alberto and Wilson in tow. Alberto wanted to witness a couple of pros in action, though he had long since become our mirthful taunter. Enrique agreed to teach me how to drink maté the next (and my final) day in exchange for a fly-casting lesson. I was all too pleased to accommodate. Our usual barren efforts to entice fish to streamer degenerated once again into a trolling exercise. By now I was holding Enrique's rod. At one point we actually had a fish on, but of course lost it before we were able to salvage some modicum of Alberto's respect. At dusk we pulled into shore and a gleeful Wilson displayed his five-pound tararira caught on the handline now wrapped around a plastic soft-drink bottle! I photographed both his fish and gear, an image that I may just put into a locket to wear around my neck should I ever need an emergency humility fix.

Next day I had a farewell lunch with Enrique and Adriana in their kitchen. He gave me my maté lesson and she a poem by Mario Benedetti. During one of our many conversations, I had expressed to Enrique my admiration of Uruguay's superb poet. We laughed over the thought that Wilson's retelling of our week in some cantina might well lead to a new folk song "El Gallego y el Gringo." We discussed the possibility of my returning next year. To the north of the Río Negro lie the Río Quequay and Río Averías, both damless, small and with rock structure. They have dorado runs. We would have to camp out. What the hell, why not?

A Guidebook

Whether fishing in a boat or on the bank, there is always a second presence—your guide. The quality of relations between the two of you can run from the boorish through indifferent to reverential. "I don't care if this is Argentina, why don't you speak better English?" "Have you heard the one about: 'What're the two toughest years in a fishing guide's life?' 'No?' (Answer: 'the third grade!')." "I don't care what you think; I'm not gonna fish Bow Channel, so take me to Woman's Key." "Can I cast now (with the implicit 'Sir')?" "Whatever you say." "The weakest link between the guide and the fish is the angler." Etcetera.

In my view, any fisherman should make the same effort to understand his guide as he expends reading the water. Failure to do so can diminish the angling experience every bit as much as a castless/fishless day. After all, at the most elementary level, your guide is in far more control of the day's angling logistics than are you. It behooves you to fashion a mutually acceptable relationship if only to avoid the angler's dreaded four-letter f-word, FROG—as in froggy rather than fishy water. Being "frogged" is akin to being "fragged," the military-slang expression for when a grunt kills his commander. Your guide possesses the local knowledge that enables him to frog you all day long without you even hearing the soughing of "rivets."

You are about to spend the day, maybe several, in more intimacy (robed to be sure) with a stranger than most of us experience with our spouses. It is a lot like a blind date, and the average Maverick flats skiff or Mackenzie drift boat affords but a few square feet, less elbowroom than an astronaut enjoys in the Mir Space Station. You and your guide are practically cell mates that must coordinate a myriad of details, right down to such mundane issues as where to store the lunches.

There is much to be negotiated and learned by both parties to this temporary union. You are the performer and he the accompanist, but without communication and practice you are only capable of making noise together not music. "There's a fish about 40 feet at 11 o'clock" seems like a straightforward, even precise, statement. It isn't. Guides can vary considerably in their estimate of distance and their reading of the imaginary timepiece. Then there is the issue of one's backcast. When fly fishing, a good guide will position his angler so that the backcast does not come straight at him. However, not all are conscientious or experienced. Hooking your guide is neither the most harmonious nor portentous form of bonding.

Another negotiable matter is the angler's casting skill. In some Florida Keys angling circles, I am sometimes quoted for my spontaneous response to John Podolsky's question the first day that I stepped on his boat: "How far can you cast, Bill?" "With or without tarpon, Johnny?" The point is that until your guide has assessed your casting distance and accuracy, not to mention your temperament under fire, you have yet to become an effective angling team. Everything else being equal, of course, it is better to cast to a fish 80 feet from the boat than 40, since there is less chance of alerting the quarry. However, it is pointless for a guide to request an

80-foot cast from an angler who either can't make it or loses control of its direction at 60 feet. Indeed, angling is nothing if not a whole series of such tradeoffs, many of which have to be recognized and implemented instantaneously under extreme pressure. You and your guide had better be on the same page, or at least in the same chapter. Yet it is not at all uncommon for angler and guide to be in different books altogether.

If you engage your guide with at least a modicum of egalitarian spirit, there is often wonderful opportunity in sheer human terms. The nature of the angling experience is itself an efficacious icebreaker. During the course of a day or several, angler and guide inevitably run out of one liners and other verbal pap. There ensues an awkward moment, a kind of watershed in which the bounds of intimacy are either firmly established, usually by a lapse into silence, or transcended. In the latter event all kinds of exchanges, largely unanticipated, may transpire. I know more, as they do of me, about the triumphs and tragedies, not to mention the fears and frustrations, of several fishing guides scattered liberally around the world than I do of most of my hometown friends and relatives.

Some might question: why bother? There are, after all, certain unstated background assumptions in play. The most apparent is the employer-employee (or possibly customer-vendor) hierarchy. There is structural imbalance in the mere fact that you are paying for a service, and he is providing it. More subtle coloration may stem from your perception of his profession, or, more accurately, lack of one. Fishing guide is at best a job, a temporary one at that and unlikely to have been recommended by his high-school counselor. Few, if any, embrace guiding as a career, as in a lifetime commitment from which one might someday retire to join other superannuated guides around the pot-bellied stove before making that final journey to Guide Corner of Kingdom Come. Guides' stated motives for guiding are many, ranging from love of the outdoors to love of people (that one is for your benefit). But the truth is that it tends to be a way station while figuring out what one wants to be when one grows up, perhaps a relatively high-paid opportunity for someone lacking other more marketable skills, or for some a respite from a recent turmoil in life like loss of employment or divorce. Given the fact that either the fishing is seasonal or the anglers are, there is little stability (as in year-round employment) to guiding. The overall recreational environment in which it devolves also poses the temptations of alcohol and/or drug abuse. In short, guiding is pretty antithetical to normal family life.

As with all stereotypes, the foregoing have some validity, though vary according to the particular case. However, if one bothers to probe beneath such surface impressions, the waters often run deep. As a small sampler of my own experience, I have been guided by several graduates of fine universities, an ex-Assistant District Attorney for the City of New Orleans, an ex-Major League centerfielder, an ex-yacht captain, a former general manager of a chain of dry goods stores, two ex-air-traffic controllers and a former pharmaceuticals salesman. Conversations with each of them have given me some insight into worlds that I would have never even glimpsed otherwise.

Gary Aka and I had come to the Florida Keys in late March to fish for permit and possibly cobia with Dale Perez. The odds of finding tarpon that early in the season were slim. However, the adage about paying your dues is true enough, and we had certainly paid ours over the years by maintaining eternal optimism in the face of adversity ranging from spotty fishing days through poor weather to our not-infrequent screwups at precisely the wrong moment. But then the fishing gods decided to smile on us. The winds and waters were becalmed, the temperature soared into the mid-80s, and the tarpon poured into the shallows. Never before nor since have I seen so many. Without exaggeration, at one point Pearl Basin was so full of basking Key West Channel fish that we were surrounded. Most were laid up or cruising almost imperceptibly. If the fishing was great, the catching was problematic. It was all but impossible to cast to a particular tarpon without spooking a tattler that spread a warning throughout the crowded neighborhood.

One fine morning, while fishing by ourselves in Mallory Basin, Gary and I had had about 50 good shots between us without a hookup. The gathering clouds on the horizon of Dale's mood thickened when Nat Raglin arrived with a neophyte angler from Montreal who promptly began to boat tarpon while his bikini-clad wife sunbathed on the bow. After his sixth hookup, Lucky Pierre blurted out, "Ees eet alwaas soo eesee?" Dale cranked up his engine.

By the second afternoon, he was thoroughly frustrated. Our only score, if you can call it that, was the 80-pounder that I had hooked blindcasting into the boat channel at Shark Key while Dale and Gary were eating lunch. About 2 o'clock we had just poled through a mullet mud in Loggerhead Basin when I spotted a tarpon out of the corner of my eye cruising in the semi-clear water of the fringe. The fish was only about 20 feet away, so, without much hope, I casually flipped my fly in its general direction. There was an immediate swirl and the tarpon was on. I bowed as the fish hydroplaned rather than jumped, and it then became obvious that she (sexual dimorphism in tarpon favors the females) was a big one. A minute later she hydroplaned again, this time maybe 300 yards away and still seemingly intent on travel to Cuba. Dale fired up the motor just in time to prevent me from being spooled.

It was the last time she was to surface, excepting the occasional slow roll to reoxygenate herself to better continue the contest. An hour and a half later I was well past the aching-muscle stage, and her back was crisscrossed with white marks emblazoned by burns from my leader. She was still pulling us at will around Loggerhead Basin, and our journey to nowhere in particular was now measured in miles. We had settled into a routine in which I'd get her on the fly line only to have her surge a short way into my backing.

Perez knows his tarpon. During his nearly 30 years of guiding, by actual count in a daily log, his clients have boated slightly over 5,000 fish. On two occasions, before Billy Pate landed his 188-

pound trophy, Dale's anglers established the world's fly-fishing record while he guided them out of Homosassa.

"Bill, that's the biggest fish I've ever had on in the Keys. It's got to be 180. When they get that big, it's easy to be off 10 pounds or so. It could even be a record."

Since at one point she had nearly beached herself in two feet of water, and we had come right alongside her with my leader almost in the rod guides, he'd certainly had a superb look on which to base such judgement.

Dale began lamenting that we didn't have a gaff and that boating the huge fish would be difficult. When I allowed that that was fine with me, since I had no intention of killing her, record or not, Dale objected,

"You don't respect your fish!"

While I struggled to process his point, the tarpon made one of its periodic surges, and for the first time in the fight, I failed to bow. My leader broke, and I will never know if I did it on purpose; it certainly wasn't a conscious decision, but I was just as glad that she was gone.

Did I have a right to be? The day's events had neatly underscored an angler-guide dilemma. For me, fishing is a sport; for Dale, it is a profession. For him, landing the world's record tarpon, if that's what she was, would be worth thousands of dollars and the incalculable esteem of the considerable bragging rights. For two days I had all but tormented him with my ineptitude, and suddenly we had a huge fish on. Was it my fish, and mine alone, by virtue of the fact that at the end of the day I was to pay him a few hundred dollars? Just whose fish was it?

The package from Argentina arrived at my wife's business while I was on a two-week bonefishing trip in the Bahamas. Her rudimentary Spanish sufficed to understand that it was from some sort of taxidermist. Caution won out over curiosity—the still-sealed mystery awaited my return.

The head that peered up at me from the gaping box was unlike anything I had ever seen before. An enormous teeth-ringed cavity revealed a large, fleshy tongue that could have almost been human. The mount was in fact mostly a mouth that terminated in two gill plates flared at right angles, and each drilled with a tiny hole to accommodate a screw should I wish to attach my gift to a wall plaque for display. I locked eyes with the monster and felt the chill of its sinister stare. The elliptical black pupils floating in yellow orbs seemed to be taunting a transfixed victim seconds before a fatal strike.

The gift was from Juan, my guide at Termas de Río Hondo during my initial attempt to catch a dorado. The accompanying missive and documentation echoed our streamside discussions three years earlier while I blindcasted interminably into the fetid waters of the inappropriately named Río Dulce (Sweet River). There were several newspaper articles detailing President Menem's recent electoral loss, heavily laced with Juan's editorial comments in the margins. At first I was confused by two articles on Argentine soccer reporting Menem's taunting of a political rival over a pending match between two bitter sports adversaries, but then I recalled Juan's impassioned diatribe against the government's ploy to spike genuine political debate by fomenting a national football craze for men while providing brain rot in the form of soap operas to the distaff side of the electorate. A comic strip and an article on jaguar encounters reminded me of Juan's passion for archery. He claims to have pioneered bowhunting in the Argentine nation.

There were three books. I had told Juan about my anthropological research among Basques and Italians recruited in Europe in the late 1950s to cut sugar cane in tropical Queensland. Two of the books regarded the sugar industry of Tucumán province. The third detailed the biographies of 12 Galician immigrants in Argentina, Juan's generous contribution to my general knowledge of southern-European emigration to his country.

His four-page letter was vintage. Juan was a Peronist, a real Peronist, outraged by careerists (like Menem) who had reduced his hero's ideals to unrecognizable pap to be served up in generous dollops to an ignorant and complicit public. While reading the missive, I seemed once again to be standing waist-deep in the Río Dulce, Juan by my side, directing my casts and thoughts,

"*Throw more to the left, Bill.* And then they came for all those brave, yet so naïve, intellectuals from the University of Tucumán. They arrested some; others fled to the hills where they formed little bands. *Cast in front of that big rock. Not to the side or behind it. Dorado always stay in front of cover.* Some of them were students, others professors. How naïve they were. Some had summer homes in the hills. They thought they would serve as refuges and links in a chain of resistance. They never had a chance. Tucumán was the only province posing 'military' opposition to the regime. The full force of the Army could be brought to bear here. *He's got it, but such a small one! We had a much bigger fish below the dam.* And so some were killed in the mountains, and others just disappeared. They never had a chance."

Juan had insisted that we stop off at his place in the city of Tucumán before moving our feast to the adjacent province of Salta. When not hunting or fishing, he was a repairman of small household appliances. He emerged from his residence/repair shop carrying an enormous tapir's skull. He insisted that I accept it as a memento of our time together on the Río Dulce. It was his most prized archery trophy. My protests, couched in terms of limited luggage space, produced a compromise. He substituted the skull of a much smaller javelina and an oripendola's intricately crafted hanging nest that he had collected on one of his jungle excursions. Juan had admired my streamer flies, so I hastened to reciprocate with as many as I could spare given our still pending several days of dorado fishing.

I read Juan's letter as his latest gift continued to stare at me in anticipation over the next twist of its improbable fate. It seems that

Casting About in the Reel World

months before my friend had gone fishing for tararira. In an all-but-dried-up backwater, he'd spotted an enormous fish and cast a streamer at it. The nearly moribund creature had taken the fly but was then incapable of any real resistance (like the intellectuals of Tucumán?). He reeled in the 43-pound dorado and saved its skull upon which to employ his considerable taxidermy skills to fashion his gift of atonement for the poor fishing that we had experienced.

The apology encompassed the shame of his beloved, now dammed and damned, Río Dulce. Prostrate and polluted, she was about to be raped by the politicians. President Menem had just approved a project that would divert her waters to his native Rioja province where they would no doubt enrich his cronies. Juan was giving up on guiding fishermen. Could I send him some American magazines? He listed *Bowhunter, Bow and Arrow* and *Archery Magazine*. The letter concluded,

> "In the base of the tongue, the dorado has a bone in the shape of a bottle stop. The people call it the little virgin or San Antonio. The Indians who fish here in northern Argentina and southern Bolivia, like the Chiriguanos or Chaguancos, string them into necklaces. The length of the necklace proclaims the dorado fishing skills of its owner. As you will note, esteemed friend, the eyes on the mount are incorrect—a serpent's eyes. They are not true, which, as you know, in the dorado are round and with a larger black iris. But what happens here in the North is that it is not always possible to find the right materials and one must "improvise" with whatever he has at hand."

Indeed!

Bob Morgart and I were walking the streets of Valle Mí in Paraguay, having just completed our ersatz camping venture on the Río Apa. The town was deceptively festive, its streets filled with a vibrant, smiling populace. One expected some procession bearing the patron saint to appear momentarily around the next corner. In point of fact, there was a serious labor confrontation in progress. The mainstay of the local economy was an inefficient, government-owned cement plant. It was about to be privatized, portending the loss of hundreds of jobs. However, the only sign of crisis was the military guard stationed at the plant itself, its young recruits no doubt longing to join in the distant gaiety.

"I guess José wasn't impressed with the gift," a sheepish Bob reasoned. On the journey out of the bush, José and I shared the same pickup cab, and I had just recounted his most extraordinary life's story to Bob. The gift in question was a thoroughly battered pair of deck shoes. It is Bob's laudable practice whenever fishing Third World venues to bring along his most used gear that he then leaves with the staff. If a bit patronizing, it is usually quite appreciated.

José is of Syrian-Lebanese descent, his grandfather having emigrated from the Middle East to Santa Fe, Argentina. José's father was an autoworker on an assembly line and owned a small estancia nearby. His better-educated son had become an insurance adjuster for a major company.

When he was 27 years old, the company transferred José to Salta. He was a dashing young man with a flashy car, a real force on the local singles' scene. Before long he was dating the daughter of the area's wealthiest landowner and tobacco exporter. One of the several flies in the ointment, in addition to the obvious difference in their social standing, was his beloved's tender age—she was 14 at the time.

Not surprisingly, her family was vehemently opposed to this particular tryst. "They suspected me of being a gold digger," he said. But apparently she was no stereotypically run-of-the-mill, father-knows-best Latin daughter. Rather, by José's account, she would have won the female lead in Shakespeare's *Taming of the Shrew* hands down. In short, they were married.

Thus began his personal campaign to convince the family of his good intentions by becoming the model son-in-law, though to little avail. His position became more entrenched by the birth of a son. Nevertheless, in many respects he felt trapped by circumstances. He respected his hardworking father-in-law, but regarded his wife's siblings to be a collection of useless drones. Life in the fast lane did have its perks, however. He traveled frequently to Miami, where his father-in-law had an enormous bank account, and to Europe. He recalls one month buying three brand new automobiles (his passion), including a $45,000 Mazda.

But it wasn't enough. One day he simply packed a suitcase and walked away from the family mansion. He moved to Asunción where, when not guiding anglers, he restores antique autos. His wife has remarried twice since his departure. At the time he was recounting his story, José had a 24-year-old Paraguayan wife and newborn child ("just to please her"). Periodically, he travels to Salta to visit his son of 10. He has some savings and a couple of pieces of property in Argentina. Life is good because, above all, his pride is intact. "In Salta they now know that the *turco** was true to his word when he denied being a fortune seeker!"

"Cast toward the croc, Bill." Geoff Hawkins and I were fishing Lower Trepang Creek out of Seven Spirit Lodge on the Cobourg Peninsula of Australia's Northern Territory. The six-foot crocodile was half-exposed, basking in the shallows just above the deep run that I wanted to probe with a fly for barramundi. Geoff handed me his spinning rod, and I made a forlorn effort. Then it was on! Not a fish—the croc. Covering about 10 feet with incredible speed, the reptile had pounced on the popper. Hooked in the side of the mouth, it was motionless, head held high, statue-like. "So what the hell do I do now?" I asked. Before Geoff could reply, the head flashed sideways, the popper exploded within crunching jaws and I was contemplating the bent swivel that was once attached to a lure.

---

* *Turco* or Turk is a pejorative term used in Argentina to designate all persons of Middle-Eastern (Arab) origin.

Geoff Hawkins is a jack-of-many-trades and a maverick to boot. If one were to pigeonhole him professionally, it would be as a dental technician. A native Queenslander and graduate of a dental program in Brisbane, he has worked periodically at that trade for others and, for the last several years, operates his own dental laboratory in Darwin. Unfortunately, or otherwise, periodically the goddess of wanderlust whispers in his ear. He has been a "bullthrower" on several Queensland "stations" (American translation: cowboy on ranches) and blaster at a New Guinea gold mine.

Unlike most of us, Geoff has two Achilles' heels, the other being fishing. He loves to be around angling so much that it seems to matter little to him whether he is doing the guiding or the casting. He is the driving force, common denominator and point man of something that he calls "the caper." Every couple of years Geoff puts out the word to a loosely knit network of Aussies scattered around their continent that there is about to be a caper. Collectively, they own some basic camping equipment stored by Geoff in Darwin and several have four-wheel-drive vehicles. The idea is to spend a week or so exploring some part of Australia's northern top end from Queensland to the Kimberlies in Western Australia. The holy grail of this particular quest is undiscovered barramundi waters.

Seven Spirits Lodge was as much a nature haven and ecotourism destination as a fishing camp. I had shared the charter flight from Darwin with Ken, an extroverted ex-journalist who reminded me a bit of an Aussie copy of Jerry Colonna, mustache and all. I knew that he and I were destined to share Geoff, and the initial banter was not encouraging. Ken was not even a crank baiter! His preferred technique was handlining while anchored up over some coral head on the Great Barrier Reef. It seemed far from clear how we were to commingle the oil and water of our polar-opposite angling karmas. As it turned out, most of the fishing was too poor for our dissonance to matter. We had not picked the ideal season. It was July, the depths of the austral winter. During the entire week

I caught our only barramundi, and neither of us managed to hook our other preferred quarry, the threadfin salmon. Ken did boat a smorgasbord of bottom fish. He was in poor health, so on the days that he stayed in, I had some great open-ocean action for queenfish and blue trevally.

If the angling was spotty, the bonding was spectacular. By week's end we were the proverbial thick thieves, true "mates" in Australian parlance. Ken was particularly full of fascinating stories. He had been a correspondent for a Sydney newspaper stationed in China when Mao triumphed. He stayed on and was quickly imprisoned and tortured, the genesis of a lifelong legacy of poor health. He was finally released and expelled. He spent the next couple of years in harrowing attempts to extricate his Chinese fiancée from the country. Bribery ultimately did the trick, and the newlyweds settled in Hong Kong where both worked for many years as foreign correspondents, co-authoring a regular column on semi-tropical gardening for a local newspaper as well. He had recently lost her to cancer and, despite his forced exuberance, was a truly lonely man of broken body and spirit.

Meanwhile, Geoff and I became progressively outrageous as the week wore on, particularly regarding our ever-present danger— saltwater crocodiles. We spotted several, many well over 10 feet long. The mud banks of Lower Trepang Creek at low tide were literally laced with the fresh slides where crocs, some wider than our aluminum dinghy, had reentered the water at the sound of our approaching engine. We knew that we were floating over them in maybe six feet of water.

One afternoon a certain call of nature became too much for me to bear, so it was necessary to go ashore. As he beached the boat, Geoff told us to stay put while he checked out the surrounding bush. It seems that crocs can attack their prey from a dry ambush as well as a wet one. Back in the boat I told Geoff that should I be taken by a croc under similar circumstances, I wanted him to erect a stone monument on the site bearing the epitaph:

By unkind fate
So cruelly mock'd
He came to crap
Instead got croc'd

By that evening the earthy little ditty was on the staff bulletin board, and Geoff had pronounced me an honorary member of the caper.

The last morning he and I took a birding stroll along one of the nature paths. All week long Geoff had probed me with questions about Nevada, particularly Virginia City and the Comstock mining district close to Reno. Since my paternal grandparents were both born there during the boom, I know something about its history. It was then that Geoff told me his implausible family story. His great-grandfather, a Sioux Indian, had also lived in Virginia City married to a Cornish woman. When the prejudice proved unbearable, he took a job as foreman on a ranch. As the Nevada range became more crowded, his employer decided to resettle on the expanding Queensland frontier. Geoff's ancestor accepted the Australian job offer, thereby becoming the founding patriarch of a considerable Queenslander clan. I regarded my friend with heightened curiosity, his dark complexion and chiseled facial features acquiring new meaning. Indeed, he could easily have acted in *Dances with Wolves*! Geoff and I touch base periodically. I am now a beknighted caperer and have returned to Australia's "Deep North" on one occasion in that capacity, sampling the barramundi fishing in several rivers of the Northern Territory. It remains one of the permanently-entered destinations in Bill Angler's GPS.

The year 1988 marked my first regular annual date on the Dean as a founding member of the Dean River Miscasts. It was also 17-year-old Billy Blewett's first year of guiding. Son of Dick, one of the original owners of the Lower Dean River Lodge, and brother of Mike, our head guide, Billy was wilderness-wise beyond his years. The one before, while deer hunting near their Bella Coola home, Billy had survived a dual grizzly-bear attack,

"I was hunting in a little box canyon and noticed where a grizzly sow and her cubs had recently bedded down. I thought nothing of it because at that time of the year they are usually moving to the high country to hibernate. I spotted a deer and stepped out on a little bare ridge to get a better shot. It was then that I saw her out of the corner of my eye. She was charging and only about 25 feet away. Since I'd been about to shoot the deer I had a shell in the chamber. But when I raised my gun I hadn't figured on the scope. At that range I couldn't sight the bear through it, so I just dropped the barrel to my hip and fired. I was really lucky because I hit her in the shoulder, at maybe 15 feet, and down she went. She jumped back up and ran away into the brush below me. But there she was again coming uphill. It was all I could do to reload in time. The slope slowed her, and when she got to me, I put the rifle to her head and fired. She went right down. The cubs were 2-year-olds and pretty good-sized. One of them charged me. I had plenty of time and dropped it at 30 feet. The other ran away. I got one shot off at about 100 yards, but missed. I spent the next two hours looking for it since I knew it probably wasn't going to survive the winter without its mom. But I never did find it."

The next season Mike Blewett no longer guided us since he had been put in charge of the lodge's upper-river camp. By then his annual cycle included both guiding autumnal bear hunters for his father Dick on his Rivers Outlet government-allotted hunting territory, followed by opportunistic carpentering in Bella Coola until the next season (June-September) on the Dean. When Billy turned 19, the minimal age for a hunting guide's license, he joined his brother and genitor in the bear-hunting operation. In truth, neither brother was particularly enthralled with bear hunting, describing it to me at one time or another as an exhausting, wet, cold miserable job—but it was a family tradition.

Meanwhile, young Billy was blossoming into an experienced fishing guide as well as both an expert angler and fly tyer. There are several rites of passage in the formation of a fishing guide, most of which transpire out of his client's sight, but not all. There was the night when "the general," a commander of a Scottish division in the British Army, asked Billy to join us after dinner in our nightly rehash of the day's fishing. Despite his streamside poise, and even brashness, Billy's face was aflame, having-been crimsoned by the cold white of the spotlight of attention. The general was an accomplished Atlantic salmon angler and spey caster. In fact, his week of futility had been the object of our gentle mirth, not to mention reinforcement of our smugness regarding the superiority of New World technology (the single-handed rod) over Old World tradition. But that day, guided by Billy, the general had caught his first steelhead. He asked us to all raise our glasses of single-malt scotch to mark the occasion, insisting that Billy join in the toast. Given the grimace over his first taste of Scotland's major contribution to world civilization, it was obvious that at that moment Billy would have preferred facing down a charging grizzly. Indeed, he would soon get his chance,

> "We were a two-client operation. Normally Dad guided one hunter, and Mike or I took turns guiding the other. However, that day we overlapped, so we were both with a client at Owikeeno Lake. We got there about noon and the wind was acting up. So we decided to cross the two-mile lake and then hike to the headwaters of a little feeder river. We planned to hunt back down it just before dark. On the way up we spotted two sows, each with two cubs, and a 4-year-old juvenile. We only shoot males, and he was too small. We were hoping to see something bigger.
>
> We came upon one of the sows, threw a rock at her, and she took off. We passed the juvenile and he was on the other side of the river. It was getting dark and that trail is pretty

bad, so we speeded up. Mike had our rifle and was in the lead. Next came the hunter. I brought up the rear with my flashlight on, trying to point the beam ahead of Mike.

Then we heard this 'woof.' We had totally surprised a bear, and it was now charging from only about 10 feet away. Mike didn't have a chance to raise the rifle, so he just fired into the ground hoping to scare it. The bear ran into the bushes, and we were relieved. But here it came again. Mike had a shell in his chamber and by then his flashlight was on. He held it against his rifle barrel, aimed and pulled the trigger. There was a click—the rifle misfired. So Mike turned the gun sideways, one hand on the barrel and the other on the stock, just to cushion the attack. He was knocked down as the bear bit the rifle near the butt, which also stripped all the skin off Mike's thumb. The hunter had jumped off the trail, so now the bear came straight at me. I threw my flashlight one way and dove the other. I curled up in the fetal position with my hands over the back of my neck. The bear just stood over me, and I felt its warm breath. It really stunk. The hunter was shouting 'shoot, shoot.' He panicked and all I could think of was 'please don't shoot!' And then it was over. The hunter was so rattled he made me take his gun. He was afraid he might hurt someone."

It was the last year that Billy and Mike guided for Dick. By then Mike was married and with little children, and Billy had a more lucrative alternative, picking mushrooms for the Tokyo market, to waltzing with bears. Brother Dean, a devoted hunter, guided for Dick until 1998 when the family bear-hunting business was sold.

Hortatory Observations
No "Guidebook" would be complete without some tips. The following are mine:
1) Remember why you hired a guide in the first place—*for his local knowledge,* which is presumably superior to yours.

2) Treat your guide as a learning resource. When I step on a guide's boat for the first time, I always make a little speech to the effect that I would welcome his suggestions if he thinks I'm doing something wrong. Most guides are excellent anglers in their own right; any experienced one is likely to have been exposed to the best. About 80 percent of what I know about fishing, I've learned from my guides. Yet most are unlikely to opine unless invited to do so.

3) Follow his lead. Your guide has as great (or even greater) a stake than do you in the day's outcome. Both his tip and reputation are on the line. It is also far more appealing to him to spend the day with a satisfied, positive client than with a whiner. Complaining, particularly excessively, does little to change the fishing and much to alter the quality of the angler-guide relationship. If he decides that you are a jerk, at the very least he has pretty much stopped trying and is just putting in his time.

4) Respect his personal space. Given the economic realities alone, a guided angler is likely to be wealthy, or at least comfortably well off, and politically conservative. Conversely, a guide is a working stiff who might actually believe that the Democrats better represent his interests than do the Republicans. He may also be deeply religious and, hence, thoroughly appalled by off-color jokes and language. It is not necessarily an icebreaker to begin your day (and relationship) with a stranger with some seamy joke about, say, Bill Clinton and Monica Lewinsky. In short, read your guide's waters before casting into them.

5) Try to understand and respect his agenda. All guides have one, and while it may overlap with yours, the fit is never perfect. You are a sojourner and therefore more fixated upon the here and now. You are going fishing today and understandably you want to catch fish, the more and bigger the better. He is a resident resource manager with a yesterday, today and tomorrow. If he is good at his job, he understands that his waters must be rested and rotated. He is also calculating such factors as weather and tides. At the end of a day, most anglers are at least curious about

tomorrow's plan and prospects. If today's fishing was slow, it is scarcely necessary to insist upon going somewhere else tomorrow since he is already way ahead of you. If you say something like, "You know, I really like to explore," it can easily come across as "Today really sucked!" Conversely, after a great today, we have all pressured our guide into returning to the same spot tomorrow. While it's only human, it's not necessarily wise. I am amazed at how infrequently my efforts to wrest control of the angling agenda actually worked out. Rather, I was back in some memorable spot casting to wary, sore-lipped fish when I could have been rolling the dice of a new experience. In short, if you start guiding your highly paid guide, you have demonstrated that there is at least one fool in the boat.

6) Select your guide well. Each of us has his own angling style and preferences. Some like catching a lot of fish irrespective of size, others prefer large ones irrespective of numbers. Some want to concentrate on a target species; others are angling opportunists delighted to sample whatever comes along. Some anglers don't mind exploring; others believe that the longer the boat ride the less time there is for fishing. Guides, too, have their styles. I probably know Florida Keys tarpon guides best. There are but a handful that meet my criteria for perfection, which is the guide who is a) willing to fish the entire gamut from the Everglades to the Marquesas, b) has a low tolerance for anchoring up to await cruising fish no matter how promising the spot, preferring instead to pole the boat and/or change locations and c) is equally enthusiastic about fishing for tarpon, permit or bonefish. I am privileged to fish with two of the best—Dale Perez and Ray Fecher—and then only after my own, nearly 20-year, process of elimination.

Burning Bright

In every life there is a certain thing fated never to happen; I was beginning to believe that experiencing Russia was mine. When I passed on Frontiers' silent auction as entrée to the angling delights of the world's largest nation, I hadn't intended eschewing them forever. But then it began to look that way. The twin Ks—the peninsular Kola and Kamchatka—exploded in Westerner angling awareness as the "in" places to pursue Atlantic salmon, rainbow trout and even steelhead. "Development" quickly eclipsed exploration. The legendary Russian penchant for bureaucracy, not to mention payola, seemed to have sewn up matters with an alacrity that only raw cupidity can inspire. Practically before the echo of the first piscine "Eureka!" had died out, access to the Kola had been routinized into the extraordinarily expensive excursion to a handful of destination lodges offering the planet's best remaining Atlantic salmon sport fishing and, at the opposite end of one country and two continents, equally pricey Alaska-like rainbow trout angling. To be sure, this being transitional Russia, firm arrangements and supposed monopolies were often precarious. Within my angling fraternity the 1990s were punctuated with the little Russian disaster stories—the confused streamside confrontations with officials and/or thugs over rights of access, the party stranded until willing to bribe a helicopter pilot for a way out of the wilderness, the IRS challenges to the write-offs of steelheaders supposedly engaged in Kamchatkan "scientific research." To my knowledge, no one was ever imprisoned or injured, let alone killed, but the angling recipe in Russia struck me as two cups of structure, mixed with several tablespoons of uncertainty and a large dollop of hassle.

It's not that I didn't have my opportunities. My China companion, Tom Earnhardt, tried to organize a reasonably priced trip to the Kola's Umba River, intertwined mysteriously with the Continuing Education Division of North Carolina State University and a nascent pro bono interest of actor Paul Newman in enhancing a fishery while benefiting a Russian charity. But at the last minute all unraveled when the key official sold our fishing access to a Scandinavian outfitter. We were to be twice as many anglers as angling spots, but it was not to worry since order would be imposed within fishermen ranks by some level of Russian policing. Tom pulled the plug.

Subsequently, Mike Michalak, out of a combination of intrigue with the emerging Russian scene and fatigue over the annual burden of hosting an increasingly bloated (20-plus anglers) tarpon week in the Florida Keys, decided to trade conch for caviar. Conveniently, his mid-June Russian window conflicted with our Florida dates. Would I like to join him on his maiden Kola voyage? It was tempting, but by then, and after a dozen or more years of inertial habit, that tarpon week had become one of the twin pillars supporting Bill Angler's temple. Even in a life as secular as mine, a few things must remain sacred. So I exited my Fly Shop's Florida chrysallis and soared on the gossamer wings of an ongoing tarpon affair, Russia pushed further off into an indeterminate future.

There were other bits of intelligence informing my Russian lethargy. Rumor had it that, save for a precious few untouched pockets, the place was overfished relentlessly. Then, too, there were the targeted species. Having but one entirely fruitless week of fishing for Scottish Atlantics in my angling memorial, the salmon were tempting. Along with Mike Coe, I have even put my name on the list for a spot on the Ponoi River—roughly a year's wait at this juncture. I suppose that when I come up, I'll show up, if only just to put it behind me. As for Kamchatka, I have long since outgrown blindcasting for big rainbows in Alaska and Patagonia, while my September's week on the Dean provides me with my steelhead fix.

The prospect of an exploratory for sea-run taimen on the Botchi River, one in a chain of 22 nature reserves collectively constituting the sanctuary of the Siberian tiger, was an altogether different proposition. It was mid-July of the first year of the New Millennium when Jeff Vermillion dangled the possibility as a hypothetical. He was in the initial stages of negotiating an assignment from the Wild Salmon Center of Portland, Oregon, to determine the Botchinsky Nature Reserve's potential to support a commercial sport fishery that would hopefully generate funding for both tiger conservation infrastructure and a research program regarding this rarest of the salmonids. Talk centered upon a late September date, but it seemed unlikely that the complicated arrangements would come together that quickly. Realistically, the trip would likely transpire in the autumn of 2001, in which case I was definitely in.

But then the slope became slipperier, and I was faced with a dilemma. The expedition was a go, and we were to depart for Korea on September 26 in order to make the once-weekly Seoul-to-Khabarovsk flight on the 27th. Our return date was October 11. Several months earlier I had agreed to speaking engagements relating to my Basque research—one in San Francisco on October 14, which was not a problem. However, the others were in Mexico City on September 25 and 27. After exploring futilely any possibility of meeting up with Jeff a few days late, I fired the last arrow in my quiver. I explained the situation to my Mexico City hosts, but with the assurance that my commitment to them took precedence. They graciously rescheduled my talks for October 16 and 18. So with dispensation from the south, I had liberation to journey west for consummation in the Russian Far East.

I was easily as intrigued and energized by the anthropological as the piscatorial prospects. The Russian Far East is one of the planet's more interesting human crossroads, an epicenter where various small groups of hunter and gathering native peoples confronted variously and over several centuries the juggernauts of many civilizations. In the introduction to his book *The Russian Far East* is John I. Stephan's succinct and masterful overview:

> Visualizing the Far East requires a tolerance for ambiguity. Located at the interstices of conventionally defined regions, it awkwardly straddles parts of the Russian Republic, Northeast Asia, and the North Pacific. Moreover, it lacks a clearly defined periphery. At once within and distinct from Siberia, at once connected with and separate from China, Japan, and Korea, the Far East is a matrix of overlapping borderlands. To contemplate the Far East exclusively through either Eurocentric or Asiacentric prisms is to don blinkers. Just as we need to use both eyes for three-dimensional vision, so we need both Asian and Russian perspectives to behold the Far East in all its manifold destinies.

Given the tight time frame (exacerbated by subtracting my annual early-September week on the Dean), preparations were more of a scramble than planned. When in Reno, I was in near daily telephone and e-mail contact with Xanthippe Augerot, director of the Wild Salmon Center and facilitator of our arrangements. She calculated my cost, faxed me the visa application and expedited it with urgency through Russian channels. Meanwhile, I was to bring sleeping bag, air mattress, tent and eating utensils. We were to float in rubber rafts for as many as 10 days, so space was limited. I bought a one-man tent and mummy bag and resolved to layer my clothing rather than including a bulky down parka. Each decision to conserve space was laced with trepidation of setting off to what I imagined to be frigid Siberia in October.

I was equally disciplined in limiting my angling gear, even leaving my fishing vest behind. Nor was I entirely illumined regarding fly selection. Following my Mongolian experience, I ordered some large Lemming flies from The Fly Shop and, for good measure, had Steve Perih, guide at the Lower Dean River Lodge, tie me up ten more rodent imitators. I added some black String and Bunny Leaches and threw in a few minnowy Lefty's Deceivers, just in case sea-run taimen remained wedded culinarily to the sea. My arsenal was completed with a handful of smaller Wooly Buggers and Humpies for the ancillary grayling and char likely to inhabit the Botchi's waters.

The week before departure I was relieved on two counts. Xan sent us a weather report in which that day's high temperature in Khabarovsk was 70 degrees. While it should be a few degrees cooler at the Botchi, we were coinciding with so-called "grandmother's summer," Russia lacking Indians. Secondly, I would not be transporting Wild Salmon Center scientific gadgetry, as agreed, since we were to be joined by Kitty Griswold, a graduate student in fisheries biology at Oregon State University. My gain, as in luggage space, was to be her loss. That small consideration brought zipping closed my two bags actually within the realm of possibility.

Jeff and I met up without a hitch at the Asiana Airline counter in the Los Angeles International terminal on the appointed evening and embarked on our red-eye odyssey to the Orient. It was then that he led me through the labyrinthine tale of the genesis of our trip. His Sweetwater Travel Company had been approached by the Wild Salmon Center as a possible joint-venture partner in developing sport fishing in both Khabarovsky Krai (province or state) and on the Zhupanova River in Kamchatka, a proven rainbow trout and steelhead stream with an existing lodge. The Wild Salmon Center had received a grant for the initial exploration of the Botchi from the World Wildlife Fund. By paying my way I was helping to finance the expedition.

Approaching Seoul the crew transitioned us to the Orient. Each of the lovely cloned stewardesses positioned herself to lead the seated multitude in a choreographed midair version of tai chi, accompanied by appropriate music.

In Khabarovsk our plane stopped well short of the terminal and we walked to it across a weary tarmac pockmarked with ancient cosmetic repairs and fresh cracks. A uniformed soldier from central casting for a James Bond movie guarded the door. He was heavy, bulbous-faced and austere. On drawing abreast I impulsively smiled and said "hi." He scowled and turned away in feigned indifference. Nor were the first two officials in the endless maze of officialdom protecting the country's ramparts any friendlier. As a veteran of this particular Russian rite of passage, Jeff advised me not to smile, link eyes or volunteer any unsolicited information. The third official, a matronly woman with a winning smile, broke the oppressive spell with a carefully articulated "hello, welcome to Russia." Bill 007 was not about to be whisked off to some grim room for interrogation.

My first sexist impression of Kitty was that she was far too pretty and poised to be a fisheries biologist, not that I had a very formed preconception of what one might actually look like. I was also suffering from a slight undercurrent of resentment over her 11th hour inclusion. My 10th hour sinecure had imbued me with a certain proprietary conviction that Jeff and I were to be the designated fishermen, accompanied by five non-angling companions. Despite her scientific credentials, Kitty was along as our third angler, seemingly to expose her to taimen as a subject species for her possible post-doctoral research. For the present, however, she was ABD and writing her dissertation on the migratory patterns of anadromous dolly varden char and cutthroat trout in Alaska's Copper River basin.

As we stood in line in Khabarovsk enduring the cumbersome process of clearing customs and immigration, any personal distance between Kitty and me imploded in a burst of "small world isn't it." She had grown up in Reno and was a descendant of one of northeast Nevada's old ranching families. Her father, Chan, had been my attorney's law partner at one time. In the far distant past, when I was but a casual angler, he had enticed me to accompany him on an occasion or two to nearby Davis Lake, then Northern California's newest impoundment, to cast black Wooly Buggers at bloated planter rainbows. It was the boat I remembered most, a cumbersome green aluminum craft. Kitty guffawed, "He got it from Montgomery Ward, and we all called it the 'Queen of the Waters'. My brother still has it." Kitty and I seemed to be instantly related through such royalty as well as the propinquity of shared people, times and place. There aren't too many native Nevadans on this planet, and it was likely the first time ever that two had coincided in the customs' line of the Khabarovsk airport. Such omens should not be taken lightly!

We met Misha that evening in the lobby of the Amethyst Hotel (another omen, perhaps, since two months earlier my wife and I had spent a delightful week cruising the Amazon out of Iquitos aboard the good ship *Ametista*). Dr. Mikhail Skopets was a fisheries biologist under contract to the Wild Salmon Center. He had recommended the Botchi and would be conducting studies during our float, particularly compilation of a species inventory. He was a small man, almost elfin, endowed with extraordinary intelligence and breadth of experience, leavened with a wry sense of humor presaged by an impish smile. In addition to becoming instantly our main authority on most everything, over the next few days it was Misha's fluency in English that would allow transnational communication to move beyond sign language. To further seal our omened fates, he was wearing a baseball cap extolling El Aereo, an air service in Elko, Nevada—Griswold Ranch country. Misha had spent a month there working on a Lahontan cutthroat trout census conducted in the Maggie Creek drainage. Poor Jeff was odd Montanan out in our evolving Nevada-insiders' discourse.

Meanwhile, our expedition's dough had been laced liberally with yeast. There were now eleven of us, including two shadowy uncommunicative figures—Russian national government fisheries biologists that our helicopter would off-load on a small tributary of the Botchi. Alexander Nikulin, chairman of the Interregional Association of Independent Tour Operators and owner of our designated outfitting company, had decided to come along, as had Steve Nelson, Russian Far East-Ecoregion Program Manager for the World Wildlife Fund.

The pervasive backdrop presence from the outset had been the Siberian tiger. I confess to having harbored certain reservations over sleeping in my flimsy tent in the forests of the night's fearful symmetry. I asked Misha if he had ever seen a tiger. "Only in a zoo." In the foyer of Nikulin's office, there was a stuffed 5-year-old tigress, so we were able to see at least a dead one. As we rode toward the military base to board our helicopter, Steve elaborated on WWF's tiger program. Initially, it had focussed all of its efforts on tiger preservation, financed by Exxon's Save-the-Tiger Fund. After World War II, there were only about an estimated 80 Siberian tigers left in the wild. By 1990 the population was up to about 250, but poaching was their Damocles sword in the wake of a collapsing Soviet system. Given the general economic crisis in the post-Soviet era, in which a man might earn 20 dollars monthly, the disparity was pathetic between that and poaching a tiger to smuggle into China, where its skin and body parts might fetch as much as $100,000. The anti-poaching brigades were of the no-nonsense variety—one of Steve's protégés had been given some sort of environmental-protector-of-the-year award by *Time* magazine. There had been violent confrontations, the results of which he chose to be vague about. In any event, recent censuses (compiled by counting tracks in the winter snow) showed that the tiger population was now in the 400 range, or about the carrying capacity of the available habitat for such a large predator.

So WWF was broadening its purview. Steve was in his second year of administering a two-year $700,000 grant from USAID to foment ecotourism. He spoke of the area's intrinsic attractions—the massive 2,750-mile Amur River system with its 110 species of freshwater fish, native peoples with their folk arts, crafts and traditions and incredible biodiversity. It is here that South Asian flora and fauna meet their Siberian counterparts, where the Manchurian ash, Korean cedar, Mongolian oak, birch, maple, larch, elms and poplars mingle with the Siberian conifer-darkened taiga, where in the Sikhote-Alin mountains the range of the Siberian tiger overlaps with that of the caribou. It might not be possible to see a Siberian tiger on one's touristic visit, but you might be shown its tracks by a guide from an anti-poaching team, visit a native village, and walk the woods for glimpses of the rich birdlife and to gather some of the more than 200 species of edible and medicinal plants. But the charge required its detonator—enter sport fishing and our exploratory. Steve was along to gain first-hand impressions of it since he was a bit out on the limb. His board of 11 locals was somewhat skeptical of supporting the $15,000 request of the Wild Salmon Center to inventory fish species on the Botchi while testing its angling potential. For some members it seemed like a bit of a boondoggle for a few fat-cat Americans, when the money might better be spent on such necessities as trails and latrines for the underfunded nature reserves. However, Steve had argued for our exploratory, and the project was one of only 12 requests approved out of a pool of 162 applications.

Botchinsky Reserve had been targeted because of its remoteness. Most of the other nature reserves had been partially degraded by logging before their establishment. Misha hoped that isolation had insulated the Botchi from the endemic overfishing (summer gill netting and winter ice fishing) that is facilitated by logging roads. He despaired over the difficulty of enforcing the game laws in Russia. The wardens are locals, and they cannot arrest their friends, relatives and neighbors without personal consequences. Misha would like to see an exchange program in which Western Europe and the United States swap game wardens with Russia.

At the military base our helicopter, commissioned from the Ministry of Rescue and Emergency, seemed enormous to me but was a runt compared to its fellow flying whales. Nevertheless, its capacious interior easily accommodated a few tons of gear and supplies, nine passengers, and three crew, which included a stentorian gentleman whose role, other than to sit with us, was unclear. His first act was to rein in an overly impetuous Jeff when he tried to enter the military base's position into my GPS! After a two-hour weather delay, we were soaring above a mixed forest, its deciduous trees touched only slightly by autumn. I would not need my parka since the only real hint of impending winter was the snow-dusted tip of the highest peak of the range dividing coastal drainages from the Amur River basin.

After two hours we landed at the mouth of the Koppi River, where we were to lunch while the chopper flew off to nearby coastal town of Sovgavan for refueling. It was at the Koppi that we were joined by Viktor Voidilov, our camptender, and his helper Nikolai Sambersky. Viktor, well-muscled yet lithely tall-timbered, exuded competence that inspired confidence. Nikolai was more reserved at first and seemed far the more rough-hewn. He was short and corpulent in a strong rather than flabby manner, and the balding pate of his oversized head, Stalinesque mustache and metal-capped dentures evoked the oafish minion of the ruthless bad guy in the Hollywood western or spy flick.

We lunched on vegetable soup and bread with red caviar and then toured the combined hunting and sport fishing camp that Viktor was building—log structures with moose- and bear-skin rugs and antler-adorned walls. The outhouse had to be the world's most elegant, with a carved wooden exterior, linoleum floor and wallpaper. Viktor handles 30 to 40 Japanese anglers annually. He also traps king crabs and heads up a 25-man team of commercial salmon fishermen. His was one of the most successful this past season, accounting for 700 metric tons and earning each of its members about $1,500 for two month's work—an enormous salary in Russia.

Steve and I took a stroll along the pier of a silent wooden fish processing plant. He'd been in Vladivostok on assignment with the World Wildlife Fund for over a year. On balance he liked Russia, but with enthusiasm that was far from unambiguous. There was the graft and factionalism that made it almost impossible to get things done. He was an environmental cheerleader, an American idealist with a fistful of dollars preaching conservation through eco-tourism to the cynical, battle-scarred survivors of the Soviet bureaucratic wars. One suspected (as indeed he knew) that it was more the short-term money than the honey of some better Promised Land that kept the cast of his particular Russian play onstage.

Probably in his mid to late 40s, Steve was a bachelor, the divorced father of a daughter now in Argentina. It seems that life in Russia for an unattached American male is wonderful, though not without its downsides. American men are godsends to females accustomed to vodka-swilling, abusive, underpaid when not unemployed, irresponsible klutzes. The women of this region were noted for their beauty. He corrected my mistaken impression, given the ostensible gender equity and human uniformity under the Soviet system, that they must be unfeminine. To the contrary, they were coquettish and flirtatious when not downright sexually aggressive, a legacy of the relaxation of sexual mores in the land of Stalin.

The cloud over this otherwise post-feminist-American-males' Valhalla was the opportunism. Vladivostok was loaded with gorgeous single mothers looking for a meal ticket of the airplane-to-the-States variety. In fact, Steve recounted what smacked of urban myth about the procession of lonely bachelors from the American Midwest who come here to seek a bride only to end up fleeced and abandoned by their Russian sweetheart once in the U.S. Indeed, you start dating someone, and the first thing she wants to know is if you're prepared to send her daughter to Yale. It makes you want to say 'but what about me? Don't you like me for myself?'

After descending gingerly into a narrow clearing on the Mulpa tributary to drop off the two fisheries biologists, we continued on

Casting About in the Reel World

to Gróssevichi, a small settlement at the juncture of the Botchi's fresh waters with the brine of the Sea of Japan. We offloaded some supplies, including a drum of gasoline and outboard motor for use in the reserve's boat on the navigable stretch of the lower river. It had been decided to devote the last three or four days of our fishing to the estuary. Even though outside the reserve *per se,* it was quite possible that our main quarry was concentrated there or was alternating between the river and the sea. We were also joined by Alexander Ilyukhin, vice director of Botchinsky Reserve, the last member of the entourage. He was to guide us through his familiar territory. For the next half hour we flew about 40 miles upriver, observing its many moods from the air while making mental notes of potential obstructions. The brilliant late afternoon sun played over the chaotic quiltwork of multiple shades of green, punctuated occasionally by the yellow or red of the odd precocious tree embracing, rather than still resisting, the impending autumn. The helicopter's shadow played across the arboreal canopy and, when the angle between sun and stream was just right, the Botchi blinded us with reflected rays. Was the semaphoric message a welcome or warning?

Given the dense forest, our landing was on an island gravel bar. We off-loaded our gear and then clung to it in the maelstrom of the man-made hurricane as our featherless stork, having delivered its babies, lifted aloft and then disappeared beyond the nearest ridge line. Our die was definitely cast as we scrambled into our waders in order to move the gear ashore.

We had but an hour before dark to set up camp, which was scarcely enough for me, since, in my usual somnolent fashion, trip preparations had not included trying out my one-man tent, purchased but the day before leaving Reno. In the time that it took me to assemble my erector set by the numbers, under Viktor's aegis, he, Nikolai and the two Alexanders had constructed a canopied dining area, chainsawed a dozen rounds for chairs and a table out of a fallen trunk, cut saplings as supports for their common canvassed shelter complete with its own woodstove, and put our kettles to boiling. My initial reading of Viktor was definitely confirmed.

In the early darkness any sense of vulnerability dissipated in the faint stirrings of genuine camaraderie as we began to touch fingers across the cultural chasm, the process smoothed by Misha's patient translations and Steve's far less symmetrical bilingualism. The dinner fare was the most remarkable element in our icebreaker. We had purchased three cases of beer and were all so armed when Viktor then poured about a shot glass of vermilion liquid into our tin cups. It was vodka crimsoned with powdered elk antler. Steve noted the Russian saying "beer without vodka is throwing money at the wind," so it was bottoms up. We then ate *chibureki,* or moose meat pies, and slabs of moose tongue.

I spent a fitful night trying to adjust to the mild claustrophobia of a mummy bag that was far too tight and a one-man tent bordering on the bivouac variety. Its ceiling was literally about three inches above my face. By morning I was faced with what would become my daily dilemma—a wet sleeping bag partly soaked by contact with condensation on the inside of my tent. However, a few minutes of careful exposure to the breakfast cook fire did the trick, so it was more of a nuisance than serious problem. I had a temperature gauge along; at dawn it was 39°, rising to the high 50s by mid-afternoon. Barring the arrival of some sort of serious cold front, any Siberian-weather fear should prove groundless.

We had five rubber rafts, two large and three small. To give Jeff maximum flexibility to carry out his river-scoping assignment, he would travel solo. I partnered up with Misha in a small raft that had to carry all of his scientific and personal gear as well. Alexander Ilyukhin also traveled solo, preceding us downstream to scout out dangerous log jams and the proper channel whenever the river bifurcated. The two larger and less maneuverable rafts carried the bulk of our gear. Viktor and Steve were in one, Alexander Nikulin, Nikolai and Kitty in the other. Fortunately, for the most part the river was easy to float. There was the occasional time when prudence dictated easing our craft through short rapids on ropes controlled from the shore, and there was one short portage when our selected channel proved to be the lesser. Periodically, we were delayed while the crew used their chain saw to cut a passage through or around an obstructing logjam.

As for the angling, there was little holding water for big fish in the upper river. A good run was of the five-foot-deep variety. However, we immediately began catching Amur grayling (about a pound) and the southern sub-species of dolly varden that weighed up to three. We started out fishing wet since dollies will usually not take a dry fly. *Au contraire* on the Botchi. By late afternoon I had landed easily 30 dollies, mostly on dries cast 45 degrees downstream and skittered across the current. It was necessary to be patient since the majority of strikes were false, the fish boiling next to my Humpy until one finally ingested it. The occasional grayling was far less tentative regarding the surface take, rewarding us with contemplation of a plump body of orange-flecked, iridescent-blue coloration, topped with a flaring dorsal fin (though not nearly as flamboyant as that of its more northerly Arctic grayling cousin). So, we were pleasantly distracted while Jeff continued to thrash unsuccessfully any likely looking taimen water, no matter how marginal, with his large Mouse imitation.

By that evening we were beginning to settle into what would be our steady diet. The focal point of each meal was either a vegetable soup, sometimes borscht, or a plate of rice or buckwheat fortified with canned meat and/or vegetables. Our bread supply was ample and remained amazingly edible after nearly two weeks. We ate it plain and also smothered in canned butter and honey. A few apples were our only fruit.

We also provisioned ourselves from the forest's magnificently variegated understory. Our main beverage was a delicious tea made from wild berries. Our soups were spiced with various gathered greens. We began eating some of our fish—grilled, in a fish soup and also pounded into fishcakes. At one point, while discussing our wild bounty, the subject of Vladimir K. Arseniev's penetration of this area (1906-1907) came up. It gave to the world the famous figure of Dersu Uzala, of the Nanai, the explorer's guide—subject of a partly fictionalized account by Arseniev and a movie by noted Japanese filmmaker Akira Kurosawa. Thanks to his book *Dersu Uzala*, Maxim Gorky proclaimed Arseniev the James Fenimore Cooper of Russian letters. According to the explorer, whenever he was without Dersu's assistance, he damn near starved. This was simply beyond Viktor's comprehension, given his own relaxed dependence upon the forest's abundance. "Didn't he think to bring along a hook and line at the very least?"

The first three days followed the same pattern. I was enjoying our preliminary bouts with grayling and dollies, but was becoming a bit impatient for the as yet elusive main event. As we descended, both the waters of the Botchi and my relationship with Misha deepened. A native of Sverdlovsk in the Urals and a graduate of Ural State University, in 1977 he decided to go as "far east and north as possible," settling in the Siberian coastal city of Magadan. "I guess I read too much Jack London," he said with a chuckle.

Misha was an indefatigable field scientist who had been systematically exploring three or four rivers of northern Siberia annually for the last 23 years. He had authored more than 60 articles and had personally discovered four new fish species: the anadromous yellow-mouthed char, the long-finned char, the small-mouthed char, and a small eel-like sea dweller that is an altogether new genus now called *Magadania Skopezi* after its discoverer. At one point we caught a six-inch salmonid, and Misha noted that it was a landlocked (as in one that had eschewed sea migration) male cherry salmon. Had it been back from the sea it would have weighed in the 10-pound range.

Misha then expanded my limited ichthyological knowledge by noting that genetic distancing places the ancestor of all salmonids in the North Atlantic. In addition to giving rise to steelhead (and rainbow trout), as well as the Atlantic salmon, one of its descendants was the cherry salmon. It seems that it was the latter that gave

Casting About in the Reel World

rise to all five Pacific salmon species about one million years ago. The Siberian taimen, the species I had sought in China and caught in Mongolia, diverged about 2.5 million years back. We, however, were after sea-run or Sakhalin taimen, one of the most ancient of salmonids, dating from roughly 40 million years ago! Genetically, it is so distant from the Siberians that some ichthyologists believe the Sakhalins to be an entirely different genus.

In addition to scientist, Misha was an accomplished angler. He characterized himself as one of only about five fly fishermen in all of the Russian Far East. He had been to the United States on four occasions and spent a total of about a year there, managing to build into his agenda angling trips to Utah's Green River and several steelhead streams of the Pacific Northwest.

For Misha sport fishing was more than a pastime. Early in the 1990s he had recognized the opportunity to fund his scientific research by combining it with catering to foreign anglers. Until recently, he had been part owner of a lodge on the Yama River, an hour by helicopter from Magadan, where there was excellent char, grayling and coho salmon fishing. However, the high operating costs and the lack of the more appealing rainbow trout, steelhead and/or taimen meant that the operation was marginally profitable. It could only command a fraction of the rates charged in Kamchatka or the Kola. So Misha had already made plans to work on the Zhupanova River in Kamchatka during the summer of 2001.

Misha exclaimed only half-jokingly that he sees his wife one or two months a year, "I told her about myself when we got married, I'm a fisherman and I intend to keep on fishing!" He added,

> "Women are one of life's few wonderful things, but freedom is the most important. Hemingway is my favorite American author. He believed in freedom. I do not want to work for anybody, and I don't want anyone to work for me."

This led naturally into a discussion of the Soviet period. Actually, Misha had an additional reason for striking a low, if independent, profile. He was a Jew. In 1982 when the Soviets were under intense pressure to allow Jews to emigrate, Misha's sister and parents went to New Jersey, after his father was terminated from his job as member of a television field team,

> "If Stalin had lived for another year, I would have never been born. He was planning a new gulag near Lake Baikal for anyone who had ever lived abroad and seen other ways of life. My father had been part of the occupation force in Germany during 1946 and 1947."

Misha favored Putin's hard-line policies, particularly in Chechnya. As far as he was concerned, anyone in Chechnya caught with a firearm should be summarily shot. The same held for armed Palestinians in Israel. Structure and civic obedience were necessary. However, he was delighted over the collapse of communism,

> "It may work for ants or bees, but it is against human nature. We are too self-interested. Besides we never had communism in Russia; it was socialism. It was organized like a monkey troupe—a strong man at the top surrounded by a few people willing to carry out any order and then the rest of us. When I was studying in the university, we had to take classes on political indoctrination every year. It was easy for me because I have a good memory, but I didn't believe any of it. We were organized into student groups, and, if there was to be a patriotic demonstration, we might be ordered to send 100 people. You went along and cheered, but it didn't mean anything. Many Russians today are like animals just let out of their zoo. They are confused. The poet Vladimir Vysotsky wrote that now we have freedom but what are we to do with it? Are we prepared? Freedom can be a great burden; a heavy responsibility."

At one point he noted that the death toll during the 20th century in the area embraced by the Soviet Union may have been as high as 100 million. Included were the two world wars, Russia's civil war, the gulags, and the forced transfers of populations. "Even if the number is only 50 or 60 million, that is 10 times greater than the toll in the holocaust." I struggled to process such mass-scale morbid information. It simply stretched my fathoming capacities and seemed to excavate an unbridgeable experiential chasm between us.

By the third afternoon, Jeff was beginning to doubt that there were taimen in the river. But then that evening we camped where a slough-like, slow-moving side channel met the main current and we spotted some large cruising fish, the largest of which was about 25 pounds. Taimen at last! Jeff quickly caught a five-pound kundzha char, a new species for us that was both a noble fighter and gorgeously colored, brindled with white spots set against a coffee-with-cream brown backdrop. I began casting at the seam where the slack waters intersected the rippling current. I had a ferocious take and strong fight from an imagined taimen that mutated into another five-pound kundzha. Around the dinner fire our hosts fashioned an elk bugle by repeatedly inserting a red-hot nail into the enlarging cavity of a carved and skinned section of a tree limb. Eventually, the forest reverberated with credible (at least to my ear) challenges that went unreciprocated. In the dark early dawn I heard what seemed to be a bugling elk in the distance. Viktor, too, had heard it and informed me over breakfast that it was actually the cry of the nocturnal fish owl.

The next morning dawned cold and bright. Misha donned his wet suit to snorkel our slough and photograph its denizens. Alas, the bigger fish were also enormous kundzha.* By then most of our gear was in varying stages of damp to wet. I spread my entire wardrobe on rocks and branches arrayed to best embrace the warming rays and then watched the steam begin to rise from my own little geyser field. We loitered half the morning while Misha com-

---

* Several months later, after studying his slides, Misha concluded that the largest fish was definitely a taimen.

pleted his inventory, removing and recording parr collected with a gill net. The lovely weather and dry gear stiffened backbones and bolstered spirits as we continued our descent. We stopped to fish the next likely looking side slough but instead were distracted by a new discovery. The standard shoreline array of rounded river pebbles was now interspersed with pieces of sandstone. Their source was evident, a nearby crumbly hillside. For the next hour we mined it by extracting the loose slabs and then breaking them apart by striking their weak fault lines. Occasionally, someone was rewarded with a fossilized leaf or seedpod.

The evening of our fifth day on the river we arrived at what had formerly been a fur trapper's cabin before creation of the reserve. It possessed a surprising and welcome amenity—a *banya* or sauna. We fired it up and washed off the grime of several bathless days. The full treatment included a whipping with cedar boughs to stimulate circulation followed by a plunge in the river. The whole process of sweating together naked, the swish followed by the smack of the leaves upon crimson flesh, and the juvenile banter all accelerated our bonding.

At the dinner table our knot was further tightened with a round of vodka and storytelling. Misha proposed that each of us tell a funny story or joke. It became an exercise in proving that humor is the most recalcitrant of cross-cultural communication. But we were all uproarious over our very futility, particularly the ever-ebullient Alexander Nikulin, who found humor in practically everything, his mirth exploding in open-mouthed, full-throated guffaws. It was that evening that Alexander Ilyukhin finally relaxed and began to smile, and gruff Nikolai Sambersky unveiled his incongruous, near-falsetto voice.

Nikolai is an experienced hunter and fur trapper. Through Misha I asked if he had ever seen a tiger. Indeed, he'd been on two hunts to capture (legally) specimens for zoos. It was impossible, not to mention highly dangerous, to go after any adults over 3 years of age. So the idea is to find the tracks in the snow of a tigress with large cubs. You then assemble five men and some willing dogs (since tigers love to eat them, only about one in 10 will join the chase). The pack is leashed until the tigress is separated from her cubs with random gunshots. The dogs are then released to run down one of the juveniles. Normally it seeks refuge under a snag, or it might try to defend itself with its back against some structure. The practice is to pin its neck to the ground with a forked stick and then truss it up, a highly dangerous business since the cub is a snarling ball of fury and its mother might return at any time. Yet Nikolai knew of only three human deaths due to tiger attacks—grizzly bears were more dangerous.

Of far greater concern than mammals were the insects, but it was autumn so we should be in the season underscored by the Russian saying " the best time of the year is between the black and the white flies (i.e. snowflakes)." Indeed, from late spring through summer, the area is plagued with the full panoply of black and horse flies, no-see-ums and mosquitoes. Most sinister are the plentiful ticks—one in 25 carries viral encephalitis. Steve advised us to check our bodies daily and not to sleep in our clothing. He had along silk thread used for an extraction procedure. We endured a scare that proved to be a false alarm. Another critter, one that is unique to the area, does a remarkable imitation of the tick. The airborne moose lice can be identified by their wings, although amazingly they sometimes shed them once having landed on their chosen host. But you can always count legs—ticks have eight; moose lice six. Even though basically harmless, the moose lice are biting little bloodsuckers in their own right and capable of inflicting pain. During the trip we each had about 10 run-ins with the critters, though only Kitty was actually bitten.

Nikolai catches as many as 100 sable every winter (his all-time high was 125) along with quite a few mink, some otter, several "raccoon-dogs" (an animal found only here) and the odd wolverine. During the Soviet days trappers worked under the license of a government corporation. They were permitted to take so many of each species from an assigned territory. It was all somewhat tenuous, however, since the head of the organization could deprive a man of his access arbitrarily. Trappers still do not "own" their territory, but now hold an exclusive guarantee under a long-term lease (25 years).

Viktor, too, was a commercial trapper and hunter during the winter, running his line on both skis and snowmobile. He used to catch about 60 sable each winter, but the population was down considerably due to habitat loss from logging. Last winter he caught only about 30. He shot and sold 10 moose and two elk as well.

In the steamy heat and shared nakedness of the sauna, the playful banter of the failed story-telling, and the exchange of life histories, any remnants of our common Cold-War legacy dissipated into the camaraderie of a bunch guys (and a gal) sharing an adventure. I fly off to each new angling destination with a set of preconceptions and invariably shed most of them along the way. It may be possible to still think solely in terms of "Brazil" or "China" having stayed in a four-star hotel in Rio or Beijing, it is an altogether different proposition to camp out for a week or more on some wilderness river with Brazilians and Chinese. It is then that national stereotypes and political systems fade into insignificance to be replaced by the flawed, faltering and fascinating process of human beings attempting to bridge a cultural chasm in order to understand one another as simply people.

I realized that, like most Americans of my Cold-Warrior generation, reconciling my Russian preconceptions was possibly the greatest of such challenges. When I was but 20, I had fallen in love with Russian literature and spent the better part of a year reading Tolstoy, Dostoevsky, Pushkin, Chekhov, Turgenev, Goncharov and Gogol in English translation. Such was my fascination that I even took a Russian course in college in the abortive attempt to access my idols in the original. I still own several (unread) Russian literary texts, purchased while a student in Oslo on a summer's study-abroad program.

The Cold War deepened into the seemingly endless wintry chill of perpetual confrontation, punctuated by such fearsome flash points as the Cuban missile crisis, Vietnam, Czechoslovakia, Hungary and Afghanistan, strategic maneuverings within the strait jacket of the omnipresent threat of planetary annihilation through intentional or miscalculated nuclear exchange. I read both volumes of Solshenitsyn's *Gulag*—arguably the most depressing (and near interminable) documentation of human capacity for inhumanity. And then there was Mr. Khrushchev banging his shoe on the podium at the United Nations while stating categorically "We will bury you." Lest we should forget, each May Day there were the images from Red Square of maybe a million Soviet citizens cheering the parading of endless cadres of troops, mountains of material and enormous missiles squatting on their mobile launchers—seemingly the Soviet system's little annual declaration of World War III. Even discounting the constant Soviet-bashing in the Western press, it was difficult for my russophile, liberal side to discern much redeeming ambiguity in such messages.

Like just about everybody else, I was resigned to live out the rest of my life in the dreadful impasse, provided with periodic updates by the clock in Times Square that was ticking down the hypothetical few remaining minutes before Armageddon. In retrospect it is really a wonder that any of us managed to get up in the morning and go off to work, let alone come home at night to procreate our descendants! And then it was over and the previously unthinkable was now possible. Here I was on the Botchi, my Cold-War ghosts finally exorcized, their weight lifted from a spirit now giddy with an incredible lightness of just being.

Parenthetically, I also gave thanks that, nuclear exchange notwithstanding, I had never had to face guys like Viktor and Nikolai as my adversaries in some kind of trench warfare. Their dazzling daily demonstration of physical prowess and ability to live off the land provided the prima facie evidence of Mother Russia's deep reservoir of strength. I could only imagine that had Napoleon and Hitler been along on our float trip European history might have been very different!

It rained hard that night and by morning I had rejoined the wet-rat brigade. Ahead of us lay our greatest rafting challenge. As its riverine valley widened, the Botchi divided into a myriad of braids, many blocked with impenetrable logjams and all peppered with tricky rapids. With Alexander Ilyukhin's local knowledge and steady reconnaissance, we charted a sound course through the maze, but it took most of the morning to negotiate about a kilometer. The two large supply rafts posed the biggest problem. We managed to flip one of them on two occasions, losing our medical kit in the bargain.

We stopped for lunch under the hastily erected canvas canopy that protected us from a driving rain. We were at the juncture of the tributary where we had been scheduled to meet up with our other two fisheries biologists. Their footprints and absence indicated that they had been and gone. As it turned out, they were miffed at a woman's participation in the expedition and were essentially boycotting us.

This spot marked the boundary of the Botchinsky Nature Reserve. From here to the estuary, a distance of about 7 miles, the Botchi was navigable by motorboat. Given the weather we decided to fish only the most promising runs during the early afternoon in the interest of reaching Grossevichi, the all-but-abandoned settlement at the river's mouth, by nightfall. There we could commandeer a building, bringing closure to the camping dimension of our trip. From Grossevichi we could use the fuel and motor that we had off-loaded on our way in to explore the lower river and estuary over the next several days.

Our first stop was at a promising side slough that we labeled the "Peat Hole," after the 10-foot thick exposed layer of peat moss overhanging the graveled cut bank. Misha and I both caught a seven-pound kundzha and Jeff had two surface strikes on his large Mouse fly. In the next run downstream, I took a second kundzha in the same weight range. The river itself had changed character. Emboldened by the strength of accumulating tributary flow and the gentler landscape, it now progressed confidently with a bank to bank force that made the wading precarious. Occasionally it paused to rest in deep pools that seemed ideal taimen habitat, though that particular species remained elusive.

Wildlife viewing was on the rise. Two low-flying, white-tailed sea eagles appeared, and a majestic Steller, the world's largest predatory bird with its eight-foot wing span, configured slow arcs in the leaden sky several hundred feet above me. The harlequin ducks, now all but extinct in much of their former Eurasian range, were as common as the pigeons in a city park. At one point a large head and inquisitive expression popped above the surface no more than 30 feet downstream from me and then disappeared. It was grayish, so I assumed it to be a wayward harbor seal, but was later told by Viktor that it was most certainly a wizened otter. Here they attain the length of 6 feet and a lightening of their guard hairs marks their dotage (as it does mine).

In late afternoon, and just about the time that shivers began to flit through soddened body and thoughts of hypothermia lurked at the margins of my consciousness, Alexander Ilyukhin appeared in a slender wooden boat that was at least 30 feet long. We hefted our raft aboard and within 20 minutes were dockside at a vacant dormitory of a seasonal commercial fishing camp in Grossevichi. Viktor had fired up both the cooking stove and the one in the adjacent room destined for drying out our clothing and gear. After a largely soggy week of one-man-tent camping, the prospect of a real bed, table, chairs and a roof overhead seemed downright waldorf-astorian.

Our angling during the next few days was pretty disappointing, our collective efforts producing the odd kundzha and sea-run dolly. Misha put out his gill nets daily and managed to catch five taimen parr and one juvenile about 18 inches long. We also learned that a 50-inch specimen had been netted in the bay a week earlier. None of us managed to catch a taimen on rod and reel. Misha was both disappointed and concerned. There are but a few healthy sea-run stocks left on Sakhalin Island. To the south of us only four mainland rivers still held taimen, all of their populations in precarious circumstances. To our north the species' range extends to only two other rivers. Misha had hoped that the Botchi would prove to be the exception. He was now prepared to join other fishery biologists this winter in preparing the report that would urge Moscow to place the Sakhalin taimen in the "Red Book" of Russia's endangered species. In theory, it would provide the species with total protection; practice and enforcement were altogether different matters. However, it was the necessary first step in the lengthy process of reeducation that might ultimately save the Sakhalin taimen. Misha believed that linking conservation to a catch-and-release sport fishery was the best approach. Residents would release their netted taimen only once convinced that they were more valuable alive as magnets for attracting the proceeds of foreign anglers into the local economy.

During our stay at Grossevichi we were visited on occasion by Nikolai Shkretov. A tall, distinguished 74-year-old man, he had come here in 1931 at 5 years of age. He seemed curious about us since he could only recall previous visits to Grossevichi by one group of Americans and another of Japanese. During the 1930s, as part of the Soviet government's incentives' policy to populate Siberia, Grossevichi had grown to 400 inhabitants, engaged primarily in salmon fishing and logging. Nikolai emerged as the leader of the community's commercial fishing. In winter, he was a trapper and hunter. The upriver cabin and banya were his winter out-camp before creation of the nature reserve. In World War II, he had served in the Russian navy. During that conflict an airstrip was built on the coastal plain 4 miles from here and, in 1945, on a few occasions Soviet aircraft used it to bomb Japan. For a while the village also hosted a maintenance station for the communications cable that ran along the coast. However, by the 1970s Grossevichi was in decline—the most accessible forest had been felled and it was proving more economical to industrialize salmon fishing aboard large trawlers seasonally rather than maintaining whole land-based communities of fishermen and their families year round. Until two years ago, the military maintained a lookout on a nearby hill (I hiked up to where there was a lone anti-aircraft gun emplacement—its structure intact except for removal of the barrel).

The population of Grossevichi was now down to six persons, including the caretaker assigned to watching over the abandoned buildings who stayed with a family that used to cook and care for the troops manning the guard-post. For the last two years they had lived off the food stores left behind by the military and the caretaker's allotment. Now they were pretty much "living off the land." It was unlikely that they would remain much longer. Nikolai was alone since he had lost his wife the previous March. This winter he planned to move to Sovgavan where he had a son and daughter. In short, Grossevichi seemed fated to become a real ghost town in the near future.

We asked him about taimen, and he remembered seeing as many as 50 in the peat-bank hole in the 1930s, and even in the 1960s and 1970s. But then the human population grew, and some residents acquired spinning tackle. They cleaned out the fish in no time. Only half-jokingly, he estimated that there might be 10 taimen left in the river, the few wily survivors. And what of large mammals? Nikolai noted that there had never been a tiger or bear attack in the entire history of the settlement. When he was still trapping, there were only one or two tigers in the area. Now he believes there are at least three or four. Last winter one morning he found a track just a few yards from his front door.

His only actual sighting was in February 1971. He had gone to Grossevichi for food supplies and by moonlight was walking back to his trapper's cabin. He came around a spruce snag, and there was a tiger about 20 yards distant coming towards him. The startled animal bolted into the woods, and when about 50 yards away, let out three deep growls. The next day Nikolai saw tracks indicating that the tiger had returned and followed him for about 100 meters before veering off for good.

As a fur trapper his main annual catch was 100-120 mink. They had been introduced (along with muskrat) from North America. While never released on the Botchi, by 1953 mink had made their way here from either the Samargá to the south or Koppi to the north. There were no limits on mink. He was also permitted to catch somewhere between 30 and 40 sable depending upon the year. He could have caught many more. He was also allowed three otter and would usually take two or three wolverines as well. It was all tightly controlled by the government. "You couldn't even keep a fur for your wife." It was the same with fish. Under the Soviets it was illegal to take a salmon home for personal consumption, and some rivers were off limit.

I thought that Nikolai was through talking, but after a pause he insisted that I listen to more. His demeanor darkened into a mixture of sadness and anger,

> "I once made 1,000 to 1,200 rubles a month. It was one of the best salaries. Then I received a 500-ruble pension as a veteran. A loaf of bread was only 30 kopeks. I had 75,000 rubles in the bank. It was enough to buy five automobiles, but then thieves took over in Moscow. I could not get my money out of the bank. It was just gone."

Misha noted that, at that same time, he made 150 rubles a month and anything over 200 was considered to be a high salary. The bank collapse to which Nikolai referred had happened at the end of the Soviet era. A combination of corruption and a vastly overvalued official exchange rate meant that, once the Russian economy entered the international marketplace, there simply were no bank reserves. At that time it took $2 to buy a ruble (the black market rate was more like 10 rubles for a dollar). Today the ruble-dollar exchange is slightly more than 27 to one. Nikolai's pension, when he can collect it, is now 1,000 rubles, or about $35 monthly—

still much higher than that of the average pensioner because of his military service. Listening to the personal woes of one man who had done everything by the book and then ended up totally ruined by circumstances put a human face on the horrible predicament of the average Russian citizen. It was so much more poignant than my impressions gleaned from faithful post-perestroika reading of *The Economist* and other journalistic accounts.

As thoughts turned to our departure, I was chagrined to learn that a) neither we nor Grossevichi had any contact with the outside world, radio or otherwise, and b) it was common for groups like ours to become stranded by the weather or other factors for indeterminate periods, the record being 42 days! The mercury in my anxiety meter shot right to the top. I now realized just how pitiful my preparations had been. I had not even thought to arrange for Jan or my office to advise the organizers of my imminent San Francisco and Mexico City lectures should I be delayed in Siberia.

October 7 was warm and sunny. Unfortunately, it was still two days until our scheduled helicopter rendezvous. That night a major front moved in and all of the next day and into the evening it poured. The weather report on Viktor's transistor radio spoke of a three-day storm. Since we were not scheduled to fly out of Khabarovsk until October 11, we did have one extra day of grace, but the sense of being trapped and helpless was palpable. We all became a bit silly in our collective nervousness. Donner Party jokes centered upon who we would eat first after our supplies ran out, Nikolai winning everyone's vote for president by nominating the villagers!

Despite the prognostication, the morning of the 9th was clear. After a flurry of packing, our gear was piled up on the gravel beach like the anticipatory offerings of Melanesian cargo cultists trying to entice aircraft out of an empty sky. The plan had been to fly further south to the Samargá to pick up another scientist, so we were expecting the helicopter by noon. By 2:30 our anguished vigil had dissolved into resignation. Viktor had already started up the stove for the evening's meal when the first faint sounds of an engine play-ing Beethoven's *Ode to Joy* reached us and then the whirlybird itself descended. Our two boycotters appeared out of some crack in Grossevichi's woodwork, and we formed a human chain to load our considerable cargo aboard.

Lest we thought that life is ever simple or just, all efforts to restart the engine failed! The malfunction was in the system that preheats the fuel. The three-man crew began to disassemble various parts while we returned to our familiar abode. The helicopter had brought along a cardboard box that we had failed to offload during our ear-lier arrival. It contained a few fresh tomatoes and cucumbers, as well as a bottle of vodka. So we munched upon our first fresh veg-etables in days (if we discount the kelp that Viktor had been adding to our fare ever since we reached the coast) and anesthetized our-selves against our growing despair. But then the engine started and it was all systems go, the side-trip to the Samargá cancelled. It would be all we could do to drop Viktor and Nikolai off at the Koppi and still make it back to Khabarovsk before dark.

One more obstacle lay in our path. Yesterday's storm was now ensconced in the Sikhote Alin range separating us from our des-tination. We began to encounter snow-dusted ridges and then flew into a genuine blizzard. For an anxious half-hour we were in a total whiteout, a weather condition later described by one helicopter veteran in our party as the worst that he had ever flown in. Once on the ground we learned that we had ducked another bullet. Two days earlier there had been a serious earthquake on Sakhalin Island, which falls within the purview of the Khabarovsk base of the Min-istry of Rescue and Emergency. Had the quake been a bit worse our helicopter would surely have been diverted there.

Despite the many close calls, we were back in Khabarovsk right on schedule and with a day on our hands. Next morning we visited the nearby fish market that Misha promised would be a veritable exhibit of the Amur's plethora of species. When we attempted to photograph a giant Chinese perch from the Ussuri branch, the several fishmongers agreed with delight but insisted on averting their faces. It was one of many species in the Red Book on offer.

Misha and Kitty, accustomed as they were to handling dead specimens, found the market fascinating. For me it was just oppressive. It would never occur to Bill Anthropologist to visit Khabarovsk's morgue in order to ascertain the variety of peoples residing in this area. There are real differences between natural and social scientists!

I fled into the wider bazaar which, despite being housed in a sprawling semi-enclosed structure, was of the fascinating flea variety. A plethora of tiny stalls and display tables, each the private domain of a budding Russian capitalist, offered everything under the sun. To my eye there was no particular organization, since the purveyors of hardware, potatoes, spices, clothing, CDs and electronics seemed distributed like cards interspersed randomly in a freshly-shuffled deck.

Amidst the cacophony and chaos there was an extraordinary island of beauty. A stately, fur-capped flower vendor sat serenely among her bouquets. Maybe it was just the contrastive effect with her wider surroundings, but she struck me as angelic, yet with a demonic, understated sensuality accentuated by a distanced air that was positively Garboesque. I caught her eye and gestured with my camera. She hesitated and then nodded. But before I could focus, she arose and posed stiffly, dissipating my fantasy of having stumbled across Bill Master's devoted Margarita.

While touring the public market, it was important to be on guard against the endemic pickpocketing. We were approached by many panhandlers, including one man carrying a couple of pieces of pipe. He wanted us to take his photo so he would be seen in America. He then told Misha that he used to be a schoolteacher but lost his post in the cutbacks. He was now a casual-laboring plumber. He had a small summer house in the forest. Would we like to buy it? No? Well could we at least spare a ruble? We spared two.

During our day some of the many complexities of this unique

city, seemingly so remote yet astride cultural crossroads, were impressed upon us. If the Soviets destroyed much of the Russian architecture of former times, in Khabarovsk there were many intricately ornamented brick structures dating from the tsarist era. If the initial burst of enthusiasm toppled many Soviet icons during the recent transition, this city's central feature was Lenin Square where strollers threaded their way among lovely flower beds and fountains under the approving gaze of the old master himself—the base of his statue still inscribed with his quote proclaiming communism to be the best of all political systems. One questions, however, how much rest poor Lenin gets at night since his stately monument is now adjacent to the B-52, a western-style discotheque that is the central focus of the city's nightlife. The action there only begins to heat up at about 1 a.m.

Part of the main boulevard leading from the square to another on the banks of the Amur is still named after Karl Marx. My imagination wandered and suddenly conjured up the ludicrous image of a humorless, hirsute Karl striding towards some dock bedecked in tarpon wear and girded with fanny pack, prepared for a day on the water with an awaiting guide. It was a surreal thought that neatly underscored the chasm between my frivolous sport and his serious spite.

If low wages and high unemployment seemed endemic in Russia, there was the anomaly of considerable construction activity everywhere both in the form of street repair and renovation of old buildings. Most of the workers were Chinese nationals imported for the manual laboring jobs. Poverty is always relative. While engrossed in selecting a piece of jewelry to propitiate my house goddess upon my return, I was warned furtively by the clerk to take note of the young man standing by me, seemingly intent on the precious stones. I looked over at Jeff, and he was similarly accompanied. I walked over to him and the two young men left abruptly and together, their obvious plan thwarted.

Our hotel was itself a little microcosm of the anguished Russian moment. Both coming and going we had shared our evening meal with a bevy of elderly Japanese men paired off and dining with exquisitely-coifed and appareled young Russian women. There was a hostess service operating openly out of an office on the second floor. Russian girls are also in great demand for six-month stints in Tokyo working as dancers. There were about 20 of them on our flight to Seoul. Other guests sharing our abode were the several childless American couples here to adopt Russian babies.

The morning of our departure Misha and I further intertwined the strands of the thread of our budding friendship by agreeing that the following summer I would return to explore with him and Jeff the headwaters of the Uda, a mighty river to our north that flows into the Sea of Okhotsk, in search of Siberian taimen. I offered to peruse and edit the partially-completed English version of the book he was writing on *Flyfishing the Russian Far East*. He planned to fish Patagonia during the winter of 2002 and accepted my invitation to join me in the Florida Keys that March on his way home. "I want you to have this. It was carved by a very talented artist in Magadan." He handed me a small cameo of what I took to be walrus ivory, scrimshawed with the image of a grizzly bear and inscribed with the word "Kamchatka." "It is 30 or 40,000 years old, Bill—a mammoth's tusk."

Frontiers

Fishing, if a fisher may protest,
Of pleasures is the sweet'st of sports the best,
Of exercises the most excellent.
Of recreations the most innocent.
But now the sport is marde, and wott ye why?
Fishes decrease, and fishers multiply.

— Thomas Bastard*

*P*rimitive Illusion and Modern Confusion—*I am standing a stone's throw from the barrier reef protecting Belize's Turneffe Island. Three-foot waves, sea-mailed from Cuba or thereabouts, monotonously assault the coral wall and are instantly reduced to the smooth swell that flows onto the flat past my ankles, raising the water level to mid-calf before ebbing towards the next incoming repetition. It is all like being inside a giant chronometer measuring infinity; the muted whooshing of the rest-*

---

* Book VI, Epigram 14: de Piscatione in *Chresteleros, Seven Bookes of Epigrames*, 1598

less tide hypnotic to my ear. A tiny black-tip shark, barely more than a foot in length, approaches and then skitters away in terror after its sighting of the anthropoid interloper. Schools of gorgeous green parrot fish, working the seam between open sea and protected flat, dissolve in each new cascade and then reappear magically and ever more magnificent against the frothy, ivory-white backdrop of saltwater just processed by nature's blender.

I spot three cruising bonefish crossing a patch of white sand and move to position myself to cast with wind and sun at my back. The osprey perched on a forlorn single branch of what was once a tree in some faraway tropical land remonstrates me for invasion of his privacy. It is midday, and for hours I have been wading but a fraction of this seemingly endless expanse without spotting human sign let alone an actual person. My mind wanders, and I imagine myself a kindred spirit of the Upper Paleolithic angler whose catch left bones in some prehistoric site in my beloved Basque Country. The apparent simplicity of it all, the back to basics, seems not that unlike his, and for a moment I savor the trans-millennial fraternal illusion.

But then I contemplate the fly in my left hand pressed between thumb and forefinger in anticipation of the cast. Purchased from The Fly Shop, it was tied by some young woman in Thailand or India from the cape feathers of a rooster possibly raised in Colorado. Attached with the finest European gossamer thread to a stainless steel hook fashioned from iron mined in Minnesota, or some such place, and then shaped in Japan, the tiny counterfeit crustacean is a microcosm of the United Nations. The plastic fly box in my breast pocket is crammed full of numerous flies and streamers. The demure browns and blacks of their animal-hair elements are accented spectacularly by the magenta, fuchsia, incarnadine, azure, silver-tinseled and phenosafranine incandescence of their manmade components bearing such exotic names as "flash-a-bou," "mylar" and "chenille." Were W.S. Gilbert an angler he would no doubt pronounce each of these cunning creations to be "a technical technological miniature modern miracle!" In my right hand I hold a graphite rod, made possible through the technology developed by the Space Program.

From head to foot I am enshrouded in wading boots, tarpon-wear pants, shirt and hat made with the synthetic fabrics of materials extracted from the primeval ooze of an Arabian petroleum deposit and then processed in an Atlantic Seaboard, state-of-the-art chemical plant.

The three wary, but as yet oblivious, bonefish employed their own energy to traverse a watery mile or so to our impending encounter; I began the journey thousands of miles away in my Nevada haunt and was whisked to this Turneffe-Island flat in taxicab, aircraft, launch and skiff. They arrive largely clueless regarding me; I have the advantage of the collective wisdom of my species concerning the behavior of theirs as communicated through the angling literature.

I'm within range and begin false casting to lengthen line and load the rod. I hesitate to try for the one tailing fish sending out semaphoric flashes of reflected sunlight, since its companions are invisibly camouflaged against the mottled bottom. I know that, if I line one of them, its panicked reaction will spook the others. But then another tail appears five feet to the left, and I sense that its owner is alone, a piscine estray. My cast lands a foot from the feeding fish, and I begin a slow retrieve. There is a swirl and then resistance; I set the hook with my left hand and raise the rod with my right. In an instant the startled bonefish is off the flat and sounding somewhere beyond the reef. With my backing now threaded through the coral heads, I know that my situation is precarious. A moment later I am reeling in my slack, hoping that I've been cut off in dispensable leader rather than precious fly line.

Jimmy threw out the anchor casually, certainly with no concern over spooking the four-pound bonefish meandering towards us. We had work to do and began wading ashore in tandem, transferring to the beach our six extra cans of gas, two ice chests, case of bottled water and assorted food boxes and camping paraphernalia. We stashed our gear near the two casuarina pines that were the only feature of what was otherwise a sparsely vegetated sand spit. Five minutes later I sat in the boat stringing my rod while Jimmy laughed at our persistently curious visitor. While still seated,

I lazily cast a #6 blonde Gotcha in its general direction, and the unelusive fish swam several feet to intercept the offering. During the next hour I had seven more opportunities, ranging from singles to a school of about 10. Seven casts had produced seven more hookups. The only blemish on my otherwise perfect record was the landing. Three of the fish had been in the six-pound-or-better range and all had taken me well into my backing, permitting them to reach mid-channel where they had niftily employed the coral-speckled bottom to break me off. By now Jimmy was using my spare rod and had a couple of fish of his own. We were in bonefish heaven!

The trip was the culmination of the previous year's scheming. For the next three days I was to camp in the Marls, a saltwater wilderness maze of uninhabited keys and shallow channels, with Jimmy Lowe, head guide at Nettie Symonette's Different of Abaco lodge. In preparation I'd brought along a tight-meshed, mosquito-netted two-man tent and a GPS. My search in several marine supply stores of the Florida Keys had failed to secure a chart of the area. The unnavigable Marls were simply off the radar screen of the boating fraternity.

Nettie Symonette, an extraordinarily gifted person in many ways and one that is certainly enamored with her own drummer, had launched Different of Abaco several years ago as an eco-tourism destination. The lodge itself is a rambling wooden structure replete with various levels of wooden walkways and decks, set amidst a fairly extensive botanical garden and series of water features, and with an evolving beach-front complex as well. Her initial plan was to display Abaco's heritage, both human and natural, by incorporating everything from local antiques in the interior decoration to caged wild pigs and rare Bahamian iguanas in the grounds. The garden was as much ornithological as botanical, since Abaco has its own unique birds, most notably a parrot whose origins may be either indigenous or piratical, and serves as a waypoint for several migratory species. So the target crowd was to be a mix of those simply seeking seclusion in pleasant surroundings and serious birders. She built it, and they didn't come, at least not in sufficient numbers to float the boat. Enter bonefishing.

Different of Abaco is strategically situated in one of the better bonefishing settings of the Bahamas. It readily accesses the inviting flats of Cherokee Sound where it is common to spot double-digit fish, although catching them is another matter given the angling pressure that they receive. However, Different's, or rather its Great Abaco Bonefishing Club dimension's, real *pièce-de-résistance* is the Marls.

When I first fished them, shortly after Nettie began catering bonefishing, it entailed taking a jarring 45-minute ride over the rutted dirt road passing for Abaco's main highway to where it intercepted the southern extremity of the watery complex. There it was possible to launch a boat. Theoretically the access was public, although in the two or three weeks that I spent at Different during those days I recall seeing another craft on only one occasion. The fishing was fabulous in terms of numbers, though not size. A five-pounder was a large catch.

Nettie would subsequently consolidate her position by acquiring the exclusive rights to a former logging road that allowed her to pierce the carapace of the middle Marls. The road ended at the edge of a brackish swamp where she bulldozed out a mooring for several skiffs. The real challenge was to link it to open water by scraping a shallow channel through recalcitrant coral rock. I happened to visit again while this process was in its final phase, a time when it was still necessary for the anglers to alight and help push the skiff while wading through knee-deep muck. It was worth it since the fishing was fabulous, it being no particular challenge to land 15 or 20 fish a day, though of an even smaller size on average than those in the southern Marls.

It was at that time that I made my first forays into Abaco's unknown. My guide was Jimmy's brother, Donny, and we began to "look around," going a bit further each day beyond the outer fringe of the areas that he had fished previously. The bonefish, if always plentiful, remained small. It seemed that we were simply too far from water of sufficient depth to support larger specimens, a good 10 miles from the main channel separating Abaco from Grand Bahama. We seemed to be in a bonefish nursery, or, more accurately, an adolescencery. We were after elusive adultery.

Jimmy and Donny are both from Cherokee, descendants of Irish loyalists to the British Crown (there seems to be a dash of irony in most history!) who abandoned their homes in western North Carolina during the American Revolution to resettle in the Bahamas— hence the seemingly bizarre and errant place name. Until the 1990s, Cherokee remained an insulated, all-white enclave that lacked even a road connection with the rest of Abaco. When I first fished Different, Nettie's guides were all from Cherokee, today none, excepting Jimmy, is. But then that's another story.

Our first night at "No-Name Key" was a pleasant surprise. Flickers of lightning, our tropical equivalent of the northern lights, outlined the several thunderheads perched like toadstools on the horizon. Fortunately, none drifted our way. At midnight a half moon illuminated the bare sandscape with such intensity that several common nighthawks stirred in pursuit of insects, the aerodynamics of their swooping simulating the sound of a distant distressed ship's hapless plea for assistance. Their flat-harmonic avian calls (ee-ee-ee) invoked a false dawn. I slept fitfully on the ground, my royal derriere acutely aware of every "pea" under the sheer tent floor. Minute by interminably sleepless minute I regretted not having brought along some kind of air mattress. But the real night miracle was Jimmy's ability to sleep outside after declaring the interior of the tent to be insufferably hot. He was able to because there were scarcely any BUGS! The no-see-ums were no-shows, and the silence was interrupted but infrequently by a solitary mosquito's whine.

Next morning we headed north along the outer edge of the Marls, in sight of the channel between Grand Bahama and Abaco islands. Since Deep Water Cay, site of one of the Bahamas's better trophy fish destinations, lay straight across the open water, I was energized by the prospect of bigger fish. We considered exploring a creek that opened out into an interior lagoon, but it seemed too shallow to chance given our falling tide. We certainly didn't want to end up beached beyond assistance on some mud flat for half the day's tidal cycle. It was then that we came upon a broad cleft between two keys that opened into an immense stretch of water that qualified as more of a bay than a lagoon. While poling us along the sand-bottomed fringe of the first key, Jimmy spotted what he first took to be a barracuda. The enormous bonefish seemed warier than the several seven- or eight-pounders fanned out across the flat behind him. My cast was a bit too long, and the retrieval spooked the behemoth, who departed with his companions in tow. Jimmy half-whispered a single expletive and for a moment I was speechless. That missed-opportunity fish was more than a mere "trip-maker," it would have been my largest catch in 20 years of bonefishing. If only there was an instant replay button on the remote control of one's real life!

The bottom was surprisingly firm, given Webster's definition of marl as "any soft, crumbly stratum," so we both waded for the remainder of the falling tide. We then spent the morning exploring a small part of this vast catchment, never going for more than five minutes without seeing fish. Several were quite large, certainly by Marls' standards, and most were absurdly easy to catch. My arm actually began to ache and by noon Jimmy pronounced that I had already landed 21 bonefish! We had one last pleasant surprise awaiting us. After lunch I waded a small flat on the ocean side of the keys ringing what we were now calling Bill's Bay and caught my biggest fish of the trip, possibly an eight-pounder. I cast to at least two others that were double-digit specimens and was given the usual lesson in how they became so.

Our second (and last) evening at newly christened Jimmy's Key was pretty much a repeat of the former excepting that I slept soundly, oblivious to beach peas (as I would have been to boulders or bamboo spikes for that matter). If the first night we'd dined on two small barracuda, now our repast began with a fresh conch salad followed by the succulent meat of four blue land crabs. Jimmy had hunted them in the pre-dawn, removing their largest claw before releasing them to grow another. With the exception of opening one can of vegetables and slicing up a few potatoes, peppers and tomatoes, we'd lived off the land quite comfortably. By noon of the third day we were back at the mooring with most of our untouched supplies, aglow with wonderful memories and filled with exquisite anticipation of our next year's foray. We both agreed that it would be for longer, four or five days, so we could penetrate even further into the maw of the Marls. That would certainly be bad news for the land crabs of Jimmy's Key.

Were I Steinbeck I might have written a book called *Travels with Mike*. My angling odyssey, like that of many others, is as much exponential as geographic—an expansion of my personal horizon into the fishing frontier of new species. My companion and guide (in several senses) at key junctures of that particular journey has been Mike Michalak. We first met in the bar of Lava Creek Lodge on Northern California's Fall River. I had booked my two-day escape from a particularly grinding schedule back in Reno through his at that time fledgling business, The Fly Shop, responding to the only ad in *Fly Fishing* magazine offering a destination within my driving distance.

I told Mike about my interest in trying saltwater angling. The winter before, exasperated by my brother John's even busier schedule than mine, I had traveled alone to Casa Mar Lodge on Costa Rica's Rio Colorado in search of tarpon. As luck would have it, I coincided with a massive cold front, dipping all the way south from the States, that brought a week of record-low temperatures and record-high rainfall. In short, I had my tropical counterpart of Babinean baptism and additional evidence that masochism may run in my family. I caught not a single tarpon (nor snook) but did see my first wild howler monkey and tree sloth.

Not to worry. Mike was taking a group in a few months to Turn-effe Island, Belize, on a bonefishing trip with the chance of a tarpon thrown in. It was then that I talked a still-gullible, newly married Jan into accompanying me to an idyllic Gilligan's Island setting (sight unseen by me, of course) where she could luxuriate daily on a palm-studded beach while I abused the bonefish. All of this was before I had expanded my entomological knowledge. I still believed that no-see-ums were native solely to the Dean River valley.

Turneffe bonefish proved more up to our confrontation than was I, besting me at every turn for the first three days. But then I scarcely cared because I had passed through the looking glass into the marine wonderland of vast sandy flats of ankle-to-knee-deep water teeming with life. I experienced the frustration of what it was like to stare at a school of 50 of the gray ghosts 50 feet away and not even see them. Such was the case when, on the fourth day and following Mike's instruction, I cast blindly and was suddenly attached to a power surge as great as that of a hot steelhead. I babied my precious catch too much, and the line suddenly went limp. I reeled in 1½ pounds of what had been a three-pound bonefish— until cut in half by a barracuda, that is.

Since I now had the saltwater virus bad, Mike urged me to join The Fly Shop's tarpon week in the Florida Keys the following summer. It was the second year of what would become an annual event for more than a decade. We were to fish with a different captain/guide each day, a melange of veteran ones such as Dale Perez, Johnny Podolsky, Lee Baker and Nat Raglin and some up-and-comers like Mike Vaughn and Ray Fecher. It was wonderfully educational since we were attending a congress rather than a class, each day's lecture sprinkled with the nugget of a different expert's experience and wisdom. It was during this annual trek that I met Bob Morgart, Gary Aka, Earl Cohen and Jerry Fitzpatrick, all of whom remain critical ribbing in my angler-life's sailboat.

It was with Mike that I went on my first real exploratory. We were scheduled to bonefish together at Los Roques in Venezuela, but

Casting About in the Reel World

something had come up. He had been asked to accompany Jim Repine ("Mr. Alaska" for his several how-to books about that fishery) on an exploratory trip in southern Chile. A new lodge had opened near Puyuhuapi. Len Leasure, its owner, was experienced in the travel business. His assisting son-in-law guided white-river rafters on the Bio Bio. But neither were fishermen. Did the new operation have angling potential? Chile sounded fine to me, so I pretty much invited myself along.

For the next week we soaked each afternoon in the lodge's hot springs, contemplating conifer-covered, wild-fuchsia and fern-bedraped surrounding hills rising to the distant glacial fields of the high Andes. If the scenery was unsurpassable, the fishing was problematic. Each morning we would go to the dock on the saltwater sound where our pilot, Bo (who, coincidentally, had flown us the summer before at Alaska's No-See-Um Lodge), awaited in the only seaplane for a thousand miles to probe one of the nearby Andean drainages. Some had been stocked near the turn of the 20th century with rainbow and brown trout, others had not. All looked marvelous, and the only way to tell was to try.

Most days we stepstaired from lake to lake up some valley, sampling fine angling along the way—or not. We would circle the lake before landing looking for any signs of settlement, and usually there were none. We would then set down at the inlet and fish the *boca,* or mouth, of the river that strung together our lacustrine bracelet.

The wall map back at the lodge was quite detailed, yet curiously devoid of place names. So like the arrogant conquistadors of yore, we agreed to name a river after ourselves, the honor going to him who caught its first fish. Thus was born the Río Douglass, duly recorded for posterity on at least one suspended parchment when Mike dawdled too long at the plane while I caught a four-pound brown trout.

Toward week's end Bo dropped us off at a particular lake while he flew back to the lodge to shuttle some other guests. We planned to explore a large nearby river, separated from us by a low range of hills. The weather was threatening. "If it gets worse, head right back to the lake when you hear my engine. We may have to bail out of here in a hurry." We followed a wild game or livestock trail to the river and an hour later Mike caught our first fish. "Hey Bill, Río Michalak," he shouted, gleefully holding his catch aloft.

As the morning progressed, we fished further downstream while the weather became more sullen. Then there it was, the sound of Bo's engine in the gloom. Mike wanted to continue downstream, believing that we were close to its confluence with the one coming out of our lake. "There has to be a trail up to it; it'll be a short-cut." I refused. I knew it would take a good hour to retrace our steps, but they were at least retraceable. Reluctantly, Mike acquiesced. Fifteen minutes later we were fording the river when two horsemen appeared, eyes agog at our bizarre apparel. "Ask them about the other trail to the lake." I did, and there wasn't any. They were father and son and had a small ranch downstream. As an afterthought I asked if this river had a name. Indeed it did. So like some Charles the Fifth imperially reining in an errant Cortés, I stripped Mike of the Río Michalak. Some tasks, no matter how distasteful, must be done!

Back at the plane Bo was anxious. He had all but given up on us, and we now faced a wall of black cloud towards the sea. The blue sky over the highest peaks beckoned, but that was Argentina with its own can of worms given the tensions between the two countries. "We'll fly over the outlet and see if there's any chance, but I doubt it." The lone, seemingly vacant, cabin across the lake was beginning to look like Home Sweet Home for some indeterminate period, since our only radio contact was with the lodge. It, too, was out of range of Chilean weather reporting, so we had no way of knowing the extent of our weather front.

To me the cloudbank appeared solid, so I was amazed when Bo suddenly ducked to near tree-top level and then began following the serpentine river down to the next lake, looking out the side window since the windscreen was literally a solid sheet of water. We landed on the large, L-shaped lake to regroup. Given that configuration, we could not see its outlet. All we could do was to fly to the crook of the L for a quick look and instant decision. Unfortunately, the lake narrowed at that point and we would be flying through a canyon flanked by sheer cliffs rising well above us. Off we went into the maelstrom, pitched about erratically like some air-borne leaf by the pulses of the incoming storm. I clutched the hand strap for a bit more purchase against the next plunge of the carnival ride. Then we were pointed skyward before banking sharply into a nosedive in order to reverse direction. Bo had aborted. I am amazed that the leather anchor survived the Herculean tug engendered by my sheer panic.

Back at the beach we waited for half an hour and then purchased another ticket. This time the clouds at the outlet seemed thinner, the horizon a bit brighter. "We're going for it, so hold on." The ceiling was actually 200 feet, so we continued our riverine descent into a much more reasonable world.

Puyuhuapi Lodge turned out to be a flash in the pan as sport fishing destination. It struggled along for a couple of years before dropping right off the angling radar screen. I have no idea what it now does when it wakes up in the morning, if anything.

"Do you believe in UFOs?" it is not the easiest question to field, particularly when in the initial throes of bonding with a stranger destined to be tomorrow's fishing guide. My inquisitor, James, sipped his after-dinner coffee, fixing me with eyes that twinkled in amusement at my hesitation before letting me off the hook,

"Well, I do. I once saw one. We were on a boat moored off a remote stretch of the South Island, where we were deer-hunting commercially. Suddenly, there was an object, an intense light really, hovering a hundred yards away. Then it took off with incredible speed and disappeared over the horizon in about 20 seconds. For awhile it left a glow."

Conversation turned immediately to my native Nevada and its notorious Area 51, where the U.S. government imposes strict security measures surrounding the testing of nuclear devices and such super-secret weapons as the Stealth bomber. For UFO groupies such activity is but a subterfuge, the real purpose being the repository for various and sundry UFOs and other extraterrestrial evidence that must be withheld from public awareness to avoid Wellesian panic.

In retrospect, it was an appropriate overture to the Stealth Fishing Ballet that was about to be choreographed next day for Gary Aka and me. It was my first angling trip to New Zealand, Gary's fifth. He had published two articles about the country's trout fishing in the newsletter of the Golden Gate Angling and Casting Club. We were at the outset of a three-week angling odyssey, a sampler of some of the most fabled waters on both islands cobbled together out of Gary's considerable experience and knowledge. I was the easy rider.

There had been a last minute change in our itinerary. The area of South Island known for New Zealand's largest brown trout had just experienced a "mouse hatch." About once in seven years the wild beech trees flower and produce seed that carpet the forest floor. The abundant food supply then triggers an explosion in the mouse and rat population, some of which ends up in the streams. The normally eight- or nine-pound trout gorge themselves on the protein and bulk up. The pursuit of double-digit trout is the ultimate angling fetish in New Zealand. Gary had one 10-pounder; he wanted more.

Our French Eurocopter levitated like a lovely mademoiselle rising confidently from her seat in a Champs Elysees café and floated over pastureland squared and rectangulated by manicured hedgerows and populated by some modern-day Noah. Cows, sheep and horses were interspersed with herds of captive red and Sitka deer, llamas, ostriches and emus. Old MacDonald clearly lacked imagination when stocking his farm.

Our pilot's lilting Kiwi accent informed us that we were to land briefly to "top up the gas and then we'll be away laughing." When not farming, he flew helicopters. Boy did he ever! His life was divided into alternating three-week stints—three here at home followed by three in either Borneo or Ecuador, though he hadn't been to the latter for several months since three of his fellow employees had been kidnapped by Colombian rebels and were being held for a $10-million ransom. "You should see my frequent flyer miles!"

Fly-out fishing, whether by helicopter or fixed-wing aircraft, is the normal modern means of penetrating the frontier—the ticket, albeit expensive, to angling paradise. Our mission was far more subtle. For the next three days, like the Stealth bomber, the idea was to remain undetected while slipping in under the other anglers' radar. Our probings would take us into undulating hill country rather than remote wilderness, where we would seldom be out of sight of railway and roadway, vehicles, out-buildings and the ubiquitous summer campers.

Angling in New Zealand is largely sight fishing. The quarry is large and scarce, certainly by the standards of the rest of the world's trout fisheries. Kiwi trout tend to be extremely wary and must be approached (always from downstream) with both caution and skill. New Zealand angling is therefore a combination of hunting and hiking, punctuated by emotional peaks and valleys. Success is elusive and subtle, predicated as much upon the fine-tuning of expectations and prospects as body count and weight. It is not for everyone, but for the right angler, it is the ultimate in trout fishing. We had hired Peter as our second guide and fourth set of eyes, thereby improving our chances of spotting a true trophy fish.

Determining that no other fishermen were working their way towards our beat of choice, we landed and rigged up. After a two-mile hike, in which we scanned several gorgeous runs and holes without spotting a single fish, like a frustrated patrol that had failed to contact the enemy, we radioed in the chopper for a move. Five minutes later we were below the confluence of the first stream with another and flying low. Peter spotted a large fish from the air that scurried to deep water at our disturbance.

"It's almost too big. It may be an early salmon, but we ought to check it out."

The morning's sunny, calm weather was rapidly deteriorating into a blustery afternoon, challenging both the sighting and casting. As we approached the indicated run, Peter and I crossed the considerable current to better approach the large fish's lie. Meanwhile, Gary and James worked the other bank spotting and fishing to a couple of decent trout.

It was when working a third that Gary had his first hookup. In the water the fish had not appeared extraordinarily large, but in the net it was a different story. If but 27 inches long, the rat-engorged trophy was shaped like a football, distended almost grotesquely into brown-trout parody. It weighed 13 pounds!

Within a few minutes it was my turn. The large fish had returned to its stand and seemed open for business. It was no salmon. Occasionally it moved sideways to intercept a nymph. The brown trout repeated the motion as my indicator passed by its head and then dipped beneath the surface. For a brief second the fish was on and then my line went limp. The little glimpse of angler's heaven was fleeting, its dissolution appropriate. To have topped Gary's fish on my very first angling day in New Zealand, as mine would almost certainly have, seemed unjust—a delict no doubt meritorious of a severe sentence in fishermen's court. My consolation came the next day when I caught a 7½ -pounder on a different small stream.

Our third and last day we resolved to return to the scene of our success. The big guy might still be vulnerable, and such huge fish are almost impossible to find. In every way, including the unfavorable weather, it was a repeat performance. No more than 100 yards from where he caught his earlier trip maker, Gary hooked another. The equally misshapen brown weighed a quarter pound more than the first. Gary had an almost unimaginable brace of 13-pounders!

Peter and I crossed over the Jordan and once again were gazing at the broad back of any angler's dream. The trout ignored one nymph after another as we tried a cast or two with just about everything in our arsenal. I then made an underwhelmingly bad one with maybe our 15th nymph pattern that landed several feet to the trout's left. Strangely, the fish flashed sideways, grabbed the fly, spit it out ahead of my startled and tardy strike and then vanished. I had not felt a thing, but the contest was definitely over.

As we awaited our pickup, again with twinkling gaze out of the otherwise deadpan face of a consummate poker player, James said to Peter,

"Bill just asked me the name of this river. Can you believe that? Is it Rock Creek or Stony River?"

For good measure he added,

"Remember now, just like the other day, we cut the numbers in half. Gary caught a 6½-pounder, right? Those chopper pilots are only interested in putting butts in seats."

Beam us up, Scotty.

It was the miracle of modern technology that rang the dinner gong that February evening at the new fishing camp on Bolivia's Marmoré River. Three weeks earlier Rob Stewart, Mike Coe, Gary Aka and I had been scheduled to join Jeff Vermillion on an exploratory for tucunaré and payara in British Guiana. Jeff had gone ahead to scope out our possible itinerary. I was still in bed reading the paper when his satellite phone jarred me out of my morning reverie.

"It's Plan B time, Bill. We have to improvise. The country's beautiful, and the people are great, but the fishing sucks. I've caught one peacock so far. The natives use some kind of plant to stun the fish for food."

The one small problem was that we had no Plan B.

"Well, Jeff, Frontiers is advertising that new lodge in Bolivia on the Río Marmoré. It's supposedly the only destination in South America where you can catch the big three, tucunaré, dorado and pacu. But it's awfully short notice."

Our instant division of labor involved Jeff contacting Frontiers while I alerted the guys. My challenge was the greater. New Englander Mike is perpetually in motion, Rob skis, hunts and snowmobiles the British Columbian interior in the winter and I knew that Gary was trout fishing in New Zealand. I left messages for all three and, amazingly, by late afternoon had e-mails back from them all, as well as a message from Jeff that Bolivia was a go. Within less than 24 hours five people on three different continents had managed to move their expedition halfway across South America!

If our very presence together on the Marmoré underscored just how pervious the angling frontier has become, at our dinner conversation we began to explore another. Mike and I are both card-carrying anthropologists and our companions were all anthropological anglers in spirit—i.e. fascinated by other peoples and cultures. Michael Coe is one of the world's leading experts on Mesoamerica, having authored both the standard textbook (*The Maya*) and the fascinating academic detective story *Breaking the Maya Code*. Nevertheless, he had not been back to the Maya area for many years, having shifted his attention to the prehistory of Southeast Asia. Jeff asked, "Hey, Mike, why don't we put together a combination trip to the Maya ruins along with bonefishing?" Why not indeed!

I found the idea particularly appealing since I missed becoming a Mayanist myself only by a whisker. During my graduate student days at the University of Chicago, I had worked for Sol Tax as a research assistant. My first professional publication had been the appendix to his article "Cultural Differences in the Maya Area: A 20th Century Perspective" (1964). Had Chicago and Harvard sorted out their joint (ultimately abortive) Huehuetenango project, I would likely have trod the Mesoamericanist career path.

The idea of combining angling with higher purpose was not altogether new to me. I had once spent a fishless summer week flailing the waters of the River Esk on the Scottish-English border. Marathon days of sheer angling frustration, prolonged well into the area's near-midnight sun, would no doubt have left me with the nadir of my fisherman's memoir had it not been punctuated by the pleasant stay with Jan at a country inn, an excursion to nearby Hadrian's Wall, firing off my bascological synapses since a contingent of Basque mercenaries once manned its ramparts and a day at Carlisle's annual outdoor sporting show attended by Prince Phillip.

Most memorable was the visit to the rustic fortified house that dominated our three-rod two-mile beat. Within the family lines of the structure's ownership, the Spensers (ancestors of Winston Churchill) converged with the Penns (as in William). I ascended the stairs to the battlement behind the groundskeeper, struggling to close the considerable gap between his Scottish-English speech and my American capacity to process it. In order to seize some control of the conversation, I pointed across field and stream to another fortified structure on the horizon and inquired about its ownership. "Oh, they'd be the black Douglasses, Sir. They once murdered everyone here." Although the little altercation had transpired several centuries earlier, fortunately we had not been properly introduced, and I was later able to finesse answering his invasive and impertinent query about my surname.

By week's end our three-week strategy was in place. One group of anglers/archeotourists would fish Boca Paila in Yucatan the first week while another fished somewhere in Belize the third one. Sandwiched in between, the combined parties would be conducted by Michael on a weeklong tour of stellar Mayan sites in four countries. I reserved all of the slots for the Belize week, and Jeff kept the other. We were about to elevate our anthropological angling to an entirely new plane.

The following February 2000 our blended group of two cohorts of serious anglers and close friends, 14 persons in all, met at Flores, Guatemala. It was really a two extended-family affair. I'd brought

Jan and my son Matt along for the archeological part only. My other slots were taken by Gary, and my two Florida angling companions, Skip Schwartz and Jerry Fitzpatrick. Jeff had filled his openings with his parents, Dale and Margaret, his brother's fiancée's parents, his aunt and uncle and their friend. Ours was a particularly stimulating and compatible group that included the former director of San Francisco's DeYoung Museum, an acclaimed East Coast painter, the director of a nature reserve on San Francisco Bay and a couple that grows native grasses for nature restoration projects. Common to all of us was a keen interest in birdlife. Several were members of the Audubon Society.

Our magical week began at Tikal, where the guides and museum staff treated Michael with the awe and respect ordinarily reserved for incarnated demiurges. The grounds of Jungle Lodge were their own nature tour, alive as they were with toucans, cassowaries, wild turkeys, howler and squirrel monkeys.

Next day it was off to the Mayan ruin of Ceibal, which required both a bus ride and boat trip on the Río Pasión. The launching point for the latter was the town of Sayaxche which, according to Michael, had once been a CIA site for training Cubans prior to the Bay of Pigs' invasion. Michael was particularly critical of a U.S. policy in Central America that had consistently sided with oligarchies against their mestizo peasants and Indians. Nor was this the knee-jerk criticism of some uninformed "lefty" academic. Michael was recruited as a graduate student by the head of Harvard's anthropology department for a patriotic stint of duty with the CIA during the Korean War—service that is documented in the book *Raiders of the China Coast.**

Our guide, Paúl, was full of local historical (and contemporary) lore. It seems that the Pasión received its name from the travails of Galván, a hapless 17th century, would-be conquistador. Well

---

* Holober, Frank. *Raiders of the China Coast: CIA Covert Operations during the Korean War*. Annapolis: Naval Institute Press, 1999.

after the Spaniards controlled the lowlands of Yucatan, it was rumored that an intact Mayan kingdom, which had been sighted by Cortés on his southerly incursion, still existed in the interior. The site in questions was an autonomous Mayan community on the island of the lake hosting present-day Flores. A group of Itza Maya offered to guide Galván there, but actually led his party to the hills of the headwaters of the Río Pasión and abandoned it. The Spaniards were saved only by discovering some springs for drinking water and then descending their trickle to a river that they followed to (Spanish) civilization, arriving back during Easter Week—hence the naming of the river out of religious gratitude.

We came to a juncture with another river and Paúl noted that a group of ex-guerrillas had settled upstream—400 or so households in all. They demand to be left alone and are highly skeptical of the recently accorded peace that two years earlier ended, at least temporarily, Guatemala's civil war. Under its terms each guerrilla was given a modest house and 35,000 *quetzales*. There are three guerrilla-controlled towns in this area, all seeking relative autonomy from the government. They have just inaugurated their own bus service that links them.

There was a continued American presence in the area. The Río Pasión is a headwater of Mexico's major Río Usumacinta. The DEA therefore maintains about 15 agents at a low-profile, nearby base to effect air and river surveillance in the attempt to interdict the flow of drugs into Mexico. Ceibal was a terminal, Classic-age Maya complex with considerable Teotihuacán (Nahuatl) influence.

Next day we flew to Palenque. For most of our group it was a novelty; for me it was nostalgia. As a 19-year-old boy bound for the Venezuelan diamond fields, I had visited Palenque, at the time accessible only by train and dirt road. Then the site itself was mainly overgrown, with only about three of its structures reclaimed out of the jungle by a small group of machete-wielding caretakers. I recall hearing snakes slither away through the undergrowth while ascending ill-defined, rubbled stairways. Now a four-lane highway leads from an international airport to excellent hotels adjacent to the manicured archeological complex. The white-robed Lacandon Maya Indians selling bows and macaw-feather-dressed arrows at the entrance to the ruins seemed like props, although Michael assured us that they were authentic semi-nomads down from the hills.

Alfonso Morales, archeologist and a graduate student at the University of Texas, joined us with the news that they were just completing excavation of Temple 19 and had found a most extraordinary burial chamber into which they had lowered cameras and a spectrometer. We would be shown the still-unannounced results the next day at the laboratory.

There was a poignant moment when Moisés, Alfonso's father and former head guide at Palenque, appeared. He and Michael had not seen one another for years, and so they retreated into the private world of shared reminiscences. He promised to lead us on the next day's tour, which would include off-limits Temple 19. He spread a map of Palenque out on the ground which detailed hundreds of unexcavated mounds. Current research seemed to be demonstrating that Palenque had once been an important city rather than simply a sacred temple complex (as previously thought).

Moisés and Michael had much to relive, since it was here at Palenque that the famous *mesa redonda,* or "round table," was held. It had gathered together some Mayan specialists to ponder the possible meanings of Mayan glyphs. Some even believed them to be a written language, which was total apostasy as far as many influential Mayanists of the day were concerned, particularly the field's grand old man J. Eric S. Thompson. It was the co-conspirators of the *mesa redonda,* following the fertile leads provided by a Soviet Mayanist, Y.V. Knorosov, who "broke" the code. Now, given our communicative capacities, when the new glyphs of the burial crypt at Temple 19 were photographed, the images were beamed immediately to David Stuart in the U.S., Mayanist epigrapher *par excellence,* and the translated transcription was already back to the Palenque team by the next day. Another 24-hour, electronically miraculous frontier penetration!

Next day at the archeology laboratory we were shown the real *pièce-de-résistance,* a several-foot-long, delicately carved frieze that may just be the best yet discovered. It remains unveiled to the world.

We were on the fringes of Zapatista country and were about to enter its core. Curiously, the entrance to our hotel was adorned by an historic mural depicting the region's history from the conquistadors down to, and including, the Zapatistas. One could only imagine that this was some kind of artistic revolutionary tax paid, or insurance policy purchased, by the affluent capitalist who owned the establishment. On our way to the Usumacinta River we were stopped frequently at military roadblocks and then ran the gauntlet of their naval equivalent on the river itself.

Our destination was remote Yaxchilán where we observed graphic depictions of a Mayan fertility ritual that entailed bloodletting in which the queen passes a barbed string through her tongue and the king perforates his penis with a ray's stinger. The guys in the group were particularly unamused. Michael showed us the temple still visited by pious Lacandon Mayas. It has a beheaded effigy of the Maya king "Bird Jaguar." It is believed that, if the nearby head is once again attached to the torso, the world will end. In addition to curious squirrel and howler monkeys checking out the rare visitors, two scarlet macaws overflew us, puncturing the silence with their raucous cries.

By late afternoon we were at Betel, a Guatemalan border post. An outside wall of the shanty serving as the bus terminal (or rather "terminus" since the road ended there) bore the greeting that proclaimed:

Welcom
Office Posada Maya
For Sale De Tikets
To Flores

We watched some local youths playing soccer, oblivious to the several dogs and pigs sharing the dirt field, until our vintage bus arrived. It took three hours to negotiate the rutted miles before reaching the asphalt. It was now after dark and it should have taken another hour to arrive in Flores. However, 20 miles shy of our goal we were stopped in our tracks, along with every other vehicle, opposite the headquarters of Basic Resources. Several hundred angry locals were on strike against the American oil company (pumping about 30,000 barrels daily), having expropriated and shut down the pipeline. It seems that they had been promised a paved road, a modern water system and extensive reforestation of their municipal lands—none of which had materialized.

Fortunately, although the strikers were brandishing clubs and machetes, their mood was rather festive. After about an hour of negotiations, the word was that we (meaning about a hundred detainees by that time) would be allowed to walk through the picket line should we wish. Our driver felt that he could then call Flores, and a substitute bus would be sent for us. We were to leave all luggage on his bus, limiting ourselves to inconspicuous valuables such as our money and passports. Just as we prepared to test the choppy waters the welcome word was that our convoy would be allowed through after making a gesture of solidarity in the form of a contribution to the strike effort. It worked out to a couple of dollars apiece. We would have gladly "contributed" 10 times as much, particularly since the next day we learned that we were the only ones pardoned. Travelers behind us had spent the night at the barrier and were yet awaiting their release.

After another side excursion by air to Copán in Honduras, which has the most spectacular of all Mayan stelae, it was off to Belize City. For the anglers the week of fishing proved spotty, but we scarcely minded. We were too energized by the new plan—a tour of Angkor Wat in 2002 led by Michael (whose book on that site should be out by then), with a week of fishing in New Zealand, Australia or possibly some Asian destination. Mahseer-fishing on the Indian subcontinent appeals to me!

* * *

There is an ineluctable and irresistible appeal to the notion of exploring new frontiers, angling and otherwise. Like modern-day Columbuses, we set sail in our mental Santa Marias disguised as metal Boeing 747s to discover New Worlds inhabited, if not by dog-headed cannibals, then by such marvels as toothy, flamboyant, fearsome fish. We are also akin to 19th century 49ers bent on beating out the competition in the rush to the gold in order to be the first to extract the best nuggets. It is that possibility that keeps me coming back for more, like the serious gambler in one of my casinos who knows that he is bucking the odds but hopeful that they just might not apply to him on this particular night. There are many ways in life to be seduced by Lady Luck, to be taken in not so much by her real charms as by one's imagining of them. In the land of the coolheaded calculators, bucking the odds is a mug's game, a fool's folly, but for the authentic gambler, including the serious angler, it is the best measure of life's zest.

Since most of us are not in a position to mount our own thrusts into the void, we rely upon the euphemistic "outfitters." As one of that hardy breed once confided to me,

> "Each new fishing destination is like a beautiful woman that everyone wants to be the first to date. Me, I'm a pimp. I want to sell her charms."

Frontiers International is the 800-pound gorilla in the fly-fishing world. In terms of sheer magnitude of bookings, The Fly Shop, owned by my dear friend and fishing chum, Mike Michalak, is the distant second. Altogether there are maybe 10 serious players in the business in North America and a handful abroad.

I once asked Mike for his estimate of the market for "exotic" or "extreme" fly fishing. I qualified the question by excluding a) the many fabled and crowded trout-fishing waters of the American West and b) the angler who saves up for years in order to take that once-in-a-lifetime, outrageously expensive dream trip to, say, Alaska. Mike placed the remaining pool at about 5,000 anglers worldwide, scarcely more than a large village.

This was consonant with my own experience. For the past 15 years I have averaged six weeks of fishing annually. About eight anglers is the usual capacity of most fishing lodges. It has been many years since I have been unable to network with at least one "stranger" that first night at the dinner table. Somewhere along the way we fished the same lodge, used the same guide or knew a mutual acquaintance within the angling fraternity. Indeed, it is usual for me to be able to connect in this fashion with several of my new companions.

The name Frontiers International neatly encapsulates the spirit of our quest. There are many reasons for embarking on a fly-fishing trip to some exotic destination, some of which are inevitably idiosyncratic, but there are also evident constellations. As the world's accessible public fishing waters become more crowded, some of us are willing to invest considerable money and effort in the search for the solitude of pristine settings. Stated more prosaically, it is also the quest for plentiful, big, dumb fish, predicated upon the notion that the angling must be superb, or at least better, beyond the purview of the madding crowd. "Seldom fished," "no pressure" or even the epiphanous "never before fished" is the standard jargon in the literature marketing back of beyond. The hell of it is, like my fellow 5,000 or so addicts, I bite frequently despite the oftentimes spotty results, rather like some lunker trout whose caution upon seeing yet another familiar artificial offering is momentarily outweighed by its hunger.

The search for frontiers is, of course, illusory, since, once penetrated, any frontier ceases to be one. And it is at this juncture that we enter the realm of the angling addict's conundrum. If he is driven ever further afield in a relentless search for angling's quintessential Elysian Fields, the quest itself is fundamentally flawed. First, it is premised upon the questionable notion that there still remains pristine wilderness on this crowded planet. Second, it is informed by the boundaries of one's horizons. My own experiences are laced with many cases in point. When Jimmy Lowe and I fished the outer fringe of the Marls, we came across the remnants of a campfire and, as if suddenly transported to the pages of *Robinson Crusoe,* at one point followed a set of footprints in the sand. During our Mongolia "exploratory," Purevdorj told Jeff and me that the next month he was scheduled to guide a large party of Czechoslovakian spin casters on the Eguur, a group of enthusiasts who had been making the trek annually since the Soviet era—our frontier, their backyard.

To say that Frontiers International is into fly fishing is a bit like stating that Neiman Marcus is a purveyor of women's clothing. Frontiers is a grandiose travel company that books golf tours, grouse shoots, boat trips on Europe's inland waterways and train trips in India and Scotland reminiscent of the Grand Tour of both the rajahs and their colonialist collaborators. As one of its many unusual initiatives, Frontiers International was among the first to perceive the business opportunity in providing exotic-destination, quality angling to affluent fly fishermen. Its ownership did its homework well and locked up four prime venues early on—Christmas Island in the mid-Pacific and Boca Paila on the Yucatan Peninsula (both primarily bonefisheries), and, somewhat more recently, Kau Tapen, a sea-run, brown-trout lodge on Tierra del Fuego's Río Grande, and the Atlantic salmon utopia on the Ponoi River of Russia's Kola peninsula. Unlike most angling destinations, which ultimately turn out to be fragile or flawed, Frontiers's big four have demonstrated considerable staying power.

Germane to Frontiers' overall success was the fact that each of the four more or less constituted a monopoly. Christmas Island was an exclusive concession conferred by the government of Kiribati, Boca Paila was pretty much the "only game" in its town, Kau Tapen's waters were the private domain of an enormous estancia and the Kola is another long-term-leased concession. At present, in all four venues, Frontiers International's empire, while not quite fallen, is certainly challenged. The competition has become fierce just as its pace his quickened.

Regarding Christmas Island, there have been periodic interruptions over the years in its once-weekly air service, and the political sands under the concession shift periodically. Boca Paila is now but one of the plethora of fishing lodges strung all along southern Yucatan. It wasn't that many years ago that the only access to now-famed Ascension Bay's remote waters was a jolting three-hour boat ride from Boca Paila. The trip was only feasible in good weather and carried a $50 surcharge for the extra fuel. Kau Tapen's monopoly on the Río Grande was broken by two local entrepreneurs who leased the lower reaches of the river from the estancia Maria Behety. And then one only has to read Fen Montaigne's description in his *Reeling in Russia* of the ubiquitous salmon poaching on the Kola to suspect that the Ponoi is no exception.

There are other ways in which the very enterprise of first finding, then penetrating and, subsequently, carving out an exclusive preserve on the angling frontier embodies the germs of its own destruction. I earlier noted that guiding is not a career. For the entrepreneurially minded, however, it can be a step of one's career path. Bob Wickwire built his lodge on the Babine River, as did Darryl Hodson on the Dean, after first serving as head guide for the first lodge operation on particular waters. A considerable contingent of the first cohort of Christmas Island and Bahamas bone-fishing guides are now "independents." For both guide and client, logistics permitting, the temptation to do an end run around the middlemen (the booking agents and lodge operators) is simply too great. Let me illustrate.

Angler's Perspective: You are at a lodge in the Bahamas thrown in with several other fishermen, mostly strangers. Your tab is several hundred dollars a day. You are being rotated daily among the guiding staff, and there is obvious disparity in the skill, enthusiasm and personality of your particular luck of the draw. You may prefer wading to fishing from the boat, but a soft-bottom area happens to go along with your assigned guide as his territory. By week's end you have the sense of having made several compromises. Then on the last day you end up with a superb and delightful guide. The chemistry between you is special.

Guide's Perspective: I do most of the work and get paid $80 and maybe my lunch. I hear that in the Florida Keys a guide is his own boss, and he gets $350 or more a day. All I need is my own boat and motor. I can borrow the money to buy them.

The Marriage—"Do you always work out of this lodge?" "No, Mon, I'm an independent guide." "Really! How interesting. What do you charge?" "Two hundred a day." "Where would a guy stay?" "No problem, Mon, there's the guesthouse right down the road. Costs about $60 a night, meals included." "OK. Let's go fishing together next March." "You got it, Mon."

In theory the guide has just more than doubled his salary, and the angler has halved his expenses. It can even work out. However, the arrangement is not without its downsides. There can be, and usually is, considerable slip between the cup and the lip. The frontier that you have just penetrated is one in which you are counting upon Your Man Friday being actually available the other six days of the week with an acceptable (as in functional) skiff and motor and with sufficient gasoline. You have foregone the backup of a lodge with its inventory of boats, engines and staff, and eschewed the insurance of a reputable outfitter willing to rectify the (frequent) egregious *faux pas* or maybe even some unanticipated "Act of God."

For his part, the wannabe entrepreneur is buying into a lot of responsibility with meager equipment, no marketing skills or contacts and probably rudimentary knowledge of business and accounting. He is also jeopardizing his steadier employment under his former employer. On balance, his leap into the void is predicated upon rosy-scenario thinking: "My boat and motor are dependable." "They will come."

As with any marriage, you have also just crossed the line into the realm of mutual obligation. You are complicit in the creation of this new reality, and much that is unanticipated may come along with it. There is the telephone call requesting financial assistance, advice or simply explaining why the agreed-upon plan won't work, probably after you have already arranged your vacation time and bought your plane tickets. There may be a gift exchange that begins innocently enough but then becomes an expectation. Some requests can become truly sticky, such as the one to smuggle some gear into his country on your next visit or to sponsor his brother's, son's or even his own immigration into the United States.

In short, developing special ties with independent guides is to enter a Himalayan kingdom that is largely peaks and valleys. I have had the exhilarating experience of seeing my picture displayed as the only decoration on the wall of a one-room dwelling because I had given its owner his "start" by being the first to book him independently. The only time that I have eaten bonefish was at the table of his parents; I was then presented at the airport on departure day with a reed wall hanging woven by his mother-in-law. But I also felt profound disappointment when my guide insisted that we go out in the teeth of a storm and then charged me a full day after we were weathered out by noon, all because he needed the money. I have also lost several days of fishing when a vehicle or boat motor failed and have been left to cool my heels because a guide was "indisposed"—as in the midst of a two-day bender. At this juncture then, and with but the occasional exception, I prefer to pay the full freight by booking through established outfitters to cowboying on my own.

And so the commercialization of sport fishing proliferates. After expending enormous effort and maybe all of his resources on building his lodge, the angling entrepreneur faces the immediate reality that any of his guides or staff member is potentially his competition, possibly with the full backing of a good client and the promised loyalty of several others. The Bahamas provides possibly the best case in point. One of its older, established bonefish destinations is Deep Water Cay off Grand Bahama Island. A few years ago its former general manager built North Riding Point Club. Shortly thereafter, several members of the Pinder family, the cream and cornerstone of Deep Water Cay's guide staff, jumped ship, first to the newly launched Pelican Bay operation in Lucaya and then to their own full service one in Freeport.

As if the potential internal schism were not enough, at this juncture the planet is prowled by hungry young aspiring operators in search of the next opportunity. Nor, as noted, are they above "riding" the skirts of another's success. So if one does find the pot of gold, he had better start playing defense immediately by a) obtaining some sort of exclusive and b) discouraging possible competition by expanding to the limits of the available resource—or both.

Jeff Vermillion has pursued such a dual strategy in Mongolia, having negotiated from the authorities a monopoly on his prime waters while constructing four lodges on them. His Sweetwater Travel Company now books 130-140 anglers into Mongolia annually. Its Asian operation operates 15 jet boats, employs 14 American guides and has an on-site staff of about 50. Despite such vertiginous expansion, there is already another operation in northern Mongolian competing through Orvis for the business of the relatively small pool of potential takers.

Even the waters of something as vast as the Amazon basin are the scene of keen angling competition. There is at least one operation that works off of a mother ship. It is therefore capable of challenging, and regularly does, any shore-based, tent-camp enterprise. It, in fact, was the bone in Big Bob's throat as he vituperatively berated the usurpers of his Taperá waters. Again, to use a Bahamian example, just a few years ago Behring Point on Andros Island was a fabled and fabulous destination. It accesses a vast saltwater wilderness. Now, during the high season, as many as 50 skiffs leave the dock and the real challenge has become to outsmart the other guides rather than the beleaguered bonefish population. The mud wrestling in the American West and Alaska is too painful to contemplate.

When I was fishing New Zealand in early 2001 all of my outfitter guides were obsessed with pressure; one likened the scramble for prime waters to war. In that country anyone can guide, and most of the water is public. So on the North Island, for instance, when the levels in the tributaries of famed Lake Taupo drop below the critical point, about 70 guides range far afield in search of angling opportunity for their clients. In doing so they are the inter-lopers who infringe upon the "territory" of a particular local guide. On the South Island no fewer than 12 independent guides scram-ble out of Te Anau for the best local waters. It is all reminiscent of the unregulated competition for pastureland in the 19th-century American West, a struggle in which my nomadic Basque sheep-men were vilified as "tramp" operators. In short, to complete our gold-rush analogy, once a particular frontier becomes a "destina-tion," its outfitters are akin to the saloon keepers in the mining camp who are never more prolific than just before the bust.

There is another anomaly inherent in today's incessant quest for quality angling venues. It is the subtle negative that flows from two seemingly benign, even laudable, positives. I refer to the combi-nation of exclusive access, however secured, to a consequently "well-managed" resource and the extant dominant catch-and-release angling philosophy. Their chemical reaction when mixed together is to produce an altogether distinct third element—the giant fish farm. One operative question becomes how "wild" is the stock of any catchment, no matter how remote or pristine, once it is man-aged to maximize angling success through a catch-and-release pol-icy (in reality catch-release-catch)? How many times has the average New Zealand trophy rainbow been brought to some angler's hand? In just the same season, how often has the average Rio Grande brown trout or Dean River steelhead been caught and released? Most bonefish of any size on the flats of any popular destination bear tell-tale tiny dark circles, scarification from previous angler encounters. Word from the northern front has it that in some Alaskan fisheries the trout are now virtually lipless after several releases. There is not a question of stupidity when the same fish is caught more than once on a particular day; it has no choice but to eat as its winter survival depends upon its ability to pork up through voracious autumnal feeding. Taking advantage of this particular opening raises legitimate dubiety over the "sporting" nature of my angling endeavor.

While I am not advocating killing our catch, I must recognize that in the days when we did so our quarry was truly wild—a single slipup signifying its instant removal from the gene pool. Nor am I overly sentimental about the fish I catch. In his recent book *A Jerk on One End,* Robert Hughes waxes near-maudlin about angling from the fish's perspective. He likens the poor creature to someone strolling along a boardwalk enjoying the day who happens to purchase a hot dog. He takes a bite, experiences searing pain in his throat, is jerked into the water and then dies an agonizing death on the bottom. A more appropriate analogy would be that of a boardwalk stroller who snatches his hot dog from a child (or the child itself) before playing out the rest of the scenario, the point being that we are only able to hook our quarry because it was bent on killing and eating something else.

I am rather more perplexed by a different anthropomorphized mor(t)ality tale. It seems that an irate British Columbia Indian at a public wildlife management meeting denounced catch-and-release sport-fishing as perverse and nefarious "playing" with the sensitive spawning process that underpins the food supply. He equated my sport to hooking a pregnant woman in her mouth, dragging her over rocks and into the water, submerging her for a panicky couple of minutes while she was sure that she was about to die and then letting her go. I guess my only (rather lame) reply is that she would still probably prefer my angling approach to the alternative of another's catch-and-kill, certain-death one. But the ice under my rhetorical logic is clearly thinning at this point!

The catch-and-release philosophy is also skewered by two other detractors and improbable bed partners. To the left there is PETA (People for the Ethical Treatment of Animals) which opposes all blood sports as cruelty to animals. They are pretty humorless and close-minded regarding the practice of persecuting fish before releasing them only to be able to "rip (the same) lips" on some future occasion, all in the name of pleasure. To the right are the larger fraternity of sport fishermen who regard catch-and-release fly fishing as elitist to an extreme. In the name of class egalitarianism, they advocate open access for all and to all angling modalities. If a resource is indeed too fragile to sustain angling pressure, then shut it down rather than reserving it for a few anglers with the deepest pockets. Such, for instance, is more or less the position of the B.C. Wildlife Foundation, a powerful association of both rod and gun clubs.

The latter raises a social issue regarding access. In Europe there is very little public water left, so quality angling is the purview and privilege of the wealthy. There is a compelling argument for what might be likened to "safari conservation," the notion that it is the hunter who has the greatest stake in his quarry's survival. Jeff Vermillion now employs 26 local game wardens to protect his Mongolian concession from trespass by other foreign sport fishermen, such as Czechoslovakian spin casters. Fragile taimen populations have been decimated throughout most of the species' vast Eurasian range and will almost certainly be over the short-term on the Eguur without such protection. Yet there remains something unsettling about converting the locals' food resource into recreation for affluent foreigners. Such are the moral conundrums lurking barely beneath the surface of my sport.

The days are largely over when men went out with impunity to trap, poison, shoot, gig, net and otherwise pillage the fellow denizens of our planet. But under this particular New World Order, as with the political one, there is much blurring of the edges. Who are we? Where do we fit in the grand scheme? Anthropocentric evolutionary arrogance is no longer our legitimate conclusion and consolation. To my mind, we catch-and-release anglers are the ultimate ecotourists, of the type A variety to be sure. We cannot just contemplate nature; we have an atavistic urge to control it. So we ritually capture, admire, touch, photograph and then release and restore our chastened quarry, and thereby reconnect with our ancestral Man-the-Predator persona. Like ancient cave painters we then adorn the walls of our homes and offices with the visual evidence of our prowess.

One can only assume that the challenges to such activity will likely increase. A new cloud on the catch-and-release angler's horizon is the recent animal rights language inserted into The Earth Charter (drafted in 1992 by the United Nations Conference on Environment and Development) by the Humane Society of the United States. Principle 15 would effectively end catch-and-release angling wherever implemented as law since it protects "wild animals from methods of hunting, trapping and fishing that cause extreme, prolonged or avoidable suffering." An alarmed newsletter, *The Angling Report,* (November 2000) issued a call to action,

> "Are you listening TU [Trout Unlimited], IGFA [International Game Fishing Association]? Orvis? Frontiers Travel? Bass Pro Shops? Cabela's?"

I recall my own reactions when first confronted about 1980 with the novel catch-and-release philosophy. I was floating Montana's Madison River with my youngest son and guided by Ed Curnow. Matt was a novice fly fishermen, so when he finally hooked a 20-inch rainbow he proudly closed in for the kill. "Why do you want to kill it, Matt?" Ed asked. "To eat." "Let's take a couple of smaller ones for dinner; it took a long time for God to make such a fish." Matt agreed, if somewhat hesitantly, mirroring my own ambivalence. Later at his tackle shop in Ennis, Ed gave Matt a button proclaiming "I released a 20-inch trout." On the drive back to Reno I mulled over that scenario and morphed into the catch-and-release Bill Angler of today. Are we now confronting the next angling revolution? Is the tiny segment of the angling fraternity that now fishes pointless as well as barbless effetely cultist or pioneeringly visionary? Only proverbial time will tell.

Virtual Angling

The serious challenge to serious fly fishermen is how to counter the doldrums and otherwise while away the wintry evenings when deprived of access to their favorite waters. Recourse to virtual angling is the antidote. Shelved anglers adjust (as in fool around with) their gear, fish vicariously by viewing, listening to and reading about other's experiences and gather together.

Gearing up: There are the purists who tie their own flies, an art, or at least craft, in which I am uninitiated. To pass through that particular portal is to enter a realm of fur and feather, gossamer and goo, chenille and flash-a-bou, a world configured by its own considerable wisdom, skill, dexterity and jargon. When I contemplate what can easily become an obsession, not to mention an enormous investment of time and money, any penis envy that I might feel for the fly-tying set is of the small variety. A smaller number of devotees construct their own rods. For the more pedestrian, including Bill Angler, there is the perusal of mail-order catalogues and the occasional visit to the local fly shop.

I do not consider myself to be a gear freak, *unlike most of my buddies.* I am prone to last minute (a few hours before flight time) scatter-brained packing before setting out on a major trip with a couple of carry-on-the-plane-just-in-case rods and a small gear bag. It usually contains two reels, each with a spare spool, a few boxes of the appropriate flies, nippers, pliers, two pairs of polarized sunglasses and some leader and tippet material. I was once spoofed in the pages of The Fly Shop's catalogue after having shown up for trout fishing in southern Argentina's chilly Andean autumn dressed for summer with a pair of leaky waders and carrying the wrong gear bag (I'd brought along my bonefish flies!). I had to be outfitted, literally from head to toe and waders to flies, out of the charity and spare gear of my companions. Fortunately, they, like most fly fishermen, had brought along two to three times more *stuff* than they could possibly use.

Having said this, and to inform these musings, I have just inventoried my gear. After a quarter of a century of acquisitiveness, I now have 14 fly boxes of varying size, some holding the tiniest and subtlest of trout flies, others ample and gaudy saltwater streamers, organized according to target species and by geography. Two are Alaska salmonid collections, although I no longer fish that state. One holds a modest selection of Atlantic salmon flies, plaintive souvenirs of my fruitless, ne'er-to-be-repeated week on Scotland's River Esk. All would fit easily into a small cardboard carton and represent an investment of several thousand dollars—Bill Angler's counterpart to Jan's jewelry collection.

I also have 16 reels with names like Hardy, Sage, STH, Fin-Nor, Billy Pate, Tibor and Abel - ranging from a Sage 503 with the lightest of lines (a three weight) for the most delicate of trout fishing to two Fin-Nors, each with a 12-weight line that I use for the big boys—tarpon and trevally.

My 15 rods range from a three-weight (for trout), through four different five-weights (for trout), four eight-weights (bonefish and steelhead), four 10-weights (permit, tucunaré, dorado) and an 11- and 12-weight (tarpon, trevally). Good grief!

Considering that each of the reels and rods cost somewhere between $350 and $700, it is clear that, had I just invested the money wisely instead, today Bill Angler's financial worth would have been a bit closer to Bill Gates' than is presently the case. The point is made not as lamentation but to underscore the big-business aspect of the fishing industry, as well as its particular version of the arms' race. Between the days of my boyhood and the onset of an angling addiction in my mid-30s, fiberglass had replaced bamboo as the base material of the standard fly rod. I still own several fiberglass ones, although I no longer fish with them, nor intend to, given that about 20 years ago graphite exploded upon the angling scene. Most of us embraced the amazingly superior new divining rods, despite the considerable escalation in their cost. Since then I and most of my fellow anglers have been played like the proverbial violin by the rod manufacturers. Almost annually, and accompanied by the slickest of professional hype, we are offered the latest toy (we have now supposedly gone through at least four "generations" of graphite) designed to overcome our (shudder the thought) 12-month-old obsolescence. Nor are our choices limited any longer to two 4½ foot pieces constituting a nine-foot wand; now we can disassemble for travel convenience into five or more sections that fit nicely into an aluminum tube easily accommodated within any suitcase.

There has been parallel improvement in reel and line technology. The 2001 Scientific Angler catalogue, for instance, offers no fewer than 24 different styles of dry fly lines, six wet ones, five shooting tapers and three shooting lines. These come in 10 different solid colors and eight color combinations. Some bear the name of a species ("Pike," "Steelhead") while others invoke Luke Skywalker monickers ("GPX," "Wet Tip Express 550gr," "Uniform Sink Plus III"). The link between line and fly, i.e. the leader and tippet, has evolved similarly from pedestrian monofilament to pricey fluorocarbon.

In short, today's angler faces complexity in properly matching rod to reel and line that would challenge an aeronautical engineer. Hear my frustration ye manufacturers, know ye that for all but the most addicted of gear freaks your offerings have become recondite. For most of us brethren of the angling fraternity, you have become as much the problem as its solution. Rather than helping us to find the elusive needle, you pile on the hay. We use the primal force of angling to get in touch with our "human nature," but you seek to bedeck prehistoric cavemen in postmodern garb.

Driving this spending spree is the quest for the perfect cast. Like most golfers, all but a few anglers have some degree of performance angst and are therefore vulnerable to the promise of the high-tech fix. What am I and my fraternity to ever do with our graphite I, II, and III rods? They are far too light and supple to support curtains. As if the plight of Bill Consumer was not woeful enough, we steelheaders are now the targeted candidates for conversion to the increasingly-popular, two-handed spey rod that is the basic instrument of European Atlantic salmon angling. The even newer news from the war front is that several manufacturers are now offering the first-generation titanium rod which costs up to $2,000 per copy. I just made a firm New Year's resolution not to buy a new stick this year, but then the Sage catalogue arrived in the mail and . . . and . . . !

Authorial Musing: There are now numerous television shows and videos to titillate those with limited imagination and/or attention span. Personally, I am incapable of getting much of a fix from passively watching the staged and edited angling successes of strangers accompanied by blither that would make even a sportscaster blush. Somewhat higher up in the intellectual feeding chain are the public lectures organized by such organizations as fly-fishing clubs and chapters of Trout Unlimited. The obvious drawback is their relative inaccessibility and inconvenience. They transpire infrequently, and you have to go to them rather than they coming to you.

Which brings me to the subject: Is there a fishing literature?

"I hope that you haven't read the latest issue of *Field and Stream*" was Jeff Vermillion's initial comment as I answered his call.

"No"

"Good, because I leave for Mongolia tomorrow and would rather be out of the country when you do!"

The magazine (August 1997) had just published an article "Leviathan," by Garret Vaneklassen, one of Jeff's Frontiers International counterparts. It was loosely based on Jeff's recounting of our Mongolian exploratory. While the liberty taken with the facts mildly offends my academic sensibility (several of the week's events described in the Taimen II chapter of this book are conflated into a single day, there is no small dose of embellishment and our four-person party becomes a single angler—me), I am cognizant and tolerant of such license given the editorial requirement of an "action" magazine; I do, however, take umbrage with the prose,

> "Far below Jeff, client Bill Douglass is on the verge of a major breakdown. 'What's going on out there, Jeff?' he calls out. 'What's that monster doing?' There is more than a hint of nervousness in Douglass's voice. Bill Douglass can't see a thing from his position, but he knows what lurks within casting distance. With his seemingly undersized fly rod in hand, he feels like David facing Goliath."

Really? Well—not really. Such livid literary embellishment, so common to one genre within the fishing literature, is akin to what might be called fish porn.

Waltonian lyricism is the Charybdis to the angling literature's sensationalist Scylla. Given the sylvan setting in which angling transpires, its texts are often poems and odes to nature. The bite is usually off at midday, so fishing writers seem obsessed with dawn and dusk. Since the angling protagonist is a solitary figure, the fishing literature is replete with introspection. Excepting possibly for his fellow anglers, it is difficult if not impossible for the author to convey convincingly either sympathy or empathy for the antagonist within the (inter)action—the fish. For most people, they are not particularly beautiful, let alone cute, members of the animal kingdom. Rather they are cold-blooded, limbless, slimy denizens of an alien maritime world, as well as rapidly putrescent once removed from it. To my knowledge, no fanciful author has ever created a credible piscine Lassie, Bambi, Br'er Rabbit, Black Beauty or Bugs Bunny.

So the possibilities of transforming the angling experience from prosaic description into poetical sublimity are definitely limited and tend to travel two treadworn paths. Consider the following distilled unadorned reality: I got up early. It was cold. I ate breakfast. I went fishing. A duck flew by. I caught a trout. The fish stopped biting. I went home.

The writer may choose to lyricize the account:

"I drifted out of the realm of slumber and from my sleeping bag, seduced by the aroma of fresh-brewed coffee and sizzling bacon skillet-dancing over a crackling fire.

"A phantom apparition sipped my tiny offering without rippling the surface or revealing its sleek, silvery magnificence. And then it began catapulting in celebration of our linked destinies.

"It was over. I had not seen a single surface-dimpling rise for half an hour. Time to share in my elusive quarries' noonday siesta."

There is always the lurid alternative:

"I cowered in my sleeping bag delaying the inevitable encounter with frigid air and cold Levis, unconvinced by the prospect of bad coffee and fatty bacon undercooked over a feeble fire.

"A perfect cast and presentation fooled my prey, goading it into a fearsome strike that shattered the still surface, startling a mallard into an explosion of unanticipated flight.

"It was over. It had been half an hour since my last take and the sudden searing pain in my left calf from a stealthy horsefly's bite pointed me toward camp and a timeout."

Of course, the better angling authors bake into their cakes a blend of both genres. But, in the final analysis, there are only so many ways of describing a person's encounter with a fish. Samuel Johnson* summed up the angling author's dilemmas:

> "There are however defects in the piscatory eclogue, which perhaps cannot be supplied. The sea has much less variety than the land, and will be sooner exhausted by a descriptive writer. When he has once shown the sun rising or setting upon it, curled its waters with the vernal breeze, rolled the waves in gentle succession to the shore, and enumerated the fish sporting in the shallows, he has nothing remaining but what is common to all other poetry, the complaint of a nymph for a drowned lover, or the indignation of a fisher that his oysters are refused, and Mycon's accepted."

Critical texts of the Western literary canon further illumine the limitations of the angling genre. Aristotle, in his *Poetics,* notes that tragedy is the most sublime of poetical expression followed by the epical. Bringing up the rear is lyricism, a mainstay of fishing writing. Horace in his *Ars Poetica* abhors purple prose, certainly a pit into which many an angling text falls. In short, most of the fishing literature is lacking in Aristotelian sublimity or Horatian elegance.

Given its rather formulaic sameness, fishing writing possesses a curious inability to hold the undivided attention of even its most natural constituency, the fishing fraternity. I have been told by many a guide and fellow angler that he finds the fishing magazines boring. The articles are either too predictably sensationalized ("there I was in expert waters!") or too blatantly promotional for a particular product or destination. Some anglers profess to read only fishing literature of the manual variety, the how-to-books regarding knot and fly tying, casting and angling techniques.

---

* *The Rambler,* number thirty-six, 21 July 1750

If I might display once again the sexist side of my nature, I also suspect that there is gender bias at play. If most anglers are guys, it is scarcely surprising, at least to me, that they are generally more enthralled by the technical than philosophical aspects of their sport. I also believe that men are less prone than women to read books. So to the extent that the angler reads at all, the short articles of a virile *Field and Stream, Sports Afield* and *Outdoor Life,* as well as those in tamer and more serious publications such as *Salt Water Fly Fishing, Grey's Sporting Journal* and *Fly Fisherman,* better match his available time and attention span than do verbose texts like the present one.

Returning to the rhetorical question with which I opened this discussion, the subtitle of *The Magic Wheel: An Anthology of Fishing in Literature** edited by David Profumo and Graham Swift is no accident. The operative preposition *in* underscores the debility of fishing writing to claim separate status as a literary genre. From the outset the two editors identify their collection of poetical and prosaical excerpts to be a "sub-literature."

This despite the fact that (for some) Izaak Walton's *The Compleat Angler* is an English classic, and piscatorial imagery has been employed by such *illustrati* as Daniel Defoe, Charles Dickens, Ernest Hemingway, Samuel Johnson, John Keats, Henry Wadsworth Longfellow, Guy de Maupassant, Michel de Montaigne, Ovid, Plutarch, Alexander Pope, William Shakespeare, Robert Louis Stevenson, Jonathan Swift, Theocritus, William Wordsworth and W.B. Yeats. Nevertheless, with the possible exception of Hemingway, we are dealing with a minor and transitory theme within the work of such titans, one that scarcely contributes a tile to some larger comprehensive mosaic that might be called the fishing literature. Even such an ostensibly angling epic as *The Old Man and the Sea* is arguably as much or more about life than fishing. I would argue that the same is true of David James Duncan's marvelous *The*

---

* I wish here to adknowledge my indebtedness to this magical text. Most of my history-of-angling asides were gleaned from its wondrous pages.

River Why and Norman Maclean's pensive *A River Runs Through It,* as well as most certainly Richard Brautigan's counter-cultural *Trout Fishing in America.*

To the extent, then, that there exists an angling canon, its gaze is decidedly inward, its musings introspective, its very language often accessible only to the initiated. The sacred texts of the angling fraternity for all but the *cognoscenti* acquire the opacity of Egyptian and Mayan glyphs. Arguably, the British are the master race when it comes to transforming the mundane into the arcane. Easily the most proficient and dedicated practitioners and scriveners of fly fishing, and with the River Test as one of their prime angling venues, it was perhaps inevitable that among the English the very nature of the sport would be contested. By the latter half of the 19th century the practice of fishing with the dry fly (an imitation of a winged insect floating on the surface) dominated and even defined the sport. It was then that monumental debate erupted between dry-fly purists, whose position was best articulated by Frederic M. Halford (*Dry-Fly Fishing in Theory and Practice*—1889), and the proponents of the technique of nymphing (subsurface angling with the imitations of the stream-bottom dwelling juvenile form of flying insects that rise to the surface like little polaris missiles, sprout wings and become air-borne) championed by G.E.M. Skues (*Minor Tactics of the Chalk Stream*—1910). Then there were the eclectics, like Francis Francis (*A Book of Angling*—1867), who believed that the complete angler would embrace both dry- and wet-fly-fishing tactics. In the unlikely event that such debate might strike one as insufficiently esoteric, it was further complicated by controversy over the relative merits of fishing upstream or down. It is no small wonder that the Brits were able to forge common cause against the Germans in World War I!

The controversy over what constitutes a "fly" (and when) continues unabated, the angling equivalent of the abortion debates. However, like most of the fly-fishing fraternity, Bill Angler is apostate, equally comfortable dry-fly fishing a Montana spring creek with a size 20 Trico that is so tiny as to require a magnifying glass to thread onto gossamer tippet as when presenting a four-inch minnow-imitation Lefty's Deceiver to a cruising 70-pound giant trevally. These are but the polar extremes of a spectrum that also encompasses emergers, terrestrials (ant, beetle, grasshopper, etc.), and poppers (fraudulent amphibians). Is it legitimate fly fishing? Who cares?

Men Gathering: Pace Robert Bly, but men have been gathering in the woods to engage in exotic male bonding rites long before you recommended it. Most of my life's intimate friendships have been forged at the dinner table of some fishing lodge. Among them are a vice president of a major oil company, a soft-drink distributor, a contractor and numerous land developers, physicians and attorneys. Had our ships crossed in some real-world context, adorned with coat and tie and flying the banner of our respective professional identities, the encounter would no doubt have been brief and transitory. But we met and continue to meet as wool-shirted and levied fellow anglers. I doubt that I would recognize any of them in their formal attire.

We share an intimacy that is truly special. In both my pressured academic and business lives, I receive countless communications from persons who all want something from me. Bill Angler, however, gets calls and e-mails from equally harried moguls and professionals who simply want to know, "How was your trip to the Bahamas?" "How are you doing?" I can circumvent their considerable defenses (a.k.a. receptionists and secretaries) by employing the secret codes of their private lines—the most privileged and intimate information exchangeable between two Trout clansmen.

If there is much gender bias in the foregoing, it is simply reflective of the demographics of my sport. I have known a few genuine and reasonably accomplished female anglers, Margaret Vermillion, Virginia Scott, and Kitty Griswold of these pages being cases in point, but the truth is they are rare. Far more common among the thin ranks of female anglers that I have encountered were younger women recently married to older anglers and manifesting enthusiasm for their spouse's passion. I believe that most were sincere, or at least were sincerely trying, but within a year or two were content to allow hubby to pursue his fishing alone or with the guys.

The statistical evidence for the male predominance in sport fishing is clear. In the year 2000 men constituted 95 percent of the 128,000 membership of Trout Unlimited. There are the four owners of Reel Women Outfitters Inc. of Victor, Idaho, who conduct fly-fishing schools for women only in Jackson Hole, Wyoming. However, if a welcome portend of things to come, they are currently the exception that proves the rule. The perception that the sport is male dominated does, however, pose an historical anomaly. Few realize that one of the hoariest texts (1496) on fishing was published but four years after Columbus' first voyage and fully 157 calendars before Walton wrote his classic. *The Boke of St. Albans* by Dame Juliana Berners included *A Treatyse of Fysshynge With an Angle,* a how-to manual. English poetry and prose provide occasional glimpses of female anglers as a part of 17th and 18th century estate life. Nor is their presence solely of an Old World aristocratic nature. Andrew Burnaby in his *Travels Through North America* (1798) states, "there is a society of sixteen ladies, and as many gentlemen, called the Fishing Company, who meet once a fortnight upon the Schuilkill." It was one of Philadelphia's most exclusive social clubs.

A willing fugitive from northern Nevada's February wintry chill, I eased my car off Highway 101 in search of the famed International Sportsmen's Exposition at the San Mateo County Expo Center. Most of my angling circle refers to this annual extravaganza as simply the "San Mateo Show"; they were the regulars and I the novitiate. 2001 marked the 25th anniversary of the immodestly self-billed "America's Largest Fishing, Hunting and Camping Show."

My provincial-rube credentials were definitely displayed when I winced over paying $6 to park my car in a lot roughly three blocks from the main event, but then my alarmed Scottish ancestors were

Casting About in the Reel World

partly assuaged when I secured a scalped $10 entry ticket for eight. The layout was perfect, or at least perfectly logical. If there were more than 700 exhibitors in all, touting everything from power boats to big-game safaris, the fly-fishing world was neatly segregated into its own pavilion. I would not have to go slumming!

For the next three hours I prowled the corridors of their show and my emotions. The raw commercialism was a definite downer. Whatever else fly fishing is to me, it bespeaks and evokes the soothing solitude and tranquility of relatively pristine forests and flats. I traversed the gauntlet of booths manned by hawkers proffering slick brochures promising the "ultimate" (as in plentiful, big, dumb fish) angling experience, whether in Northern California, Alaska or Africa. Interspersed among the outfitters were the manufacturers displaying their latest gewgaws.

But then the air was heavy with authentic bonding as clutches of buddies and paired fathers and sons weighed the many options on offer while crafting their next angling adventure. As I passed Sweetwater Travel's booth, Dan Vermillion was too engrossed with a client for me to interrupt; a few steps further along I disappeared into Mike Michalak's bear hug. The Reno Fly Shop guys were there in force and we worked through the somewhat artificial exchange of next-door neighbors who suddenly run into each other on Fifth Avenue. Where's Gary? Fresh back from New Zealand, Gary Aka and I had agreed loosely to get together at the "show." We didn't.

Not being a fly tyer, I did not dawdle in the crowded theater where attentive eyes transfixed some master at his vise (or is it vice?). His running commentary was beamed to one and all through his lapel mike. In an act of magical corporeal detachment, his magnified fingers filled the screen of a nearby television monitor.

Far more magnetic for Bill Angler was the casting pond where first Gary Borger and then the legendary Lefty Kreh performed as part of the non-stop casting clinic. Listening to his banter, I quickly understood why people either love Lefty or don't. The black humor of his pointed putdowns was laced with wisdom delivered with words that could easily wound. To volunteer to be his guinea pig was akin to asking to be seated at a ringside table for a Don Rickles' show. Nevertheless, in a few short minutes from Borger I learned a new way of holding the rod so as to avoid a droopy back cast and from Kreh a delivery that obviated a trailing loop and hence wind knots. Heady stuff indeed! With such a valuable information chiseled indelibly on the marble of my memory, I could virtually feel the approval of my Scottish ancestors. It was worth *at least* eight bucks. But, of course, that damn brochure about the Okavango will no doubt compound that damage a thousand-fold at some time in the not too distant future.

A Tale of the Dean

A **Pioneering Generation**
Bob Stewart was back from the war and prematurely gray. Flying 50 missions over Germany as a tail gunner in an RAF fighter bomber had left its physical mark on the young man who had used his brother's birth certificate to enlist at 16. He was now 19 and looking for a place to forget the memories of his maimed and dying buddies. He soon married his childhood sweetheart, Virginia Harvey, and they homesteaded property under the Veteran Lands Act in Winfield, a small community near Kelowna, British Columbia, where they built a house and lived for five years.

However, Bob's dream was to one day own a ranch and, possibly, a fishing or hunting lodge. He also had a consuming fascination with aviation and wanted his own airplane. So he worked for two years in the Alaskan commercial halibut fishery and then during the off season in Seattle as a gas-station attendant and gunsmith—saving every spare penny.

In 1951 Bob's wanderlust and desire for wilderness adventure took him back to his native British Columbia. He staked out a claim to a government tract at Nimpo Lake and, the following March, bought a one-ton truck and a few wooden boats and moved his young family to the property. Today's nearly effortless trip from Williams Lake to Nimpo took the tiny expedition two days. That summer, Bob and Ginny lived in an Army surplus tent with their children while constructing the first of many log cabins.

For the next five years the family spent winters at the Winfield orchard and summers at Nimpo, hosting a few intrepid guests in their emerging "lodge." In the mid-1950s Bob made his way over the newly constructed, yet atrocious, road to Bella Coola on the coast. There he found two of his acquaintances from his hometown of Summerland, B.C.—Al Elsey and Dick Blewett. Elsey owned Talcharko Lodge, a king salmon and bear-hunting operation, and Blewett worked for him as a guide when not plying his trade as a carpenter.

Bella Coola was love at first sight. The following autumn Bob moved his family there. The Stewarts lived in an abandoned school, purchased an uncompleted house and hired Blewett to help them finish it that winter. Stewart and Elsey entered into several abortive ventures together, the main result being that Dick ended up working mainly for Bob when not guiding bear hunters for Al.

According to the *Kimsquit Chronicles,** Elsey was the first to recognize the potential of the Dean River's fishery, taking the occasional client there (an eight-hour boat ride in good weather) beginning in 1954. In the Stewart-family version, Bob was the first to become really intrigued with the presence of the spring and fall steelhead runs in the Bella Coola River. He thought that the steelhead was a more interesting sport-fishing quarry than the salmon. Elsey's brother-in-law was a commercial fisherman so he knew that steelhead were being taken as incidental catch in the Dean Chan-

---

* James Sirois, *Kimsquit Chronicles: Dean River, British Columbia.* (Hagensborg, B.C.: Skookum Press, 1996).

nel by the salmon fleet. It was reputed that one boat had caught a 42-pounder. However, the species was still largely disparaged by local anglers; recognition of its sport-fishing equivalence to the Atlantic salmon still lay in the future.

There was a conundrum regarding the timing of the Dean steelhead run. Stewart and Elsey made several short exploratory trips to the Dean at different seasons over the next three years. In the spring and summer they caught nothing, in the fall a few coho salmon. They were acting on the likelihood that the Dean's steelhead run was in summer and prolonged, when the ones in the other local coastal streams were springtime and of short (one-week) duration. Andy Siwallace, Elsey's employee and local Bella Coola Native American who had grown up on the Dean, was the likely source of this information.

In any event, Stewart and Elsey failed to catch steelhead on any of their early visits. However, it was said that an intrepid angler, Eddie Cyr, had landed his floatplane somewhere upstream and taken a large steelhead. For the time being, Stewart contented himself with erecting a cabin on the Bella Coola property to house a few anglers that he began guiding during the spring and fall steelhead runs. In the summers he ran his expanding Nimpo Lake trout operation.

By 1958 Blewett was Bob's partner at Nimpo and their mutual dream was to have an airplane in order to establish spike camps in the vast lake country beyond their base. Enter Dick Poet, a skilled crop duster. Dick was from Oregon and married to Bob's first cousin, Helen Stewart. In 1958 Poet bought a wrecked Cessna floatplane and rebuilt it. It was the first aircraft in what would ultimately become Wilderness Airlines, Ltd. In 1959, at Bob's invitation, Poet based his plane at Nimpo Lake Lodge. He also bought a ranch near Kleena Kleene.

Bob convinced Dick to link their fortunes into a combined hunting and fishing operation. The efforts were complementary since the autumn hunting season begins about the time summer sport fishing ends. They joint-ventured a string of packhorses and Stewart became a licensed hunting guide (moose, caribou, mountain goats and bear). The whole package was overly ambitious and undercapitalized. However, it did have a good mix of skills and resources—Blewett's master carpentry and guiding experience, Poet's aircraft and ranch, Stewart's Nimpo Lake and Bella Coola operations.

A River to Build On

The Dean River flows out of Nimpo Lake and wanders for about 50 miles across the Chilcotin Plateau before plunging into a wild and inaccessible canyon. Sixty miles from saltwater, it descends through a series of cataracts that form an insurmountable barrier for steelhead returning from the sea. In its lower reaches the Dean is fed by several glacial tributaries, notably the Sakumtha. Two miles inland from its terminus, there is another frightening stretch of water called the Lower Canyon. Below it the river meanders through relatively flat countryside before entering Kimsquit Bay at the head of the Dean Channel.

In 1961 Elsey sold Talcharko Lodge and pretty much dropped out of the Dean River picture. That summer, Poet, Blewett and Stewart landed by floatplane on the Dean near its confluence with the Sakumtha, still intrigued by the possibility of discovering a summer steelhead fishery that might then become one of Nimpo's options. On August 19, Poet flew Blewett, Stewart and their first two clients to the river. While their guests fished (one caught a 26-pound steelhead), Stewart and Blewett looked for a permanent campsite near a better place to land the floatplane and settled on the present site of the Lower Dean River Lodge. The plan was for the four men to raft downstream to the tidewater of the Dean Channel where Poet would pick them up. On that journey Blewett floated through the hair-raising waters of the Lower Canyon, probably the first man to ever do so! Meanwhile, Anson Brooks, while making a fuel stop for his airplane, saw the beautiful fish and immediately commissioned his own trip to the Dean. He was the third and last paying guest that first season.

Stewart and Blewett formed an equal partnership to establish a permanent Dean River camp, initially a tent one. At the same time, since he would spend the summer on the Dean, Dick sold Bob his interest in Nimpo. For the 1962 summer season Bob was to market the Dean option to his Nimpo clientele, Poet would fly the guests and supplies, and Dick was to run the daily operation.

The operation required a boat. In 1960 famed boatbuilder Glen Wooldridge of Grants Pass, Oregon, had built a variation of his Rogue River wooden craft for Elsey. So, in the spring of 1962, Blewett visited Wooldridge, who generously shared his shallow-water boat construction ideas. Dick had already constructed several wooden boats and incorporated Wooldridge's ideas into a Dean River prototype. It would become the crucial technological advance in the development of the Dean's sport fishery. The completed 24-foot craft was towed to Kimsquit Bay and then transported past the Lower Canyon on top of a logging caterpillar.

In June 1962 Blewett and Rob Stewart (Bob's 14-year-old son) went to the Dean to build the necessary infrastructure, using flown-in prefabricated tent platforms that Dick had made. Blewett arranged to have a smaller version of his boat helicoptered in. Meanwhile, Bob Stewart had hired Darryl Hodson (of Ocean Falls) to guide for his Bella Coola operation, then at Nimpo and, finally, the summer of 1963 on the Dean (where he ran the camp's second boat). So the Lower Dean River "Lodge" was now a reality.

Initially, the operation was both tenuous and star-crossed. In October 1964 Dick Poet crashed his Beaver at Fenton Lake and was killed. His widow sold the nascent Wilderness Airlines logo and sole remaining aircraft, a Cessna 180, to its pilot, a young Bella Coola resident, Dan Scheutze, and his partner, Darryl Smith, who today owns Pacific Coastal Airlines. Then in January 1965 a flood obliterated the Lower Dean River Lodge's infrastructure. The Stewart/Poet/Blewett dream of a fly-out fishing and hunting empire was in serious disarray. The camp on the Dean was rebuilt by Blewett, Rob and a hired hand in time for the summer season. By then Bob had a floatplane and did the flying.

That year Dick, Darryl and Rob each operated a boat, catering to three anglers, and so the camp could accommodate a maximum of nine rods. However, there were several weak links. Bob and Dick had no means of regular communication (not even radio contact), and there was neither a set schedule nor a fixed clientele. Rather, Bob continued to try to interest his guests at Nimpo in the Dean option and would often show up unannounced with the takers. Few knew about the emerging steelhead Valhalla, and those that did learned by word of mouth.

There were, however, two notable exceptions. First there was Seattle's Anson Brooks, scion of the Powell River Ltd. papermilling fortune, a company that had been sold to MacMillan-Bloedel. Brooks fell in love with the Dean during the inaugural 1962 season and remained a regular for the next 30 years. He had access to company aircraft and an extensive circle of acquaintances. It was his assignment to entertain company clients, such as Otis Booth of the Times-Mirror Corporation. Brooks' "word of mouth" clearly counted for much more than the run-of-the-mill variety.

Then there was Dick Shannon, one of the California Central Valley's most prominent farmers. A regular at Nimpo and early sampler of the Dean's charms, from mid-July to mid-September *every weekend* he would fly his own plane from California to his favored British Columbia fishing destinations accompanied by a different set of guests. He divided his attentions equally between a weekend of trout fishing at Nimpo followed by steelheading the next on the Dean.

Nor was Shannon a mere client. In 1964 he left a supercub at Nimpo for Bob's use, a loan that proved critical when Poet was killed that autumn and Bob became the flying link between Nimpo and the Dean. The relationship was further complicated when Bob crashed the aircraft and was unable to replace it until the winter of 1966. Consequently, during the mid-1960s the Stewarts were in Shannon's debt, and he was also by far their most significant customer, two realities that gave the Californian considerable influence over the operations.

The Competition

In the fishing world it seems that news of opportunity travels more quickly to potential competitors than to likely customers. Almost immediately the Lower Dean River Lodge lost its monopoly. In 1961 Elsey had sold Talcharko Lodge on the Bella Coola to Don Siegel and Bill Brohan of Sun Valley, Idaho. The reality, as opposed to the romantic idea, of running a fishing lodge prompted them to hire a resident manager. They did, however, construct personal residences on the property, and their Sun Valley connections helped expand the lodge's clientele.

Siegel and Brohan hired Vancouverite Robin Fisher to manage their operation, and he soon commissioned a riverboat from Blewett, ostensibly for use on the Atnarko River, a branch of the Bella Coola. Not only did Fisher not pay for the boat, he immediately moved it to the Dean where he moored it just above the Lower Canyon. Initially, Talchako housed its anglers on a larger "mother ship," the Calypso, which they moored in the Dean Channel. When this proved to be too crowded for the clients' tastes, Fisher established a houseboat at Kimsquit.

By the mid-1960s, Charles Morse, of the Fairbanks-Morse fortune, had purchased Rimarko Ranch at Charlotte Lake, 15 miles from Nimpo. To compete with Bob Stewart, he wanted Rimarko to offer its guests similar amenities. To have a steelheading option, Morse constructed his own Kimsquit land-based camp and placed a boat above the Lower Canyon as well.

There were two other commercial sports fishing initiatives on the river during the 1960s. Ivan Tallio, a young ambitious member of the Bella Coola Band, secured a government grant, rumored to be some $90,000, to launch his own short-lived effort on the lower river. In 1965 Ray MacPherson, a fishing tackle shop owner from Kamloops, worked in August for Blewett, substituting for a restless young Rob Stewart who took a month off to find out what summer might be like in wider worlds. "Ray Mac" left abruptly, and Blewett called Rob to request that he return to guide for the remainder of the season. It would be 35 years before Rob would again leave the Dean in summer for more than a few days. The next year Ray Mac appeared as Fisher's camp manager. When that didn't work out, the following season the undissuaded Ray Mac established his own tent camp above the Lower Canyon.

Commercial sport-fishing access to the Dean was limited by more than just physical isolation, imagination and capital. It required persistence and, above all, expertise. All four of the competing operations proved abortive, and, in any event, their activities limited to the waters just above the Lower Canyon. Even there (the easiest stretch to negotiate) the boating proved more than challenging to the wannabes.

All four failed within a couple of years of one another, and each left in its wake a clientele anxious to continue fishing the river. Some did so by making ad hoc private arrangements; others asked for dates at the Lower Dean River Lodge, requests which, by the late 1960s, were difficult to accommodate given the camp's by-then full dance card. Conditions were ripe for schism.

Family Affair, Family Afar

In the autumn of 1963 Darryl Hodson married Nancy Poet, Dick's daughter. He would continue to work for Blewett and Stewart over the next four seasons as their head (salaried) guide. Rob Stewart, Nancy's second cousin and about five years Darryl's junior, was also a salaried guide and at the bottom of the camp hierarchy. However, while still a teenager, Rob clearly had at least the potential of becoming Bob's heir apparent.

Darryl was an accomplished outdoorsman. He also had a good streamside manner in his dealings with clients and was ideally situated to bond with them. By then, the Lower Dean River Lodge had its own fall, coastal bear-hunting operation under Dick's direction, complete with a mother ship. Dick employed Darryl as a hunting guide.

Meanwhile, Rob was working through the usual challenges of late adolescence, which included the sporting of a beard, an uncompromising rebelliousness and a holier-than-thou embrace of the emerging catch-and-release/artificial-lures-only angling philosophy. He was wearied and ambivalent over the weekly routine whereby nine anglers killed their limit of steelhead (81 fish) that Rob was then expected to clean, chill and load onto the outgoing plane. No one knew much about the fishery, and Rob was beginning to have qualms regarding its survival. All of this, of course, placed the Young Turk on a collision course with the camp's more traditional, harvest-oriented lure fishermen, particularly Dick Shannon.

Darryl Hodson had his personal vision and ambitions. While still working for Blewett and Stewart, and with the financial backing of one of the camp's clients, he purchased an aluminum boat to start up a coastal bear-hunting business. By 1967 he had picked out a spot for his own fishing camp less than a mile downstream from the Lower Dean River Lodge. Shannon was impressed with the young guide's entrepreneurism and negotiating skills when purchasing from him a used airplane, and he certainly preferred Darryl's personality and philosophy to those of the brash Rob Stewart. For Shannon, Hodson represented the stable and amenable future. Without quite burning his bridges at Nimpo, Shannon tilted towards Hodson on the Dean.

There is a Hodson-family version of the story, written by Geoffrey Norman and published in *Forbes FYI* magazine (March 13, 1995), based upon an interview with Darryl's daughter Jill. Accordingly, Darryl was making $500 for the season when Bob Stewart, in desperate need of more help, hired an inexperienced guide for $800. Darryl protested in hopes of getting a raise, but Bob refused, saying that "a deal is a deal." So Darryl quit. As Jill noted,

"In a way, he was doing my Dad a favor. He was too ambitious to just be a guide for someone else. He had so much energy."

So in 1968 Darryl and Nancy built their own camp. Given the growing demand for Dean River slots, there was ample business for both operations. After several years of apprenticing with Dick, Darryl also constructed his own boats. He was eventually the first on the Dean to create an all fiberglass design. Darryl's brother, Randy, joined the operation as a guide.

The External Threats

To the casual eye Deanland is a pristine wilderness. That impression is somewhat deceptive. Since the 1960s, the Dean Valley has been logged heavily. By mid-decade there was a gravel airstrip at Kimsquit, a logging road and a bridge across the river at the head of the Lower Canyon. In the 1970s a second bridge was built below the confluence of the Sakumtha and Dean to abet additional tree harvesting. During the logging years, on a still summer's day, dust hung heavily in a valley jolted periodically by the mechanical cacophony of chain saws and logging trucks.

The logging ceased more than a decade ago, and both bridges are now in ruins. In their wake, the commercial timber interests left another controversy—a reforestation plan that favored conifers over native deciduous species. For several years the two fishing camps opposed (before finally prevailing) the provincial plan to spray herbicides on the spontaneous growth in the conifer seedings.

A constant problem throughout the 1960s was the growing fame and popularity of the Dean as an angling destination. Camping anglers began to arrive in exponentially increasing numbers by boat, seaplane and even helicopter. The enhanced angling pressure was being played out against the backdrop of near total ignorance regarding the Dean's fishery.

In the late 1960s Blewett responded to the river's growing popularity by opening a helicopter camp in the Dean's upper reaches. However, after three years of operation, it was closed by the provincial government, arbitrarily and without explanation, underscoring for Dick the vulnerability of his toehold.

Dick Blewett became politically pro-active. In the early 1970s, the Dean, like every other B.C. river, had a three-fish-daily, three-day limit (or a maximum of nine per person). More than a thousand steelhead were killed on the river annually. Without any hard data, the Department of Fisheries and Oceans estimated that there were 15,000 steelhead in the river, a population that could easily sustain the existing sport-fishing harvest. However, to veterans like Dick, Darryl and Rob it was evident that the fishery was being overly challenged.

Blewett started agitating for a lower limit and a ban on bait. Influenced by literature from the California chapter of Trout Unlimited, he also began to advocate the emerging catch-and-release approach with his clients, several of whom were now fly fishermen. Many of the lodge's guests began writing letters of support for tighter regulation of daily limits, angling techniques and access to the Dean. In 1972 Dick embarrassed the director of the Department of Fish and Wildlife in front of his staff over the excessive limits. New measures were promptly put into effect. For the next few years the limit on the Dean would be two-fish-daily for two days and bait was banned, as were multiple hooks on artificial lures.

Another, even more sinister, sword was hanging over the heads of Dean lovers. In the 1950s the provincial government had entered into an agreement with Alcan Aluminum Company to build a major plant in British Columbia. Deemed the Kemano Project, phase one dammed the Nechako, a tributary of the mighty Fraser River, to provide the needed hydroelectric power for a smelter. Kemano II, conceived earlier and announced in the early 1970s, called for interdicting the Dean in its headwaters for diversion of much of its flow northwards to the project's reservoir.

Kemano II threatened the very survival of the Dean's fishery, triggering a zero-sum game in which compromise was fatal. However, given the times, halting an already half-completed major development project seemed unlikely. To join the struggle at all, proponents of the Dean needed sound data on its fishery.

Thus, in the 1972 season the lodge's guests were asked to contribute to a fund for a fish-tagging study. Many were skeptical ("Progress is inevitable. You guys are just squatters here anyway."). While some refused, one client, Jim Cox, responded with enough support to cover the field expenses of Dennis Hemus, a graduate student fisheries' biologist and Lower Dean River Lodge guide, during the 1973 season. The effort was complicated by an immediate personality conflict between Hemus and the provincial Department of Fish and Wildlife biologist. Perhaps embarrassed that such a study required private funding, the DFW insisted that it be conducted by one of its own employees.

The compromise was that Hemus wore a MOE (Ministry of the Environment) uniform while funded by the private contributions. He proposed to tag 500 fish in the summer of 1973, a goal regarded by MOE officials as preposterously ambitious. What the professionals failed to consider was the complete support of the guides and guests at both lodges. The fish were tagged, scale-sampled and weighed on the spot. The stomach contents of killed fish were also noted. Camping anglers did their part as well, releasing fish into strategically located pools, where they were held until Hemus could make his daily round to tag and liberate them. In all, 678 fish were tagged, which produced the most extensive study of any wild steelhead population to that time.

The effort attracted the attention and support of federal fisheries' biologist, Dave Narver, who assisted Hemus with fish-scale analysis. Narver had more than a passing interest in the Dean, having published his own article on it in 1970. The Dean's notoriety was growing, and the British Columbia Steelhead Society joined the fray. About the same time a Vancouver-based angling club, called

Casting About in the Reel World

the Totems, established a tent camp above the Lower Canyon for its members and added their voice to the Dean's chorus.

The Kemano II challenge evaporated, almost miraculously and in story-book fashion, when Tom Ladner, one of the Lower Dean River Lodge's influential and devoted Canadian clients invited Englishman John Hale, chairman of Alcan's board, for a week of "see-for-yourself" angling on the Dean. Soon thereafter it was announced that the river was to be excluded from the project. More recently it was scrapped entirely and unilaterally by the B.C. government after Alcan had invested more than $500,000,000 in phase two, a subject of ongoing litigation.

Changing of the Guard

Business acumen was not a prominent part of Dick Blewett's otherwise impressive arsenal of life skills. Under his management the Lower Dean River Lodge turned a meager profit. Indeed, by the early 1970s it was debt-strapped, its main accomplishment having been to outfit the mother ship of the company's coastal bearhunting operation—Dick's first love. He was essentially tired of managing the many financial and political challenges on the Dean. His wife, Rose, was fed up with the several months of raising the five Blewett children alone.

Rob Stewart married Rayma Bryant in 1970. She became the camp cook while Rob worked as Dick's head guide. With each passing year he had assumed more responsibility, particularly since Dick began leaving before conclusion of the fishing season to guide bear hunters. In 1972 Rob purchased his own airplane, giving him critical mobility that Dick always sorely lacked. At the time, Rob, Rayma and their infant daughter Wendy had no home of their own. In winters they rented an apartment in Williams Lake where Rob worked as a carpenter between guiding bear hunters for Dick in the late fall and boatbuilding under Dick's tutelage in Bella Coola in the spring.

Rob was in his mid-20s and wanted more opportunity. Given

his carpentry skills and airplane, he approached his father with the proposal of running the out-camps at Nimpo, but Bob was too strong-willed and independent or wise to let go. By season's end any wilderness fishing operation is a cauldron of pent-up tensions. For the staff, months of constant encounters of the close kind tend to blow minor slights all out of proportion. Trying to run a class operation in a wilderness setting, and with only the thinnest of lifelines and safety net, is enough to make any operator paranoid regarding the Fates. Small disasters are a daily occurrence, big ones a constant fear.

So that fateful fall of 1973 Rob was impatient and Blewett unhappy. Rob announced that he would not return to the Dean the following season, putting additional pressure on Dick. This prompted a summit meeting of the two senior partners, each of whom offered to buy the other out. Bob had asked Rob to be present and told Dick to state his price. It was $40,000 for his half. Bob wanted 50. Dick countered that he'd sell his share of the company's fishing operation for $25,000 if he could keep the boat and the bear-hunting business. Rob secured a bank loan and purchased Dick's interest in the fishing camp.

A Chinese sage might have concluded that Rob had wished without being careful. The camp was dilapidated and small (a third of its present size), and the equipment was worn out. The only real asset was the business itself. The company had some extraneous debt, which Rob assumed as well.

Undercapitalized, Rob and Rayma tried to get through the 1974 season on a shoestring. He hired his sister, Wendy, and brother-in-law, Doug Clarke, as help and cut back to eight rods with four clients per boat. He also instituted a fixed three or four-day schedule. Fortunately, another couple, Earl and Sue Buller, came to visit and stayed for the season. It was a tough year, but the Stewarts made a little money.

Meanwhile, there was another development on an unexpected front. In the early 70s, Bob and Dick had opened an "upper camp" to accommodate the three anglers displaced by the close of the helicopter camp. After Rob bought Dick's interest, Rob's younger brother, Duncan, ran this satellite operation. Legendary Peter McVey, an expatriated Englishman, was the cook, a role that he continues to play each summer, more for the fishing opportunity than the money. In the mid-70s, Duncan talked Bob Stewart into selling him his interest in the Lower Dean River Lodge for $40,000, to be repaid out of the profits. This produced its own tension, since Rob wanted to reinvest in infrastructure, while Duncan needed a regular distribution to make his payment.

In 1975 the lodge went back to the three-boats and nine-rods program, which worked out better. The following year there was high water all summer long, with many lost days and cancellations. Rayma was discouraged and wanted out of the Dean; Rob believed they were too far in debt to extricate. In 1977 she did not return, remaining instead in Bella Coola working for Wilderness Airlines. It was the beginning of the end, not to mention Rob's and my streamside commiserations over divorce.

Fortunately, that summer he was able to hire a young couple, Dave and Debbie Fort, who had worked at Hodson's. Debbie saved part of the day by replacing Rayma as cook, while Dave shored up the guiding. It was a successful summer, capped off by Rob's buy-out process of Duncan's interest. Duncan also agreed to remain on as the paid operator of the upper camp.

It was our first trip to the Dean and our second steelheading experience. My brother John and I were veterans of a frigid week during mid-October the year before on the Babine further to the north and inland. Since we were far from hard-core anglers, the wonder was that we were attempting another week of steelheading at all. In six days of angling on the Babine neither of us landed a fish, and our combined strikes' total could be tallied on a single hand.

Now John and I were fishing the Dean in the pleasant warmth of early September days. Following veteran advice we were equipped with spinning rods rigged with Okie Drifters. We each lost our steelhead virginity and experienced the excitement and awe of handling and then releasing our first fish. But as the week wore on I became impatient to break out my fly rod. Rob Stewart urged me to be patient since it was difficult to mix spin casters and fly fishermen in the same water. He promised that the last day he would arrange a trip far up river for me and the only other fly fisherman in the group—the young angler of a father-son combo.

The awaited morning at breakfast my would-be companion's father insisted that they spend the day together, throwing in a pretty pathetic "I'm-paying-the-tab" combined power play and guilt trip to boot. A chagrined Rob told me to remain behind as the others left the dock. Both Bob and Duncan Stewart happened to be in camp, having wound down their Nimpo Lake, trout-fishing season the week before.

The three of us soon headed for the upper river as the first rays of the morning sun commingled with the rising mists of an early autumn chill. The few precociously golden leaves in the still hesitantly greenish canopy were dislodged from their summer's perch by the day's first thermal breeze, parachuting lazily down to the surface film where they formed little fleets to be launched seaward by the mighty Dean.

Bob caught two fish by noon and declared his angling to be over. Satiated, he was content to be our raconteur and sidewalk supervisor. By the time we had reached our furthermost destination, Anchor Hole, I remained fishless if far from unhappy. By Stewartian consensus I was to fish the promising headwaters by myself. On the third cast of my Scarlet Skunk fly she was on. Half an hour later I released my trophy a good 200 yards downstream from where I had made her acquaintance. It was September of 1978. I know because there is a tradition at Lower Dean River Lodge of recording any steelhead over 36 inches in length—most seasons a couple of dozen fish in all. My first, and hence very special, wet-fly-caught steelhead, had made the grade by half an inch.

After several seasons on the Dean, I was ready to graduate from wet-fly underclassman to dry-fly doctoral candidate. However, the decision did not come easily and was fraught with procrastination. Conventional wisdom held that steelhead would rarely take a dry. Once in freshwater they ceased feeding, so it seemed unlikely that they would bother to negotiate the several feet between their stream-bottom lair and the surface to strike something that was presumably of little interest.

At times I would rig up a dry line and float a #8 Humpy over a likely lie, but my resolve would quickly wilt before the realization that it might be a fool's errand. It was then that I would recall the words of Trey Combs in his classic book Steelhead Fly Fishing and Flies (1976). It describes his encounter in 1973 with a mighty (23 lb. 2 oz., 38½ inch) Dean River buck. Rather than release his prize, "It now hangs on the wall of my fly shop at my home in Black Diamond, Washington. When I look at the fish, it is with a feeling of fulfillment because I realize that taking everything into consideration, it is just about impossible to catch a steelhead of this size on a dry fly." With such allusion to the exceptional nature of the dry-fly steelhead encounter in mind it was difficult to stay with the Humpy program, particularly since even fishing (more conventionally) wet, when steelheading it is common to go several hours and hundreds of casts between strikes.

But then one fine autumn morning, like a serious drinker resigned to attend his first AA class that very evening, I decided to fish dry all day long come heaven or low water. My first surprise came at Shannon's Run on about my fifth cast. A small hen sipped my offering and then cartwheeled downstream in sheer outrage. A few minutes later I released my personal angling landmark with mixed feelings of elation and suspicion. Now that I had proven my point, was it really necessary to belabor it? In my heart of hearts I believed that I had just been the beneficiary of a fluke.

At the Bridge Hole, our next stop, I was assigned one of my favorite stretches of water and the temptation to fish it wet was overwhelming. I was sitting in my car in the parking lot just outside the AA's meeting place wrestling with second thoughts. No, damn it—a deal is a deal. For the next half-hour I fruitlessly worked the lovely run. I was a bit down-in-the-mouth and down to the last few feet of fishable waters in the tailout when its surface exploded and the tiny Humpy that I had

been studying so assiduously morphed into a 12-pound steelhead punc-
tuating the atmosphere with serial jumps.

I have never quite experienced before nor since the warm glow of sat-
isfaction and wonderment pervading my being that afternoon as I walked
from the dock to the lodge. I felt far more humbled than egotistical as I
prepared to recount to my angling companions the magical day in which
the planet stopped rotating on its axis and was stilled within its orbit as
Bill Angler caught five steelhead on a dry fly!

But did Rob Stewart really own anything at all? In 1978 the province
informed him that all pulp leases on the Dean had reverted to the
public; consequently, Stewart's arrangement, which was with the
timber company, had no validity. The government announced its
plan to auction the fishing camps on the Dean—Rob was free to
bid! It was his first of many wakeup calls ("I finally realized that
it was a very unfriendly world out there. Also, that I had bought
a wheelbarrow full of smoke!"). Gradually, he and Darryl were able
to convince provincial officials to grant them a non-transferable,
ten-year lease (to be paid retroactively). It would not be until the
early 1990s that Rob managed to secure a long-term, transferable
one that gave him a true shareholder's stake in his own life's work—
in short, an asset.

In 1978 Rob married Pegge, his present wife. Soon thereafter
they bought 90 acres on the Bella Coola River within Tweedsmuir
National Park. There they built their own house, barn and work-
shop. Rob planted pasture as well, which today supports a few
cows. The Bella Coola property is the critical backup for the Dean
operation, the place where in the winter Rob constructs his river-
boats, possibly rebuilds a floatplane and just generally hones his
equipment for the next season. Rob and Pegge have now owned
the Lower Dean River Lodge for more than twenty years. His sons,
Scott (by Rayma) and Robertson (by Pegge), have both guided on
the Dean, providing the third generation of the Stewart presence
on the river.

Birth of an Activist

Rob purchased Blewett's interest in the Lower Dean River Lodge the same year that Hemus conducted his landmark study. Rob was perplexed by the politics surrounding it. He was still naïve enough to believe that the conservation goal was sufficient to overcome all resistance. The following year the Department of Fish and Wildlife coopted the Lower-Dean-River-Lodge/Hemus initiative, spending ten times as much as the $2,000 raised for the original work while tagging only 145 fish.

The fact of the matter was the whole initiative had underscored an anomaly in Canadian fisheries' management. The federal and provincial governments are frequently at cross purposes. The federal Department of Fisheries and Oceans, a powerful agency with a large budget (rumored to be currently greater than the value of the annual netted salmonid catch of the entire British Columbian fleet), is charged with both protecting fish stocks in the ocean while regulating commercial fishing. Meanwhile, B.C's Department of Fish and Wildlife is a grossly underfunded, weak agency that has ostensible jurisdiction over freshwater fish stocks and guiding—setting license fees, limits, length of seasons, rules of access—yet always subject to federal approval. Thus, when steelhead are at sea they are under direct DFO jurisdiction, and, when in a river, under the purview of the DFW. Not surprisingly, there is a low-key, ongoing turf war between the two agencies—the one powerful and paternalistic, the other paranoid and petulant.

The DFO's prime concern was to sustain the commercial fishery and industry which in terms of sheer dollars is far outweighed in significance by British Columbia's sport-fishing interests. The DFW tries to balance conservation with the desires of the largest number of anglers. Clearly, over the years the Dean's very notoriety as North America's premier steelhead stream and demonstrated capacity to generate powerful advocates have posed serious problems for both agencies.

In 1973 the commercial fishermen went on strike, thereby failing to net the Dean Channel. That season the steelhead run in the river was noticeably better, confirming the suspicion that many Dean-River fish were being intercepted in the salt water by the commercial interests. Shortly thereafter, Dave Narver was appointed Director of Fisheries (the "F" in DFW, part of the British Columbia Ministry of the Environment). He implemented a more conservation-minded policy regarding the steelhead fishery, drastically reducing the limits province-wide and to zero on Vancouver Island. Eventually, there would emerge Special Waters Legislation whereby the province's rivers were ranked according to class. The Dean would emerge as the first class-one stream, subject to severe limitations on public-angling access.

In part these decisions were influenced by Rob Stewart's activism. Throughout the 1970s he was diligent in writing letters to all of the powers-that-be and made the first of many trips to Victoria to lobby in defense of the river. He indeed learned well the lesson that the Dean's future survival depended at least as much on political as environmental considerations. Darryl Hodson was equally convinced that, whatever their rivalry in other contexts, the two original lodges had a mutual interest in making common cause within the fray. Rob had Darryl's proxy as he entered the political arena.

In the early 1970s Rob organized most of the Bella Coola and Dean River sport-fishing operations into the Central Coast Guides Association. In the winter of 1973-74 he affiliated it as a sub-chapter of the larger Guide Outfitters of British Columbia, mainly a hunting guides' organization. For awhile Rob was vice president of the GOBC, attending its annual winter conventions. Through this involvement he was able to secure influential GOBC support for the Special Waters Legislation that has become the lynchpin in the current management program for the Dean.

In the early 1980s there was a new challenge. Under international treaty with the U.S., the Canadian DFO had agreed to limits on the annual wild king salmon harvest. However, both nations were free to enhance runs with hatchery stock that would then be excluded from the quota. Under Canadian law commercial fishermen needed to fish for a certain number of weeks annually in order to qualify for coveted unemployment compensation in the off-season. Chinook was the only salmon species caught in the month of June, so clearly (from the DFO's standpoint) a "terminally-excluded" chinook run was desirable. In 1982 the DFO's hatchery began releasing chum and chinook salmon into the Bella Coola River.

Given the cataract in the Lower Canyon, the Dean has never been much of a salmon stream (it does have small runs of chinook, coho and a handful of sockeye). Consequently, the number of steelhead smolts in the Dean is superior to the salmon ones, an unusual situation and the main reason that the Dean is such an outstanding steelhead fishery. Therefore, the hatchery program was more of an indirect than direct threat to the Dean's steelhead fishery. Or so it was thought until 1984, when there was a huge chum-salmon run in the Dean Channel that attracted much of the B.C. commercial fleet. It took 400,000 fish there alone, and that summer far fewer steelhead than normal came into the Dean. Dennis Hemus was the sport-fishing representative to the Sport Fishing Advisory Board. He sounded a strong cautionary note that the ecological balance was being upset in the Dean Channel. The equivocating governmental response was that the record salmon run was aberrational rather than directly attributable to the new hatchery's activities.

In 1986 1.4 million chum salmon, the hatchery's main focus, were caught in the Dean Channel. Again the steelhead run was interdicted at midseason. It was evident that they were being intercepted in commercial nets as by-catch, though a subject about which commercial fishermen were understandably close-mouthed. Eventually, there was consensus that 13,000 steelhead had been lost to the netting.

That same year Rob replaced Hemus on the Sport Fishing Advisory Board of British Columbia, appointed by the Canadian Minister of Fisheries. This enabled him to make common cause with the numerous and influential Skeena drainage sport-fishing outfitters. He was also named to the Central Coast Advisory Board as the SFABO's sitting member. The CCAB had an influential voice in determining pre-season regulation of the commercial fishery.

It soon became evident that steelhead are surface swimmers when negotiating the saltwater channels during their migration to their home rivers. MOE and sport-fishing interests argued successfully for a "weed-line" system whereby the commercial gill nets had to be suspended a minimum of a meter beneath the surface. Later there was also a regulation that called for the seine fleet to "brail" and sort their catch in order to release steelhead unharmed. While the new measures improved steelhead survival rates, they require a capital investment, take more time and effort to manage and also reduce the commercial catch by some factor. Many commercial fishermen ignored the regulations (but at risk of punishment), while others began to avoid the Dean Channel. Rob's activism on this front caused some tensions with many of his commercial-fishermen former schoolmates and neighbors in Bella Coola.

For the time being, market forces have mitigated the hatchery-stock issue. In part due to recent record sockeye salmon catches by the American fleet in Bristol Bay, Alaska, as well as other factors such as growing competition from the relatively-inexpensive salmon produced by the accquaculture industry, the price of chums has fallen at times to an uneconomic 15-30¢ per pound for females with roe. There are lingering issues from the recent major dispute between the American and Canadian governments over ownership and management of Pacific-salmon stocks which further clouds the future of commercial fishing in British Columbia. In 1998 the DFO prohibited all coho harvesting in B.C. waters. Ironically, the firm policing of this regulation also provided the first effective enforcement of the rule requiring incidentally caught steelhead to be returned to the sea.

Despite such developments, the future of the Dean's steelhead run is far from clear. It seems likely that many of the fish are still being intercepted farther at sea before reaching the Dean Channel, possibly in part by foreign fleets. Also, steelhead runs in British Columbia in recent years have been spotty, prompting speculation that El Niño may have upset the balance of nature for some indeterminate period of time.

Rob's second agenda item was to secure some sort of limited angler access to the Dean itself. The need to do so was brought home to him almost immediately upon purchasing the lodge. His first season one of the guests of the upper camp brought along a representative of Fishing International, a major U.S. booker of sport-fishing destinations. He proposed an arrangement with FI that Rob and Duncan rejected. So Fishing International began to introduce guided anglers onto the Dean in various fashions, culminating in the late 1970s when it moored a mother ship to Rob's offloading dock at Kimsquit and refused to move despite being asked to do so by the Royal Canadian Mounted Police.

FI then teamed up with another would-be operator, Tony Hill, at Kimsquit. Hill's position was tenuous at best, and, initially (1984), limited to the public waters below the Lower Canyon. But then he put a boat above it, claiming that it was only for ferrying passengers across the river. He also provided his guests with ATVs so they could use the logging road to "fish themselves" (i.e. unguided).

The Tony Hill challenge, combined with the increasing rafter/camper traffic from the Bella Coola-to-the-upper Dean helicopter connection, underscored the need for clearer regulation of the resource. After many years of lobbying, a political compromise that balances the private interests of the historic operations with those of the general public was reached. Fifty rods per week are allowed on the river above the Lower Canyon. Twenty are reserved for the existing operations: including 12 for the Lower Dean River Lodge (nine at the lower camp and three at the upper) and eight for Hodson's (six at their lower camp and two at an upper helicopter camp). The remaining 30 rods on the river above the Lower Canyon are made available to Canadian nationals on a first-come basis. Those which are unsubscribed enter a lottery in which non-Canadians (mainly U.S. citizens) are allocated river access. Successful winners in the lottery must guide themselves. Subsequently, two rods without boating rights were allocated to the Tony-Hill Nakia Lodge operation (which, given that the formula calls for a 60/40 spilt between public and private interests, means there are now 55 rods per week on the Dean).

In theory, such are the rules; in reality, they are slightly bent. There is at least one group of perennials from Kamloops that seems but a thinly veiled guide operation and a certain U.S. "angler" appears on the river with regularity bringing up the rear of a flotilla of rafters like some mother hen watching over her chicks. However, by and large the system has brought a modicum of order to the river.

One final challenge, a modern echo of ancient sounds, deserves mention. The 1990s have witnessed Native-rights' activism throughout the province, and the Bella Coola Band is no exception. It claims traditional ownership of the Dean River, and, in the summer of 1998, established, for a time, a steelhead-netting operation on the lower river. The results were disappointing, and the initiative was dropped in 1999, but it could be reinstituted in the future. Nor can anyone's crystal ball foresee the ultimate resolution of the Bella Coolas' claims. This is potentially the wildest of the Dean's many wild cards.

Oh Romeo!

When Darryl Hodson left Dick Blewett in 1968, to set up his own competing operation, there was not the schism that my brother John and I had experienced on the bitterly divided upper Babine. Through his marriage to Nancy Poet, he was, after all, related to the Stewarts. Darryl always respected Bob Stewart, seeking out and then following the near-fatherly advice freely given. Bob counseled Darryl to maintain a small and manageable operation, which he did, complementing his fishing lodge with a fall bear-hunting business. Until 1976 Hodson's Lodge accommodated but four rods on the river.

A noticeable shift occurred in Deanland chemistry when Rob Stewart took over the Lower Dean River Lodge. Darryl was Rob's senior and, as noted, had been Dick Blewett's top guide until making his move. In many respects Darryl was a mentor and role model for Rob during their years together. But there was also the undercurrent of a near-sibling rivalry for Dick's approval in which Darryl held the obvious immediate high hand, whereas, Rob, an owner's son, possessed the future's trump card (as subsequent events would prove).

As an operator, Darryl was a risk-taker and visionary. He incorporated helicopter fly-out options to the upper Dean and, eventually, to the Kitlope River into his operation—but with only loose cost accounting. In 1976 Darryl increased his rod numbers to six on the lower Dean, and in the 1980s argued, successfully, for a two-rod, tent-camp permit on the upper river. Rob is a conservative businessman, one virtually obsessed with cost-benefit analysis. He has also concentrated his energies upon infrastructure, making capital improvements each and every spring to his operation (whether it be construction of a new cabin, a shower house, or expansion of the main lodge).

Over the years the two lodges have collaborated in a variety of ways whenever mutually beneficial. These include buying supplies together to realize bulk discounts, hiring a barge to move them to Kimsquit, sharing ownership of the truck that carries clients of both above the Lower Canyon and their common cause on the political front. Nevertheless, there is also the legacy of the earlier personal rivalry that has fed the myth or reality of two distinctive camp cultures. The Hodson version of the difference emphasizes the smallness of an operation that can thereby offer its guests more intimate attention. The contending view is that the original camp pioneered voluntary catch-and-release angling and was first to move to a nearly all fly-fisherman clientele. Therefore, the Lower

Dean River Lodge caters to a more relaxed, conservation-minded guest. Periodically, a test of wills breaks out on the river over daily schedules and distribution of anglers (in order to control the greatest amount of prime water). Even the very boat colors seem to underscore differing philosophies—our fleet is painted baby blue while Hodson's boats are a piratical black with yellow trim. Each morning, while we dawdle over breakfast, Hodson's boats pass by in the gloom of impending daybreak to lay first claim to prime stretches of our common waters.

While the anglers of neither lodge were ever involved directly, for many years the two camp cultures translated into a certain stiffness or aloofness streamside. We exchanged few words and only the occasional gesture, while motoring slowly and courteously past one another in the eternal leapfrogging quest for the day's as yet unfished riffles and pools. Such were our compartmentalized worlds, at least until the season of 1989 when our affable guide Bob Hull and Jill Hodson fell in love.

Jill is one of the Dean's most experienced guides, a widely known path-breaker for her gender in a predominately male world. Bob and Jill Hull continued guiding for Hodson's, and for us old-timers the competition between the two lodges has relaxed, though without disappearing altogether. The anglers' code still does not quite demand "after you!"

Mortality

One day of my week in the 1993 season Rob was guiding me when Darryl Hodson appeared by boat with two of his anglers. His helicopter was disabled, so he had been unable to ferry them to the upper Dean. He wanted Rob to be aware of the predicament to avoid any misunderstanding of the presence of two extra anglers on the lower stretch of the river. I continued fishing while they talked, and Darryl left to retrieve his float plane for the trip to Bella Coola and the needed helicopter part. Rob later expressed his concern over Darryl's stress. Not only did he have anglers to move at his upper Dean camp, others were scheduled to be shuttled to the Kitlope. When Darryl flew over us a short while later, Rob remarked, frustratedly, "If he's going to kill himself, I hope that we can have the memorial service on a Thursday so I can be there!" Thursdays were Rob's day to fly to Bella Coola for groceries.

The next morning Hodson's boats failed to make their usual dawn appearance during our breakfast. As we prepared to leave our dock, Bob Hull arrived to inform us that Darryl had been killed the previous afternoon. After repairing his newly leased Hughes 500 helicopter, Darryl had flown his anglers to the Kitlope. Apparently, he had decided to clean his windshield while the rotary blade continued to rotate. Unaccustomed as he was to the height of the counterweight, it struck him in the head, killing him instantly. The following Thursday there was a memorial service for Darryl in Bella Coola.

Later that fall Tony Hill contracted to ferry timber cruisers engaged in site assessment work back and forth across the river above the Lower Canyon. On a rainy day with the Dean near flood stage, Tony was running late to pick up his clients. He started across the river at dusk. It is Rob's rule of thumb not to navigate it for 12 to 24 hours after a crest, given the floating debris. There is a particular danger of it clogging one's engine. Rob believes that is what must have happened to Tony. A two-week air search turned up 50 pieces of the shattered craft, but the body was missing. It wasn't until the following June that Rob happened upon the intact bow, its anchor rope wrapped around a leg bone, which suggests that Tony probably became entangled as he threw out his anchor to try and keep from being swept into the cataracts of the Lower Canyon.

Ernie Renzel and Fred Anderson were fishing partners, sharing a week on the Dean for many years. I met Ernie one season by being included in his group during my stint as a last minute substitute. He was retired from the grocery business and was the ex-mayor of San Jose, California.

Ernie must have been in his 80s and seemed to be pretty much along for the ride. He would rise about 10 o'clock, eat breakfast, fish for a maximum of a couple of hours in the Camp Hole (less time if he caught a steelhead) and then try to talk one of the two young camp domestics into playing a game of dominoes (they adored him). He would then read, nap and await our return to share vicariously in the day's stories. Ernie was sweet, mellow and the perfect gentleman, a man who never swore. I thought maybe it was all a reflection of his age, but Rob insisted that Ernie had always been the most laid-back angler imaginable.

Fred Anderson was the camp legend. He, too, was from the Bay Area, where he owned a furnace business in Orinda. He was a chemical engineer by training and had helped develop napalm during the Second World War. He was gruff, short-spoken and given to swearing.

Fred was a fishing machine, all throttle and no brake. He would rise before anyone else and fish through breakfast. He preferred fishing two or three holes all day, ones where he could make 100-feet-plus casts with the special lines and shooting heads that he commissioned directly from the manufacturers before today's far-more-advanced technology. Fred kept a rubber ball on the front seat of his car to exercise his casting hand whenever delayed in traffic. He belonged to the San Francisco Fly Fishing Club and became a tournament-quality caster through endless hours at its Golden Gate Park practice pond. Fred invented a system that allowed him to urinate without shedding his waders, and another that let him put on his raincoat without leaving the water.

On one memorable day Fred caught 23 steelhead in the same hole. I have probably averaged about 1.5 fish per day over my many years on the Dean. He kept an extensive journal, recording the details of every fish he ever caught. In addition to the Dean, he fished other notable steelhead and trout destinations, and is reputed to have introduced the single-handed rod and shooting heads to New Zealand.

By the time that I met Ernie, Fred no longer fished the Dean.

He was incarcerated in a hospital for the criminally insane, having shot his wife to death and then wounding himself. He blew away part of his face, but survived. As one of his fellow fishermen observed, "It was the only time Fred ever missed!"

Afterglow

My wants are simple. I have no desire to latch onto a monster symbol of fate and prove my manhood in titanic piscine war. But sometimes I do like a couple of cooperative fish of frying size.
—John Steinbeck

Fishing largely consists of not catching fish; failure is as much a part of the sport as knee injuries are of football
—Robert Hughes

Fishing is a delusion entirely surrounded by liars in old clothes
—Don Marquis

Life is nothing if not transition. My friend Julio Caro Baroja, noted Basque social historian, once told me that its purpose was to gather memories for old age. In my fondest recollections the planet has become piscatorial. The real natives of *my* South America are the dorado, pirarucú, tucunaré, payara, jacunda, arowana, pacú and tararira. Its immigrants are the rainbow and brown trout of Chile and Argentina rather than their Basques that I have studied, lectured and written about when not otherwise more seriously engaged in antipodean angling. The voice of Australia whispers "barramundi," and Asia speaks to me in Taimenese.

I took early retirement from my university position at 12 midnight December 31, 1999, in order to prepare myself for the next thousand years and to be able "to go fishing," an explanation that elicits near universal derision among my colleagues, friends and family. They long ago concluded that my life is but one continuous effort to polish my fishing-bum credentials. So be it. And now the former enthusiastic grandson, bamboo pole in hand and hectoring his elder to be taken fishing, is the impatient grandfather surveying his once removed brood for the first signs of a serious fledgling angler to mentor. Transition!

The reliable bookends of my variegated angling life are the week each June that I fish for tarpon in the Florida Keys and the other spent at the Dean in early September. The monitor measuring my mortality is the annual deterioration of a wrecked ship and two logging bridges. Before there was snow on his mountaintop, a dark-haired Bill Angler first contemplated the beached vessel near Boca Grande Key that looked almost like it could be salvaged at the next high tide. Today three mangroves have sprouted from the rusted cormorant perch. The two logging bridges violating the Dean's pristine pride were serviceable when I first saw them; they have long since collapsed and been swept away in the spring flooding, leaving behind twin pilings on opposite shorelines—Scylla and Charybdis of human technological arrogance overwhelmed by the infinitely greater forces of nature.

Next Monday I leave for my annual trek to the Lower Dean River Lodge to be hosted there by one of its new owners, Jeff Vermillion, and two of his investors, Gary Aka and Jerry Fitzpatrick, my former guests. For years, on our winter getaway, Rob and I had discussed his exit strategy, or lack of one. He was beyond satiated and seemingly without much light at the end of his tunnel. But then there were Jeff and his brothers, energized and intent on stringing together a fine necklace out of choice angling pearls. They already had the Copper River Lodge in Alaska's Lake Iliamna watershed and, of course, their Mongolian lodges. It was my pleasure to introduce the couple—I was now about to attend the wedding. Transition indeed!

As I pen these words, scattered across the top of my desk and segregated into neat geographically discriminated piles, ready to be filed away, I'm not sure where or for what purpose (maybe to one day bore the attendants in the retirement home?), are the photographs composing Bill Angler's lifetime gallery. The hundreds of images certainly could not be segregated by pose. In each the angler holds his trophy, a predictably triumphant, if somewhat forced, smile beaming ivory-white out of the darkened matting of hair too long, beard unkempt and Stevie Wonder sunglasses. The backdrop of alabaster sands, verdant vegetation and azure waters changes but little from place to place or by period. The fish themselves, if a bit confounded and vanquished, are eternally young. But the angler?!

In the earlier photos he reminds me of my son or nephew. Over time he metamorphizes into my fraternal companion. The most recent photos are definitely paternal. The eternal young lad who still resides in Bill Angler now fishes disguised as his own father. This boringly static, yet constantly evolving, visual record underscores for me the extent to which we are all soulmates of Dorian Gray!

Yet it is but my 60th year, and my race is far from over. I look forward to closing the circle by taking my ageless self fishing once again with that grandfather who will stare at me out of future photographs. I may now wade with greater caution and need the magnifying glass attached to the brim of my hat in order to thread delicate tippet through my hook's tiny eye, but I am far from through gathering the memories for my old age.

Socrates once said that we cannot escape our problems through travel because we take ourselves along. While that sounds good as sound bite, and captures a certain reality, it is also quite obfuscating. Maybe we don't change in some fundamental sense, but we certainly evolve within our individual parameters. I can state with confidence that Bill Angler is far more laid back today than when he first began his angling quest. He no longer measures the success of any trip in terms of size and numbers of fish. Don Starr, a dear fishing companion who has passed on to his eternal reward, once challenged me when I speculated that I had become so committed to the catch-and-release angling philosophy that I would liberate a world's record. "You'll never know, Bill, unless you have the opportunity." It was years later on a March afternoon in Loggerhead Basin that I resolved that particular question about myself.

Today I fish both more and less than ever. More in the sense that the frequency of my trips and their duration are both increasing, less in that their angling focus has blurred. My journeys are now less to Outer Mongolia, though there is an element of that as well, and more to my inner self. In Socratic terms the challenge has become one of learning as much as possible about that invisible Siamese twin that I take along. What I do know is that the voyage is never more enlightening, both as regards anthropological and personal knowledge, than when taken alone. I have long since ceased to predicate my angling excursions upon the availability of a buddy. Indeed, even when accompanied there is a piece of me that is always solitary—the unrelenting observer of myself. I have learned much from the royal road to travel adventure books of Richard Halliburton, Paul Theroux, Peter Mathiesson and Fen Montaigne (not to mention Marco Polo and Ibn Khaldun), becoming privy to their intriguing worlds, ones fashioned out of their observations during solitary perambulations undertaken in remote corners of the planet.

When he was 55 years old, Teddy Roosevelt embarked upon an exploratory expedition in the Brazilian highlands, accompanied by his son, Kermit. After the customary "grand-safari" slaughter of numerous animals for both pleasure and the taking of scientific specimens, the venture turned sinister. Father and son descended a previously unexplored stream known as The River of Doubt, a headwater of the Amazon. It was a journey into hell that nearly cost both of them their lives. Teddy barely survived and returned to civilization an old man, his health broken. When asked why on earth he had done it, he answered, "It was my last chance to be a boy again!" Each time I prepare for my next foray in international angling I think of Halliburton and empathize with Roosevelt.

In strictly angling terms, while not entirely extirpated from my inner essence, in the main my personal feeding frenzy is over. I can scarcely relate to the 10-year-old boy fishing for bluegill at tiny Potts Lake in the high Sierras, out of salmon eggs yet told by a passing game warden to catch and kill as many of the stunted fish as possible because the pond was over-populated, who then proceeded to bait his hook with the plucked-out eyeballs of his prior catches. I am certain that I killed a couple of hundred bluegill that day.

As a 40-year-old angler I was waist-deep in the frigid waters of the Ugashak during my fourth trip to Alaska, catching a near-record Arctic char on practically every other cast, when I was suddenly awash in ennui. I sat out the remaining two hours before our flight back to the lodge, ruminating over my other Alaskan experiences, days basically punctuated by high counts of released, four to six-pound rainbows taken almost effortlessly by fishing a Single-Egg pattern behind spawning sockeyes. I compared this with the near-masochistic satisfaction of finally landing a Dean River steelhead after hours of futility. On my return to Reno I renewed my contact with Rob Stewart after a several-year lapse; I have never been back to Alaska.

Similarly, I severely wounded my Amazonian enthusiasm that morning while at Lago Refugio when Mike Coe and I encountered the school of ravenous tucunaré. Before our and their feeding frenzies were over, I was reading a book, overly satiated with angling.

I may one day again pursue tucunaré, but it will be only after a considerable period of healing.

Now, when fishing the Dean or the Río Grande, the anticipation is far more exquisite than the consummation. After the thrill of landing an enervated silver apparition fresh in from the sea, I am likely to replace my adrenaline with caffeine. Rather than wading right back into the fray, I would rather savor the moment with a steaming cup, pleasant conversation with my guide and contemplation of the scenery. At some point I might stroll the streambank or beach in search of an unusual pebble, seashell or piece of coral. For 20 years it has been my practice to bring back one such offering from each trip, the detritus that now overflows a wicker basket atop Jan's dresser.

This is not to say that my angler's enthusiasm has diminished. It is now simply more refined. The thought of catching my 4,073rd bonefish is depressing, the anticipation of catching the next one exhilarating, no matter its size. I far prefer the quixotic quest of the impossible dream, not to mention questionable angling prospects, the Bikini atolls and Botchi rivers, to the near-guaranteed action of the tried and true. But that is only possible once one ceases to measure success in terms of weight, length and body count. At this juncture I demand far more than many encounters of the scaly kind. Rather, I want a genuine anthropological experience that is as deep as it is wide. Such is now my requirement of the rivers flowing into my mind's memory.

Nor am I being either entirely altruistic or humanistic. Rather it is an exercise in practicality at this juncture. Given the juggernaut of humanity extruding into every corner of this particular planet, the only real remaining frontiers are of the personal interior kind. It has always been true, yet never more than now, that the quality of the angling experience depends entirely upon the angler self that accompanies one. There remains considerable latitude for profound satisfaction, but only insofar as one's expectations do not outstrip reasonable prospects. The challenging encounter with a single fish under the right conditions far transcends in memory value the white noise of hauling in a surfeit of big, dumb fish.

In sum, I would like to think that I have learned something from both Fred Anderson and Ernie Renzel. Like Fred, I do take my fishing seriously; like Ernie, I try to keep it in perspective. For, in the commonest cliché of our angling literature, fishing is about much more than catching fish. Indeed, for me angling has been a life's tale and a spirit's poem.

September 2000
Reno, Nevada